PROFESSIONAL

Offshore Jurisdictions & Services

GUIDE

Simon Evans
General Editor

FT
LAW & TAX
Asia Pacific

Published by **FT Law & Tax Asia Pacific**
An imprint of **Pearson Professional Asia Pacific**

Suite 1808
Asian House
1 Hennessy Road
Wan Chai
Hong Kong
Tel: (852) 2863 2600
Fax: (852) 2520 6646
Internet: pphkg@hk.super.net
Web: www.pearson-pro.com.hk

First published 1997
Printed in Hong Kong
ISBN 962 661 042 5

Preface

This book is not unique in what it sets out to do, and that is document the features and benefits of key offshore jurisdictions, by defining in a clear and easily digestible way the vehicles available to international investors in such jurisdictions and the legal and regulatory environment within which such vehicles must operate. However, it is unique in the way it attempts to do this, by recognizing the 'offshore business' and the vehicles and jurisdictions which support it, as a 'capital flow' business. Thus, not only does the book contain all the usual information one would expect to find about relevant trust and company laws but also commentary from leading practitioners who have deep insights into their workings. Regulatory and tax issues which need to be considered where 'offshore' and 'onshore' meet are also highlighted.

The term 'offshore' has come to mean many different things to different people over the comparatively short period that this business has existed. Moving offshore – or investing offshore means nothing more than investing capital or moving physically outside one's country of origin. However, it has through common usage, come to mean more than this and in the context of 'offshore jurisdictions' has come to mean territories where the tax climate is advantageous to nonresidents, and where confidentiality laws are attractive to 'low profile' investors.

The ever increasing tide of 'copy cat' legislation between competing offshore jurisdictions over the last decade, in an attempt to attract a greater share of international offshore funds, has resulted in, what seems at first sight greater homogeneity in the regulatory and legislative environment. In many respects, this may tempt the practitioner to be less discerning in the choice of jurisdiction for the establishment of investment vehicles. Nothing however, could be further from what the truly professional adviser should be doing. A closer inspection of relevant legislation, scrutiny of the infrastructure of the jurisdiction, and greater attention to the more specific requirements of the client and or the transaction should more strictly determine the choice of jurisdiction.

The publishers have not in this first edition attempted to grade each jurisdiction and critically evaluate its merits. Inclusion of details does not necessarily mean that the jurisdiction meets all the relevant criteria of the discerning practitioner. This is perhaps the next phase. Some jurisdictions have been omitted, most notably Hong Kong as the publishers felt that the main use of the book would be in Hong Kong, and there are more complete sources of reference on the SAR.

Greater global ties between revenue and regulatory authorities, the increasingly aggressive attempts of many revenue agencies to apply ex-territorially the revenue laws of their own particular jurisdiction, and the rightful skepticism with which global law enforcement agencies regard transactions which even suggest money laundering activities, make it absolutely critical that the offshore jurisdictions and those who operate within them have the right attitude to global compliance. Attitude is difficult to determine but 'effective' legislation is a significant indicator that a jurisdiction has accepted the right approach.*

The previously clear lines between offshore and onshore continue to become increasingly blurred. If offshore jurisdictions and the clients and advisers who utilize them are to bring stability to international capital flows, resulting in acceptability by those who must police them, the choice of jurisdiction and vehicle is of paramount importance.

As the offshore world matures and the likelihood of litigation in respect of offshore vehicles increases it is critical that the forum for such dispute resolution has an adequate legislative framework and experienced practitioners to staff it. Knowledge of the framework is a valuable tool for the adviser and we hope this book will contribute by providing an effective and practical source of first reference.

Simon Evans
Hong Kong
Nov 1997

*'Effective' means not slavishly 'accommodating the perceived demands of the market place but facilitating client requirements within acknowledged standards of legal theory and practice'.

Contents

INTRODUCTION

Offshore Trusts and Companies:
A Consumer's Guide
by Peter Willoughby

Offshore Trusts and Companies: A Consumer's Guide

Peter Willoughby

The use of offshore trusts, usually in association with offshore asset holding companies, has become more and more common with increasing personal wealth around the world. The purpose of this paper is to review the use of offshore trusts and to highlight the main reasons for using them, some of the pitfalls to be avoided and some of the dangers that lie ahead.

Offshore Trusts

There are many reasons for using an offshore trust. For most people, the reason which springs instantly to mind is tax planning of one sort or another. While it is true that the origins of the trust lie in the avoidance of feudal dues and therefore from the earliest days, were concerned with tax mitigation, there are many other, possibly stronger, reasons for using trusts. What follows next is a discussion of the main reasons for using trusts.

Advantages

Prudent asset planning

Most wealthy people prefer to decide for themselves how their assets are to pass on death. For example, a wealthy individual will normally wish to provide for a source of income for his spouse, for the education of his children and perhaps also safeguards for any children or other relatives who suffer from disabilities. Such a person will probably wish to make gifts not only to relatives but also to charities and for other public purposes. Arrangements of this kind are best made before death even though they are intended to continue to have effect after death. While a will can achieve some of these objectives, a trust involving the transfer of ownership of assets to trustees with defined objectives as to how and for whose benefit the assets are to be held and administered provides a confidential and flexible basis for asset planning.

There may also be special problems for certain individuals governed by laws which dictate how assets are to pass to relatives at death. This is usually referred to as 'forced heirship'. Forced heirship occurs under Sharia law in Moslem countries and also in civil law countries mainly in continental Europe where the concept of a trust is not always recognised. Forced heirship also occurs in Japan.

A trust can be a useful way of overcoming forced heirship rules although, as recent litigation in the Cayman Islands (*Lemos v Coutts Co (Cayman) Ltd* unreported on the main issue but see (1992-93) CILR 5) has shown, reliance on the provisions of local trust laws which provide that forced heirship rights are not to invalidate a trust, may be of limited or no effect insofar as assets are in the forced heirship jurisdiction of the settlor or in a jurisdiction which is sympathetic to the forced heirship jurisdiction of the settlor. It should also be remembered that many jurisdictions which are not ordinarily regarded as having forced heirship laws nevertheless have legislation under which dependants can claim on the estate of a deceased person. This is the position in, for example, the United Kingdom and Hong Kong.

Providing for continuity after death

The death of a wealthy individual, can, and very often does, cause major disruption. In the absence of a trust, it will be necessary to obtain probate of any will, or if there are assets in more than one jurisdiction several wills, or in the case of intestacy a grant, or grants, of letters of administration. This is a bureaucratic process which normally involves delay, expense and publicity. Where an individual owns assets in several jurisdictions any will has to be proved for probate purposes in each jurisdiction. Alternatively, the individual may have left separate wills dealing with assets in each jurisdiction in which case probate in each jurisdiction will be necessary.

The problems of obtaining a grant, or several grants, of either probate or letters of administration can be overcome by the use of a trust. If properly drafted, the trust can provide for the enjoyment of income and other assets during lifetime and then the passing on of the enjoyment of the assets to other members of the family following the death of the settlor. The trust can therefore achieve continuity without the public process of obtaining a grant and also without the delay, bureaucracy and expense which so often occurs following death.

Care is, however, essential when setting up a trust designed to circumvent the need for a grant of probate. The risk is that where a trust allows the settlor to retain effective control until death after which the trustees are intended to administer the assets, the trust will be construed as an attempt to provide for a will which, if not executed according to the formalities required for a will, will be invalid (*Re Pfrimmer's Estate* [1936] 2 DLR 460).

This is a dangerous trap for many so-called trusts under which the settlor retains effective control. Apart from being an invalid will such a trust might also be set aside as a sham as in *Rahman v Chase Bank (CI) Trust Company Ltd* (1991) JLR 103 or the settlor might be treated as still the equitable owner of the trust assets (see *Grupo Torras SA v Sheikh Fahad* (Supreme Court of Bahamas No. 72 of 1994-1/9/95)). The trust assets would then fall into the estate of the 'settlor' and the trustees would be acting unlawfully if they administered the assets without the authority of a grant of probate or letters of administration.

Tax planning

Trusts are often a useful way of mitigating income, capital gains and inheritance taxes. In some jurisdictions, however, such as the US and the UK, the scope for avoidance of most taxes through the use of offshore trusts is now severely limited for persons domiciled in those jurisdictions. Moreover, as governments switch the emphasis of their tax systems from direct to indirect taxation, trusts and other forms of direct taxation planning become less effective. The trend towards the taxation of expenditure through sales and value added taxes will make the use of offshore jurisdictions less and less relevant for those who do not actually live in those jurisdictions. It should be remembered that in the eighteenth century, when taxes were levied on goods and services and not directly on income or capital gains, there were no offshore jurisdictions with low taxes. The effect of modern comprehensive valued added and sales taxes in the context of private wealth planning does not yet seem to have been appreciated by tax advisers or tax authorities conditioned to think only in terms of direct taxation.

Providing for minors and those with disabilities

Trusts are frequently used to protect members of the family who are below the age of majority, who suffer from mental or other disabilities or who are thought to be irresponsible and not to be relied upon to look after assets given to them outright. Again, a trust can provide a useful way of providing for the needs of such individuals.

It should be added that where a person suffering from a disability such as mental illness is of full age it may be necessary to ensure that the person receives independent legal advice where a proposed trust affects property in which the individual already has a vested interest. This will be important where, for example, an individual suffering from a mental illness is to be persuaded by other relatives to settle his own property on protected trust for himself for life with a remainder to any spouse or children.

Protection from potential creditors

In recent years, offshore trusts have been used quite commonly in an attempt to protect an individual from the claims of future creditors. This has been, to a large extent, a development peculiar to the United States because of the huge awards of damages sometimes handed down by juries in civil cases. While there has been some interest in the use of trusts to provide protection from future creditors in other jurisdictions, asset protection trusts designed to frustrate creditors remain to a large extent a development driven by widespread and excessive litigation in the United States. A few jurisdictions, such as the Cook Islands, have gone out of their way to provide for legislation (described as 'ineptly drafted' by the Cook Islands Chief Justice in *515 South Orange Grove Owners Association v Orange Grove Partners and Others* (CA 1/95 6/11/95)) which will facilitate the protection of private assets of US citizens in particular, from creditors. Unfortunately, it sometimes appears that there is no clear line drawn between establishing a trust to provide protection against possible, but as yet unidentified claims and the use of trusts in an attempt to defraud existing creditors or creditors whose claims can reasonably be anticipated. It is becoming clear that asset protection trusts of this kind are not popular with judges, even in the Cook Islands. In the *Orange Grove* case the poor drafting of the two year limitation period enabled the Cook Islands Court of Appeal to uphold a Mareva injunction in favour of the creditors because the Court was able to commence the two-year period from the date of the California judgment for the creditors rather than the date when the cause of action arose. Further proceedings in the *South Orange Grove Case* (No 2) (1997/98) 1 OFLR 3 were also successful in establishing the ineffectiveness of another asset protection trust (debtor protector trust?) in issue.

Those jurisdictions which have promoted trust legislation specifically designed to protect assets from creditors have attracted widespread criticism and in practice it may well be that such trusts will often be disregarded by courts in other jurisdictions at the behest of creditors. Indeed, where, as in the Cook Islands and a few Caribbean jurisdictions, legislation permits the settlor to retain control over the trust assets, it is doubtful whether a trust, as generally understood, will exist and it is possible that a nomineeship, bailment of chattels or an agency will have been created. If this is so, and the trust assets are not physically situated in, say, the Cook Islands, the trust could well be disregarded or characterised as creating a different legal relationship by a court in another jurisdiction. A different approach was indicated in the Bahamas case of *Grupo Torras SA v Sheikh Fahad* (1994 No. 72, 1/9/95) where the court indicated that it would be possible to bypass arguments based on limitation of actions or the validity of a trust and treat the assets as in equity still owned by the settlor so that a tracing order could be made. While this decision has been criticised as not reflecting the true facts, the principle that has emerged is one of general application.

What, therefore, is likely to matter most in practice is the location of the assets rather than the location of the trust and the particular law governing the so-called trust. This is illustrated by *Duttle v Bandler & Kass* (1992 U.S. Dist. 23/6/92) where the US District Court for the Southern District of New York decided that it had jurisdiction over a purported Liechtenstein trustee holding US assets, despite the fact that the trustee refused to appear before the New York District Court. This was because, said the judge, it would be inequitable for a fraudulent settlor to keep assets from the jurisdiction of the US courts by selecting a foreign trustee who would not submit to the jurisdiction. In two other recent cases in the US, trusts have been set aside as the *alter ego* of the settlor (see *Deryll Wayne Pack v United States* and *United States v Reinhard P Muller*). The *alter ego* argument was also applied in the Bahamian case involving *Sheikh Fahad*.

If the assets are not in the jurisdiction where the creditor brings proceedings but the debtor is physically present, the court might threaten to imprison the debtor for contempt of court if the assets are not repatriated by the trustee (see *Re Larry Portnoy* 201 Banker 685 1996). Thus the debtor settlor might have no alternative but to direct the asset protection trustees to return the assets.

The choice of a jurisdiction for an asset protection trust is no longer an easy one and before making a decision it should be remembered that trusts have always been concerned with protecting assets. It is only in the last ten years or so that the term 'asset protection trust' has become a cliché meaning a trust set up with actual or potential creditors in mind. Such trusts do not enjoy universal support, indeed many trust companies and trust jurisdictions have deliberately decided to have nothing to do with them. An individual who is concerned about possible creditors' claims is probably most unwise to choose a jurisdiction which advertises itself as having asset protection trust legislation. Such a choice is likely to raise a presumption that the trust was an attempt to defeat creditors. A wiser approach is to use a straightforward trust jurisdiction with a reputation for sound trust law without any predisposition for particular types of trust business. Those jurisdictions with one or two year limitation periods designed to make it easier for debtors to escape their creditors will, when used, incur the wrath of judiciaries in other more conservative jurisdictions.

Ensuring that family assets endure through several generations

There is an old saying that a family can go from 'shirt sleeves to shirt sleeves in three generations'. In other words, the wealth generated by a self-made entrepreneur will have been dissipated by the third generation. There is no doubt that a trust can help to preserve a family fortune by preventing later generations from dissipating it. It is, however, essential to ensure that the trust is properly set up and that the assets have passed into the ownership of the trustees and are under their control. Failure to achieve this can result in the trust being set aside as a sham following proceedings by the second or third generation. This was illustrated in *Rahman v Chase Bank* [1991] JLR 103, a decision of the Royal Court of Jersey (Channel Islands). The *Rahman* case has been a salutary reminder of the dangers of allowing a settlor to retain direct control of assets which allegedly have been transferred to the control of trustees. There are many trusts where a similar situation exists and therefore these trusts are at risk not only from other members of the family who claim the assets but also from tax authorities and creditors.

Very often the asset to be preserved through future generations will be a family business built up by a successful entrepreneur. While the entrepreneur will want the business to continue after his death, it may well be that the second or third generations will wish to liquidate the company which owns the business, distribute the assets and then squander the proceeds. By transferring a controlling shareholding in a family company to trustees and restricting the circumstances in which the shares may be sold by the trustees, it will often be possible to ensure that a family business will continue on through several generations. The wishes of the settlor are often indicated in a nonbinding letter of wishes and further controls may be imposed on the trustees by the use of a protector whom the trustees must consult before taking any major decision, such as a significant change in the nature of the business, sale of the business to a takeover bidder or liquidation. However, the equitable rules affecting trustees and protectors in this sort of situation must be carefully observed. The trustees holding the majority shareholding must act responsibly and interfere if the directors contemplate a risky venture unsuitable for a company whose shares are held in a trust for the benefit of future generations. If there is a letter of wishes or protector the trustees must nevertheless exercise their proper and independent discretion in administering the trust and the protector must take into consideration the interests of the beneficiaries before exercising his powers. A protector does not usually owe any duties to the settlor and therefore where a protector regularly takes instructions from the settlor which are then slavishly followed by the trustees there is a serious risk of the trust becoming void as a sham. Alternatively the protector and the trustees could be sued for breach of duties owed to the beneficiaries.

Confidentiality

One of the major advantages of a trust is confidentiality. While the legal ownership is in the trustee and this will appear on various public records, the beneficial ownership and the various rights of the beneficiaries will not be a matter of public record because, unlike companies, there is no public register of trusts or beneficial interests. Indeed, most records of ownership such as those at a land registry or at a register of members maintained by a company, are usually prevented by statute from recording details of beneficial ownership. Some jurisdictions however, now provide for registration of trusts but this does not usually require registration of particulars and is mainly used as way of recording the date of creation of the trust. The practice of requiring registration of trusts is not, however, widely used because it may erode confidentiality, or be thought to do so, and usually results in additional government registration charges and is wrongly seen as comparable with the incorporation of a company. Any such view is wholly misguided because it conflicts with the fundamental equitable principle that a trust arises whenever a trust relationship exits between a trustee and a beneficiary and not from the administrative action of a registrar.

Disadvantages

Political risk

It is important to think ahead when a trust is to be set up. Some of the offshore jurisdictions which now offer modern trust laws are not free from political risk. In the past 20 years, several small offshore jurisdictions have suffered political upheavals of various kinds. Cyprus, Liberia, Malta and Panama are examples. It is therefore important when preparing a structure which is intended to last for many years, to choose a jurisdiction which has a good record of political stability. In the case of Malta it is now clear that the political problems in the years shortly after independence are now very much in the past and the jurisdiction is setting very high standards of regulation.

Potential for scandals

Many offshore jurisdictions have been anxious to attract business in order to generate revenue. Some in their anxiety to generate revenue, have not established scrupulous systems of regulation and have enacted legislation which provocatively overrides fundamental trust principles in an attempt to be unduly user friendly. As a result, there are risks in some offshore jurisdictions that those who have established trusts, and also incorporated companies, have done so for the purposes of money laundering, unacceptable forms of tax avoidance, tax evasion and the defrauding of creditors. Where this has happened, it is inevitable that eventually there will be scandals and the jurisdiction used will be criticised. It is then likely that criticism will taint all users of the jurisdiction.

There is a further problem now that the OECD countries, together with a few other large countries, have formed a Financial Action Task Force to review those offshore jurisdictions which are regarded as underregulated and uncooperative. This could lead to two tiers of offshore jurisdictions, those that are acceptable to the major countries of the world and those that are not acceptable. Those that are not acceptable could be excluded from the world's banking system and financial markets, and their users pressured into moving to other jurisdictions. Clearly, it is very much in the interest of a person establishing an offshore trust, or incorporating an offshore company, that the chosen offshore jurisdiction is within the first tier.

Letter of Wishes and Trust Protectors

Reference has been made already to letters of wishes and to the appointment of protectors and it may, therefore, be useful to summarise briefly some of the considerations that are involved with the preparation of letters of wishes and the appointment of protectors together with the duties and obligations which might be imposed on such persons.

The commonest way in which a settlor will try to influence the decisions taken by the trustees is by a letter of wishes. This should be a nonbinding confidential document which merely expresses the wishes of the settlor without binding the trustees to follow those wishes if the trustees feel that they should exercise their discretion in some other way. It is also prudent to prepare any letter of wishes some time after the trust deed has been executed in order to exclude any argument that the letter of wishes is in reality part of the trust instrument. This might be a possible inference if both documents are executed at the same time or within a short time of each other. Indeed in *Hartigan Nominees Pty Ltd v Rydge* (1992)

29 NSWLR 405, it was suggested in a minority judgment that a letter of wishes was a trust document because it was used by the trustees when deciding upon their duties under the trust deed. While this argument was not accepted by the other two judges, the dissenting judge presented a compelling argument which might be followed in later cases.

A letter of wishes should be expressed to be a confidential document between the settlor and the trustees so that its contents should not normally be disclosed to the beneficiaries or to a third party. There are, however, occasions when a tax authority will make inquiries about the existence of or contents of a letter of wishes. Provided it has been drafted carefully there should not be a problem in providing details, indeed refusal to cooperate is likely to add to any suspicion the tax authority may already have. Nevertheless, disclosure of the contents of a letter of wishes, whether to a tax authority or a beneficiary can cause problems for a trustee. It may assist a beneficiary in litigation against a trustee, particularly in the case of a beneficiary who wishes to challenge the validity of the trust or its proper administration.

A prudent alternative to a letter of wishes is for the trustee to record the settlor's wishes in a file note. This will be a confidential and wholly informal record that is not signed by the settlor. It will not be a letter of wishes as normally understood although it may have much the same effect. It is also difficult to see how it could be regarded as part of the trust deed or as fettering the discretion of the trustee.

A settlor who wishes to take matters a little further might consider appointing a protector. That person might be a family professional adviser, such as a solicitor or accountant, a member of the family or an old friend of the family. The normal role of a protector is that of liaising with the trustee to ensure that in general terms the settlor's wishes are followed through the exercise of negative controls. It is, nevertheless, essential that the protector's powers do not have the effect of removing from the trustees their overriding discretionary powers in relation to the administration of the trust. Where this is either provided for or can be shown to be the way the trust is in reality administered, the result may be that the trust is a sham or that in substance the protector is a trustee. Protectors are sometimes given powers which involve arbitrating in disputes between trustees and beneficiaries, reviewing the trust administration, advising on the migration of the trust to another jurisdiction and making decisions on the appointment of new trustees.

In general, a protector will have a duty to keep the trust under review. This duty probably does not have to be expressly set out in the trust deed because it arises from the fiduciary duty owed to the beneficiaries. A protector should keep a professional trustee up to the mark and, if not satisfied, will often have power to require the trustee to retire and be replaced by a new trustee. In exercising any power to dismiss a trustee and appoint a new trustee the protector will be under a fiduciary duty to exercise the power in the best interests of the beneficiaries and not for any other reason such as meeting the wishes of the settlor (see *Von Knieriem v Bermuda Trust Company Ltd and Another* (1994, Supreme Court of Bermuda, Civil Jurisdiction No.154)). More recently in the Isle of Man High Court (*Steele v Paz Ltd* (1995, Unreported 10/10/95-CH 1992/95)) the fiduciary role of a protector was also confirmed. It is therefore dangerous to assume, as is often the case, that a protector is the agent of the settlor. Like the trustees he does not have duties owed to the settlor unless the settlor is also a beneficiary. This runs contrary to the assumption that the appointment of a protector provides a method of enabling the settlor to exercise control over the

trustees, although it may in practice achieve this unless a dispute arises when the protector may be sued for breach of fiduciary duty owed to the beneficiaries.
It is very important that the protector's role remains advisory only. If a protector is given powers which enable him to direct the trustees in matters relating to the control and distribution of income or capital so that he is in effect the agent of the settlor this could render the trust void under the *Rahman* principle or result in the protector being treated as a quasi trustee. If such a protector is resident in a high tax jurisdiction an attempt might be made to tax the trust income and gains in that jurisdiction.

A practical disadvantage of having a protector is that the appointment can add another significant layer of cost if a professional protector, as opposed to a member of the family, is selected. Where the protector is incorporated and in the same ownership as the trust company there is a greater risk of both the trustee and the protector being sued for breach of fiduciary duty.

In general, it appears that letters of wishes and protectors are less popular than they were in the 1980s and are now seen by many as creating potentially serious problems. A prospective settlor is probably best advised to select a reliable professional trustee rather than to try to retain control of the trust assets and administration of the trust through a letter of wishes or a protector.

Choice of Jurisdiction

There are a number of factors which should be considered when deciding where to establish a trust. The main considerations are as follows.

Favourable tax environment

It is prudent to choose a jurisdiction for the trust which has a favourable tax environment. In general, the larger jurisdictions such as the United States, the United Kingdom, Australia, Canada and the Republic of Ireland do not have favourable tax jurisdictions although they do have excellent trust laws. In contrast, New Zealand has excellent trusts law with tax exemptions for the trust and the trustees provided that the settlor is not a New Zealand resident and the trust does not have New Zealand source income. If the beneficiaries are also not New Zealand residents there will be no New Zealand tax liability for them. A New Zealand trustee of a foreign trust has no reporting obligations in New Zealand and can claim the benefit of New Zealand's network of double taxation agreements for the beneficiaries.

Satisfactory trust law

It is most important to choose a jurisdiction with a satisfactory trust law. As the trust concept developed first in England as part of the law of equity, it is sensible to choose an equity law based jurisdiction. There are, however, some uncertain areas in English trust law which is one of the reasons why a number of offshore jurisdictions have introduced their own trust laws. These tend to consolidate many of the principles of English trust law while at the same time attempting to clarify areas of doubt and trying to deal with special problems such as those affecting settlors whose dispositions are subject to forced heirship rules. There are dangers in seeking to modify the traditional rules of equity in relation to trusts if a trust law goes beyond clarifying grey areas and seeks to change or repeal some of the fundamental principles of the law of trusts. In this regard the trust laws of some jurisdictions appear to be defective in that the trusts for which they provide do not always comply with what are traditionally regarded as fundamental requirements such as control and ownership of the trust assets vested in the trustees to the exclusion of the settlor.

This is particularly so in the case of those jurisdictions which have set out to attract so-called asset protection trusts by giving settlors wide powers of control over the trust assets which are inconsistent with the control that must be exercised by the trustee of a valid trust. It has also been suggested that a trust law can provide for a trustee to delegate all its discretion as well as its powers. If, however, a trustee were to delegate discretion the probable result is that the delegatee would become a new trustee because a trustee cannot, as a matter of equity, delegate all discretion and remain a trustee. There may also be problems for those jurisdictions like Jersey, Guernsey and Malta which are not equity based and whose trust laws, some have suggested, exist in a vacuum. The main difficulty appears to arise from the fact that a trust is a relationship between a trustee and a beneficiary which is recognised by and if necessary enforceable under the law of equity. A trust is not 'formed', 'incorporated' or 'created by registration' like a company. Moreover, as a trust is a creature of the law of equity which has developed over more than 800 years, it is not clear that a trust that is recognised by statute in a jurisdiction which has never formally adopted the law and principles of equity, is necessarily governed by all the same principles and can be enforced by all the same remedies as a truly equity based trust. It should be said that although the law and principles of equity were first developed in England they are now followed and developed in many jurisdictions. It follows that where a jurisdiction has adopted the law and principles of equity it will have adopted worldwide equity principles and therefore can follow the latest developments which are not necessarily the current English version of equity (see *Cusack & Cotter v Scroop Ltd* (1997/98) 1 OFLR 68 and *Cusack & Cotter v Pannell Kerr Forster & Crowe* (1997/98) 1 OFLR 409).

A trust that is recognised by the Jersey or Guernsey trust law will be regarded as a trust for the purposes of those statutes in any legal proceedings brought in Jersey or Guernsey but such a trust might be regarded as something different from an equity based trust by the courts of an equity jurisdiction. Provided, however, that the basic principles of equity trust law have been followed there should be no problem. The lack of equitable remedies for the enforcement of trusts may also be a problem. While these concerns may be academic and it may be that in practice there is unlikely to be a problem, it has to be remembered that many trusts are coming under attack from disappointed relatives of settlors, creditors and tax authorities with the result that the trust laws of the world are coming under closer scrutiny than ever before. Moreover, the user-friendly trust laws of some jurisdictions which have tried to make trusts achieve objectives that are inconsistent with the essentials of a trust are causing some advisers to question the validity of trusts recognised under such laws. Jersey, Guernsey, and certain civil law jurisdictions like Malta, have not made the mistakes of some offshore jurisdictions in this regard but nevertheless their trust laws do raise the question of whether they necessarily create trusts which will always be recognised and enforced as trusts by other jurisdictions. On the other hand, it should be said that the Jersey and Guernsey trust laws expressly preserve whatever trust law existed previously unless inconsistent with their trust laws. There clearly was some trust jurisprudence in Jersey and Guernsey before the Islands enacted their trust laws (see eg the Guernsey Royal Court decisions in *John Edward Lihou* (10/6/1837); *Priaulx Le Marchant & Co v Brehant* (9/2/1839); and *Ahier v Le Mesurier and Le Cocq* (17/6/1843)). The main difficulty with the trust concept in Jersey and Guernsey is that the Islands' legal systems have not apparently developed a range of equitable remedies for the enforcement of trusts. This could be important because ultimately trusts are about enforcement by beneficiaries using equitable remedies.

Good judiciary

This is extremely important. There are occasions when trustees need to apply to the court for directions and it is essential that they can instruct competent counsel to appear before a judge who understands trusts and the principles involved. A further matter of importance is that from time to time there are disputes between trustees and beneficiaries, and others such as tax authorities, when again it is necessary that the judiciary can cope with what are sometimes very complicated legal proceedings. The older trust jurisdictions such as Jersey, Guernsey, the Isle of Man and Bermuda are all well able to cope, indeed much modern trust case law has been developed in these jurisdictions. There are, however, inevitable doubts concerning the judiciaries of some of the newer jurisdictions. In a few cases trust jurisdiction is in the hands of what are in reality lay magistrates without formal legal qualifications.

Good professional services

This is also essential. It takes many years to develop trust expertise within a jurisdiction which is backed up by adequate legal, accountancy and banking services. Again, the older jurisdictions are very well served in this regard but some of the newer jurisdictions less so.

Good communications

Good communications are important where a trust is based in an offshore jurisdiction. If the settlor and beneficiaries are in other parts of the world, they must be able to communicate quickly and easily with the trustees. The settlor and beneficiaries may also wish to travel to the jurisdiction of the trust from time to time and therefore adequate telecommunications alone may not be sufficient: there should be adequate means of transport to and from the jurisdiction.

Political and economic stability

This has already been mentioned. It is of fundamental importance when putting together a structure involving a trust or trusts in offshore jurisdictions and the use of offshore asset holding companies.

Reputable and prudent supervision

Some of the older jurisdictions are well supervised and for that reason have long standing reputations for prudence and respectability. Jurisdictions such as Jersey, Guernsey, the Isle of Man and Bermuda are preeminent in this regard. Malta has also become a highly reputable and well regulated jurisdiction. Some of the newer jurisdictions, however, do not yet have reputations for thorough and prudent supervision of their users. Some are known for trying to attract business by being too user friendly at the expense of prudent supervision.

An up-to-date and user friendly company law

Most trust structures involve the holding of assets in companies the shares of which are held by a trust. In choosing a jurisdiction for offshore property holding companies, it is important to select one that has an up-to-date and user friendly company law. There are now many jurisdictions which have modern company laws and in most cases the bureaucracy has been reduced to a minimum. Unfortunately, the trend has perhaps gone too far in some offshore jurisdictions with much emphasis on being user friendly and little or no emphasis on regulation. This could result in courts around the world disregarding the separate corporate existence of such companies, indeed this process has already started. It should be added that proper regulation is costly and therefore results in higher incorporation and annual fees. In the long run incorporations which are cheap but unregulated may prove costly.

Which Trustee to Choose?

The choice of the right trustee depends very much on the nature of the trust and the particular circumstances. Clearly, it is important to choose an individual or a corporate trustee in whom the settlor can place absolute confidence. For a small trust established for family purposes, such as a trust to provide for a member of the family who suffers from a disability, there are strong arguments for choosing a member of the family or perhaps a professional adviser who is well-known to the family. In the case of a trust which is set up for the benefit of a number of beneficiaries, perhaps a discretionary trust, there are good reasons for using a bank trustee company or some other large institutional trustee. Such a trustee will have the backing of a large organisation, a substantial (and one hopes) well trained and intelligent staff, and ultimately substantial financial resources that can provide compensation if anything goes seriously wrong.

When choosing a professionally qualified trustee or a trust corporation, it will be necessary to take careful account of the cost. A professional trustee such as a solicitor or accountant will normally charge by reference to the time involved. Very often, a firm of solicitors or accountants will provide a separate trust company but this is unlikely to affect the basis for charging. In the case of a trust corporation, such as a trust company which is part of a banking group, charges may be related to the value of the fund or consist of a fixed charge when the trust is established, an annual fixed charge and a charge by reference to time for work involved. An institutional trustee should normally be expected to provide a set of annual accounts in return for the basic annual charge. A few corporate trustees still charge an 'exit charge' on retirement, a practice which is widely regarded as unsatisfactory. It may be acceptable to charge for administrative expenses when a trustee retires but a fixed or ad valorem charge which is not related to the cost of any work involved might be seen as designed to discourage a change of trustee. If that is what is intended such an approach is inconsistent with the fiduciary obligations of a trustee even if apparently permitted by the trust instrument. Overcharging is a breach of trust. In general, most corporate trustees no longer charge fees on an ad valorem basis.

It is usually more satisfactory, and generally cheaper, if there is a fixed charge when the trust is set up together with an annual fixed charge and an additional charge for any special work done. The better corporate trustees will treat the fixed annual charges as covering their role as a trustee and the provision of annual accounts. Any additional work will normally be charged out on a time basis. Some large trust companies are prepared to quote a fixed annual fee without the addition of charges for time expended once they have considered the nature of the trust, the complexity of the administration and the amount of the funds involved.

The fees charged by corporate trustees vary a great deal, but it does not necessarily follow that those charging high fees always provide better service. It is sometimes the case that large fees reflect the costs of a large and costly organisation as well as the additional compliance costs which can affect very large trustees whose aggregate trust assets require them to disclose their interests in listed companies because the trigger point for disclosure is passed. Smaller trust companies do not have the same overheads and compliance costs to pass on to their customers and they often have excellent back offices capable of coping with the large quantities of paper work and computer records that trust administration can generate. When assessing the fees charged by a trustee company and making a final decision on the choice of a trustee, it is always important to ensure that it has a back office capable of coping with the proper administration of the trust. 'Cubical' trust companies run by another entity may not be able to meet the administrative requirements of some trusts and will also be subcontracting the administration to another person. The fact that the chosen trustee is not actually administering the trust but has delegated this to another organisation is far from satisfactory and may, in itself, amount to a breach of trust.

In choosing a trustee, particularly a bank trust company, it is important to discover whether it is assumed by the banking group that other bank services such as general banking and investment management facilities will be used by the bank trustee company. Not all banking groups understand the nature of a trust and the fact that it involves a special relationship between the trustee and the beneficiaries. There have been cases where banks and other large institutions have 'sold' trusts as though they were 'products' with the intention of charging additional fees for providing banking and investment management services. Unfortunately, the pressures of modern marketing techniques are often incompatible with the relationship which is required by law to exist between a trustee and the beneficiaries of a trust. A bank trustee company which uses other services within the banking group should always make this practice clear to the settlor and provide details of the charges involved before the trust is set up. If this is not done there may be a conflict of interest resulting in a breach of trust by the trust company which could be sued by the beneficiaries.

Where the practice of a bank trustee company is to use other services within the banking group, great care should be taken by the trustee to ensure that the fiduciary obligations owed to the beneficiaries take priority over the understandable loyalty that may exist to other companies within the banking group. If the trust company is run in disregard of the fiduciary obligations of a trustee, and regard is had only to commercial considerations, the likelihood is that sooner or later the bank trustee company will be sued for breach of trust. In recent years, there have been a number of successful actions brought against bank trustee companies (see, for example, *Bartlett v Barclays Bank Trust Co Ltd* [1980] 1 All ER 139 and *West v Lazard Brothers Co (Jersey) Ltd* (1993) Jersey Unreported Judgments 136 (18/10/93)).

Offshore Companies

There are now many offshore jurisdictions offering company incorporations. Some of these jurisdictions, in a frantic effort to obtain business copy each other and sometimes enact new laws with only the short term objective of marketing their companies in mind. At first sight, it is difficult for a professional adviser to decide how the choice of jurisdiction should be made although like sharks in a feeding frenzy most turn first to the British Virgin Islands for an international business company.

In general terms, it is possible to divide the jurisdictions offering offshore company incorporations into nine categories. These are as follows:

1. The Caribbean international business companies' jurisdictions

The most active are the British Virgin Islands, the Bahamas, Barbados, Belize, St. Kitts, Anguilla, Cayman Islands, Nevis, and the Turks and Caicos Islands. Of these, the British Virgin Islands is by far the most popular although some of the other Caribbean jurisdictions offer an equally good and sometimes cheaper products with, in some respects, more attractive legislation. It is, however, necessary to sound a warning note about the concept of the international business company, simple, quick and cheap as it may be. In essence, the concept involves a jurisdiction with two company laws, one for those who wish to carry on business within the particular jurisdiction which is subject to wide ranging disclosure requirements and the other designed for those who do not wish to carry on any business or do anything at all in the particular jurisdiction. Indeed, the basis of an international business company is, or seems to be, that the jurisdictions offering this product usually take no interest in who the beneficial owner of the company is going to be or the purpose for which the beneficial owner intends to use the company, provided that nothing is done within the jurisdiction itself!

For most traditional company lawyers, there is an uneasy feeling that this is not really what company law is all about. Indeed many are left wondering whether the House of Lords would have reached a different decision in the celebrated case of *Salomon v Salomon & Company* [1897] AC 22 (which confirmed that a company run by one person was a separate legal entity and not a mere agent of the owner) had the case concerned an international business company. Given that in some of the Caribbean jurisdictions there is very little attempt to control who owns international business companies and in none of the Caribbean jurisdictions is any attempt made by a regulatory authority to discover beneficial ownership as a condition for incorporation, it is probably only a matter of time before the larger jurisdictions, which make up the members of the International Fiscal Task Force, bring pressure to bear on those jurisdictions offering unregulated international business companies forcing them to introduce disclosure of beneficial ownership and other forms of regulation such as public registers of directors and shareholders.

2. The new Pacific and Indian Ocean international business company jurisdictions

The main jurisdictions are the Cook Islands, Western Samoa, Vanuatu, Labuan and Mauritius. These jurisdictions are as yet largely without track records in relation to their international business companies.

3. The Channel Islands and Isle of Man tax exempt companies

Jersey, Guernsey, Alderney and the Isle of Man provide for a special category of tax exempt company which, although resident, is treated as nonresident in relation to offshore activities. A fixed annual fee of £500 is payable for this status although there has been discussion in Jersey of the abolition of this fee. The principal advantage is that an exempt company can be managed and controlled from each island and can still be treated as nonresident so that it is not necessary to arrange for directors' meetings to be held in some other jurisdiction in order to achieve nonresident status. The exempt company fee was introduced to discourage the use of Sark, another Channel Island, as a place for the holding of board meetings and the avoidance of Jersey and Guernsey income tax. While this ended the 'Sark Lark' mark 1, the mark 2 version involves the use of Sark as a provider of directorships for Carribean international business companies which operate in Jersey and Guernsey with little or no regulation. Alderney has power regulate foreign companies operating in the Island and is expected to introduce rules requiring the filing of information by such companies.

4. The European international business company or international company

These are provided for by Jersey, Guernsey and Alderney, the Isle of Man and Gibraltar. These jurisdictions do not offer equivalents to Caribbean, Indian Ocean or Pacific Ocean international business companies. The European concept, which began in Jersey and Guernsey, is largely tax driven. Although the concept varies a little from jurisdiction to jurisdiction, the basic idea is that these jurisdictions offer variable tax rate companies. For example, in the case of an Alderney or Guernsey international company, it is possible to negotiate a tax rate with the Guernsey Tax Administrator of between something over 0 per cent and not more than 30 per cent. This is then fixed for five years. These companies are useful for the purpose of tax treaty planning and for avoiding the effects of controlled foreign corporation legislation in the jurisdiction of a parent company. These companies can also be used for offshore treasury functions and captive insurance.

5. Jurisdictions catering for special purpose companies

This includes insurance or ship and aircraft registration companies. In the category of insurance, Guernsey is at present the fastest growing centre for captive insurance companies but the Isle of Man, Bermuda and the Republic of Ireland also have extensive insurance and captive insurance company business. Jurisdictions well-known for ship and aircraft registration include Bermuda, the Bahamas, Liberia, Malta, Panama, the Isle of Man, Guernsey and Jersey. Guernsey has very recently developed a new concept which allows a company to be divided into separate self-contained compartments or cells which operate independently of each other. The companies are particularly attractive to the fund management and insurance industries at whose request they have been provided. There may be other situations in which cell companies can be used but it is too early to judge what they might be. The essence of a cell company is that each cell is separated with its own cell assets. If a cell is wound up the liquidator and creditors have no rights as to the assets of other cells.

6. Jurisdictions offering guarantee companies and hybrid companies

These are used for tax planning purposes and as alternatives to trusts. The main jurisdictions include the Isle of Man, many of the Caribbean jurisdictions, Alderney and recently Guernsey. A hybrid company is a guarantee company with shareholders as well as guarantee members.

7. Jurisdictions offering limited duration or limited life companies

These are known in the US as limited liability companies. These corporate bodies are in substance a form of corporate partnership in which all members must be involved in the management. Despite corporate personality they are 'transparent' for all tax purposes, that is to say all income, gains, expenses and credits are attributed to the individual members on a pro rata basis. These corporate entities effectively provide for a simple form of corporate entity with limited liability for domestic use by small traders or as a simple asset holding entity. They can be used in much the same way as the Caribbean and other international business companies and have great attractions for US persons because they avoid the heavy tax liabilities affecting conventional non-transparent offshore subsidiary companies. This form of incorporation is now possible in the Bahamas, the Cayman Islands, the Turks & Caicos Islands, Nevis and the Isle of Man.

8. *Jurisdictions offering tax treaty benefits*

Although most offshore jurisdictions do not offer tax treaty opportunities because of their low tax rates, there are a few which nevertheless are able to do so. Thus, Cyprus has an excellent double taxation treaty network with Eastern Europe, Madeira has advantages through its connections with Portugal and therefore the European Union as a whole, Malta has a wide range of useful tax treaties and Mauritius has useful double taxation treaties with China, India and South Africa.

9. *Jurisdictions offering geographical advantages*

Various offshore jurisdictions offer geographical advantages, eg Jersey, Guernsey, Alderney, Isle of Man and the Republic of Ireland (Europe), Cyprus (Eastern Europe), Bermuda, the Bahamas, the Cayman Islands, Panama (USA), Mauritius (India), Hong Kong, Singapore and the Philippines (SE Asia and in the case of Hong Kong, China).

Having considered the nine categories into which offshore company jurisdictions can be divided, the choice of a category will normally be indicated by the particular requirements of the client. These may involve political or image considerations, a particular business sector such as shipping, aircraft, captive insurance, or guarantee or hybrid companies or quantity and cost where a large number of companies are required as asset holding companies for a major international group structure. Usually once the requirements of a client are taken into account, it is relatively easy to arrive at the appropriate category from which to choose a jurisdiction.

Before making the choice from within a particular category, it is most important to exercise prudent judgment. Reservations concerning the future of the international business company concept have already been expressed. The main problem is that the enormous success of the British Virgin Islands international business company registry could well result in scandals in the absence of prudent regulation. Many British Virgin Islands international business companies have been set up for artificial tax planning purposes and this has given the jurisdiction a questionable reputation with many tax authorities. It is possible that some BVI IBCs have been set up as fronts for international criminal activities. This is particularly so because many have been incorporated with bearer shares so that tracing beneficial ownership is almost impossible. Without some control over the beneficial ownership of these companies, the risk of international business companies falling into the hands of undesirables is significant, bearing in mind that in 1996, for example, 32,000 BVI IBCs were incorporated (with in total 210,260 companies on the register at 31 December, 1996). It is only a matter of time before scandals involving BVI companies occur and the danger then will be that bona fide users of the jurisdiction could be tainted by association. One only has to look back at the flight of companies out of Panama in the 1980s to see what might happen in the absence of adequate supervision. The danger of taking BVI companies and those connected with them for granted without first making careful inquiries was illustrated in *Shanghai International Capital Ltd v China Finance Trust and Investment Corporation* 1995, No A994, a decision of the Hong Kong High Court. The case concerned a Mareva injunction to freeze the assets of the defendant, a company with assets of US$10 million. The solicitor acting for the plaintiff failed to make proper inquiries as to the bona fides of his client and obtained the injunction in the belief that the plaintiff company was a reputable merchant bank. In reality it was a BVI company with assets of HK$55 and US$180. The upshot, when the truth emerged, was that the plaintiff's solicitor was ordered to pay the whole of the defendant's costs as damages for the inconvenience caused.

There may be other serious problems that will emerge with time in relation to the use of international business companies. An example arose in 1991 in relation to a case decided by the Chief Justice of the Cook Islands Sir Clinton Roper. In *Century Insurance Ltd v Credit Lyonnais Bank Nederland NV* (1991) Plaint No. 4/91 (12/4/91) it was held that for technical constitutional law reasons a Cook Island's international business company registered as an insurance company could not obtain leave of the Cook Island's court for service of legal proceedings outside the Islands.

There appears to be a willingness on the part of many judges to disregard companies incorporated for tax planning purposes or for the purpose of avoiding liability to creditors where the use of a company is contrived and artificial. This is illustrated by a number of recent cases. For example in *United States v Reinhard P Muller* (US Court of Appeals for Eleventh Circuit; 77 AFTR 2d Par 96-457, No 94-3617), a case which involved tax evasion, the judge ignored the separate personalities of the individual (for whom the company had been incorporated) and the company which was held to be the *alter ego* of the individual. The judge commented that the 'observance of the fiction of separate existence would...promote fraud or injustice'.

In *InverWorld Inc v CTC* (Memo, 1996 301), another US case, an aggressive tax avoidance scheme involving the use of a foreign company to separate foreign from domestic activities so as to restrict US tax liability to income from domestic activities was successfully challenged by the IRS. This was achieved largely by challenging the scheme as artificial.

It should not be assumed that attacks on the artificial use of companies is confined to the United States. Recently in Hong Kong, a parent company and its wholly owned subsidiary were treated as one and the same in deciding the liability for profits tax of the parent company (see *CIR v Magna Industrial Ltd)* [1996] HKRC 90-078. This decision was reversed on appeal ([1997] HKLRD 173) but the danger of a judicial attack on the artificial use of companies remains a real one. It appears that in cases involving tax avoidance or evasion, and in cases involving fraud on creditors, the courts of several jurisdictions are prepared to lift the corporate veil or apply the *'alter ego'* theory. It seems likely that the next decade will see a large number court decisions in which corporate veils will be lifted.

In addition to the particular requirements of a client, there are, of course, standard criteria which are relevant in selecting an offshore jurisdiction for incorporation of a company. Thus in choosing a jurisdiction for the incorporation of a company, one will need to take account of such things as political and geographical considerations, time zones, the availability of professional expertise, judicial expertise, reputation and the likelihood of scandals. There are also matters which relate specifically to company law such as disclosure requirements. The attitudes to disclosure vary a good deal among offshore jurisdictions. Some require disclosure of registered shareholders, some require disclosure of beneficial ownership to a licensed agent, some require disclosure of directors, some, such as the Channel Islands and Malta require *confidential* disclosure of beneficial ownership *to a regulator* and others require no disclosure of any kind.

Where no disclosure is required, an offshore company jurisdiction may have sown the seeds of its own destruction. In contrast, although confidential disclosure of beneficial ownership as required in the Channel Islands (Alderney, Guernsey and Jersey) has not proved good for business from South East Asia, it is interesting to note that a recent survey of European independent financial advisers rated Jersey and Guernsey (together with Alderney) as the second and third most confidential of offshore jurisdictions. There are many in South East Asia who have been unhappy with the prospect of having to disclose beneficial ownership, even confidentially, to a faceless regulator on the other side of the globe and have therefore rejected the Channel Islands and incorporated their companies in places such as the British Virgin Islands. However, it should be stressed that confidential disclosure of beneficial ownership is precisely what it is stated to be, confidential. Confidential disclosure of beneficial ownership is, therefore, no problem for an honest person, indeed it is a hallmark of respectability to be accepted as a suitable beneficial owner of a Jersey, Guernsey or Alderney company. All that is involved is disclosure of the name or names of the beneficial owners to, in the case of Jersey, the Registrar of Companies and in the case of Alderney and Guernsey, the Financial Services Commission, in order that the names can be run through a computer data base and checked for any record of dishonest or criminal activities. Ironically the reputable and well-regulated offshore company jurisdictions are, because they are reputable and well regulated, favourite targets for money laundering and organised crime.

Another matter to be considered when choosing an offshore jurisdiction is administrative regulation. Matters such as the making of annual returns and returns of other information for inclusion on public or private registers can be time consuming and expensive. Most offshore jurisdictions now realise that much of the information which formerly had to be returned for small companies was of no real use and can result in serious storage problems for the registry. In consequence many filing requirements have either been removed altogether or greatly relaxed. The lack of a public register of charges to protect the priority of a lender's interest is, however, a disadvantage because banks are reluctant to lend to companies incorporated in jurisdictions which do not provide for formal registration and protection of creditors interests. This is a weakness with some of the international business company jurisdictions which have tried to oversimplify their legislation.

It will also be necessary to consider the flexibility of the constitution permitted for a company incorporated in an offshore jurisdiction. Again, most offshore jurisdictions have taken this into account. For example, most provide for single member companies, have a requirement that only one director is necessary, provide for no par value shares, allow share purchase and redemption, provide for flexibility as to names (together with a procedure for reservation of names) and have abolished the *ultra vires* rule. Many allow names in another language and some allow the memorandum to be in any of a number of specified foreign languages.

Not all offshore jurisdictions permit bearer shares. The advantages of bearer shares have been greatly exaggerated, particularly in South East Asia, with little or no attention being paid to the dangers. Bearer shares can create serious problems. If lost or stolen, the control of the company can pass to third parties. But most important of all to professional advisers, it is not possible to comply with due diligence obligations where bearer shares are issued unless the bearer share certificates are retained by the adviser on safe deposit. In general, many of the advantages of bearer shares, without the disadvantages, can be achieved by using nominee shareholders or by using guarantee or hybrid companies.

Another matter which is regarded as important is corporate mobility or migration which is often misleadingly called redomiciliation. This has become fashionable and most international business company jurisdictions provide for it, as does the *New Zealand Companies Act* 1993. Some jurisdictions also provide for merger provisions which enable a company in one offshore jurisdiction to leave and merge with a company in another. It should be said that not all the problems which these concepts create have been solved. In the case of a merger of, for example, a Panamanian company into a British Virgin Island company, there can be problems where shares are held by the Panamanian company in a Hong Kong company. How does the Hong Kong company register the change of shareholding? Have the shares been transferred or have they passed from one company to the other by transmission? This is important for Hong Kong stamp duty purposes and also for the purpose of completing the entries in the register of members of the Hong Kong company. There is also the difficulty that some foreign courts might not recognise the concept of corporate mobility. For example, a French court might decide that a migrated company has in substance been put into liquidation in the jurisdiction of original registration and reincorporated in the jurisdiction of so-called immigration. This will be important where the assets, or some of them, are in France. There is also a view that a company which owes its existence to the fact that it is recorded on a register in a particular jurisdiction will cease to exist when it is removed from that register and therefore there is nothing to transfer to the other jurisdiction. It may be that this problem can be covered by an express legislative provision but until tested in the courts it is difficult to say for certain that migration is technically possible.

In conclusion, something should be said about certain special types of companies. Reference has already been made to guarantee and to hybrid companies. Guarantee companies are companies which do not have limitation of liability by reference to shares but by reference to sums which the members have guaranteed to pay to meet the companies' debts in the event of a winding up. Hybrid companies are companies with members whose liability is limited by shares and also with members whose liability is limited by guarantee. Although guarantee companies have been widely used for many years in several jurisdictions for charities, university colleges and clubs, until recently both ordinary guarantee companies and hybrid companies were thought to be of little other use.

Guarantee and hybrid companies have, however, become important recently in hitherto unexpected ways. Guarantee companies were thought to be useful in connection with capital gains tax planning in the United Kingdom and in other jurisdictions where taxes affecting companies have been drafted in such a way that they only apply to companies limited by shares. It may, therefore, be possible to avoid the effects of certain tax legislation by simply not having a share capital. This particular loophole was, however, closed in the United Kingdom by the *Finance Act* 1996.

Hybrid companies have a number of other uses not related to tax planning. The first concerns the use of a hybrid company to achieve many of the objects of a trust without establishing a formal trust which will be subject to the strict equitable rules requiring the control of assets by trustees and governing trustees in the way they exercise their fiduciary duties. For example, it is possible to establish a hybrid company in such a way that the shareholders effectively own and control the assets for the benefit of beneficiaries who are the guarantee or 'beneficial' members. It is possible to draft the articles of association so that additional guarantee members (beneficiaries) are introduced from time to time and also to provide for a 'protector' by giving one shareholder special powers. If necessary, the person who is the effective 'settlor' can be given a controlling shareholding or controlling directorship. This approach is useful where a settlor wishes to retain more control than the trust concept will permit or where the settlor is domiciled in a jurisdiction which either does not recognise trusts or has forced heirship rules. Since all jurisdictions normally recognise companies, wherever incorporated, the problems caused by a formal trust disappear. The Isle of Man, Alderney and Guernsey hybrid company legislation is particularly useful where an alternative 'trust' structure is needed. Amendments are in hand which should make Alderney guarantee and hybrid companies even more useful.

Other advantages of hybrid companies include the achieving of confidentiality for beneficial ownership through guarantee membership which is not recorded on a register of shareholders (this has many of the advantages of bearer shares without the disadvantages), achieving transparency for US tax purposes and exchange control planning because the creation of new guarantee members (ie new beneficiaries) does not involve the transfer of any cash or the use of a security.

Conclusion

The uses of offshore trust and company jurisdictions are now complex and varied. As the wealth of individuals increases, there is an increasing tendency for the control of their wealth to move away from the larger jurisdictions. Some large countries may view this development with alarm and wish to take preventive action, but it is probably now too late for the process to be stopped altogether. While many countries have agreed on the need to control international activities involving money laundering and the more extreme forms of tax avoidance, and they may be successful in limiting such activities, the uses (and abuses) of offshore jurisdictions will continue to multiply. Nevertheless, as most offshore jurisdictions are small and unable to resist serious pressure from large and powerful countries, and some are potentially unstable, professional advisers would be wise to exercise caution in selecting a jurisdiction for a trust or company. The possibility that the trusts and corporate products of some underregulated offshore jurisdictions will be excluded from access to the international banking system and financial markets should not be overlooked.

Peter Willoughby OBE, JP, LL.B., LL.M., TEP, is a consultant with Deacons Graham & James. He is also a Visiting Professor of Law at the City University of Hong Kong, a Visiting Professorial Fellow at the University of London and an Honorary Lecturer at the Universities of Hong Kong and Macquarie. He is a regular contributor to various international journals on taxation and trust matters.

THE OFFSHORE JURISDICTIONS

Alderney
Anguilla
Antigua & Barbuda
Bahamas
Barbados
Belize
Bermuda
British Virgin Islands
Cayman Islands
Cook Islands
Costa Rica
Cyprus
Gibraltar
Guernsey
Isle of Man
Jersey
Jordan
Labuan
Liechtenstein
Luxembourg
Madeira
Malta
Mauritius
Netherlands
Singapore
Switzerland
Turks & Caicos Islands
Uruguay

ALDERNEY

Peter Willoughby

Introduction

General

Alderney, which is the third largest island in the British Channel Islands, lies 25 miles north east of Guernsey and 8 miles north west of France. The island is approximately 4 miles long and 1 1/2 miles wide and, in relative terms, is far less heavily populated than Jersey or Guernsey. The island has a large deep water harbour with berthing for small freighters and oil tankers, a fishing fleet and moorings for 100 yachts. A modern marina is planned for 200 yachts. Alderney has one small and attractive town, St. Anne, which has good facilities such as hotels, shops and offices. Five UK clearing banks have branches in Alderney as does one UK building society finance company. There are locally qualified advocates, two international lawyers who provide services for offshore investors, accountancy firms and several trust companies based in the island. Guernsey advocates and accountants also practise in Alderney.

History

Alderney, like the other Channel Islands, has been part of the Duchy of Normandy since before the Norman conquest of England in 1066. It was from this date that the link with the United Kingdom was established. Alderney, although British, is neither part of the United Kingdom nor a member of the European Union, the island having developed its own laws and customs over the centuries. Until the second world war, Alderney was an entirely separate jurisdiction. Alderney was evacuated immediately before the German occupation of the Channel Islands and by 1945 the island had become derelict. It then became clear that the prewar autonomy was economically impractical and in 1948 Alderney assumed dependence upon Guernsey for certain core services. It is for this reason that the Guernsey Income Tax Law applies to Alderney. Since 1948, Alderney has retaken control of a few core services but only time will tell whether the island can resume complete autonomy.

Constitutional

Under the 1948 legislation those functions of government which were not transferred to Guernsey were transferred to the then newly established States of Alderney. The States comprise an elected President and 12 elected States Members. As a consequence of the transfer of responsibility for core services to Guernsey, two members of the States of Alderney represent Alderney in the Guernsey States of Deliberation. Alderney's 1948 constitution also provides for the holding of People's Meetings each month before each meeting of the States of Alderney.

The Legal System

The primary source of common law in Alderney is, in theory, the customary laws of Normandy. The customary laws relating to real property and succession have, however, been replaced by statute law. Alderney is unique in the Channel Islands in having a statutory system of land registration. In practical terms, and particularly in the case of offshore finance centre operations, Norman customary laws are of almost no relevance to the modern legal system. In many areas of civil and commercial law, the Alderney legal system is separate from that prevailing in Guernsey. Thus, Alderney has its own legislation governing companies, real property, arbitration, building and development, wills and employment. Trusts in Alderney are governed by Alderney customary law, which takes into account the principles of the English law of Equity in the absence of a choice of law provision indicating that the law of some other jurisdiction is to apply. There is no statutory trust law but consideration is being given to this and to the express application of the principles of Equity.

The courts

The Court of Alderney has 7 Jurats, who are appointed by the British Home Office. The Court has unlimited jurisdiction in civil matters but its criminal jurisdiction is limited to non-indictable offences. Original criminal jurisdiction over indictable offences committed in Alderney resides with the Royal Court of Guernsey. Appeals from the Court of Alderney lie to the Royal Court of Guernsey and thence to the Guernsey Court of Appeal and to the Privy Council in London.

Taxation

There are no capital gains, inheritance, value added or sales taxes. Income tax is levied at 20 per cent on the worldwide income of residents by the Guernsey Income Tax Authority. Alderney and Guernsey levy separate property taxes (rates) on Alderney property owners, but the combined total is low by international standards. Excise duties are charged on alcohol and tobacco. A form of stamp duty is levied at 5.5 per cent on the value of real property on sale or on the value of shares sold in a real property holding company. This is payable by the purchaser in addition to Land Registry fees.

Economy

Alderney's economy is based on tourism, agriculture, fishing and financial services. The island is becoming very popular with private fliers both as an interesting place to visit and as a cheap refuelling stop.

Recreation

Alderney has an attractive golf course with spectacular sea views and views of the French coast. Other sports include sailing, fishing, tennis, cricket, football and snooker. The island has its own unique flora and fauna and receives many visitors interested in bird watching. The cliff walks are popular and the beaches clean. There are bird sanctuaries on Burhou island and on two rocky islets which are within Alderney's jurisdiction. There is an interesting and well laid out museum with exhibits dating from the bronze age and the Roman occupation. Alderney has the only working railway in the Channel islands, which carries stone from the quarry to repair the breakwater and tourists to the quarry for barbecues.

Communications

Alderney is well served by Aurigny Air Services with frequent daily flights to Southampton airport which has an express rail link to London, together with many daily flights to Caen, Dinard, Guernsey and Jersey from which there are connecting flights to London, Paris and other European cities. There is an express rail link from Caen to Paris. At present, there are no regular ferry services to and from Alderney other than for carriage of weekly freight. However, a regular passenger ferry service to and from France may start in 1998. Cruise ships visit Alderney in the summer.

Time Zone

The time zone is the same as for the United Kingdom although there is pressure to adopt the French time system of GMT + 1 hour in winter and + 2 hours in summer.

Language

The language spoken is English although many islanders also speak French.

Alderney as a Community

The island is fortunate in having a happy and united community which is free from most of the problems which affect larger countries. There is an almost complete lack of bureaucracy and serious crime. Houses and cars are rarely locked. There are some 800 vehicles on the island, which is free from traffic congestion and air pollution. The People's Meetings held monthly ensure that matters to be debated in States Meetings are understood by the electorate which has an opportunity to comment.

Alderney's Offshore Services

Although a small and less well-known jurisdiction than Jersey or Guernsey, the island has had its own company law since 1894. In addition, for many years there have been a number of trust companies administered in Alderney. Alderney is not, therefore, a new jurisdiction, even if it is perceived as such by some who until recently had never heard of the island.

For over twenty years, there had been pressure to update the companies law and in 1992 consideration was given to the establishment of an International Business Companies Register along the lines of the registries in the Caribbean. It was, however, decided to replace the 1894 statute with modern legislation that would meet the needs of those requiring local incorporation while also offering attractive and well-regulated companies for sale in the international market place. The idea of an IBC register was therefore abandoned. Alderney is governed by Guernsey legislation with regard to money laundering.

Corporate Law

New Companies Law

The *Companies (Alderney) Law* 1994 was passed by the States of Alderney in July 1994. By coincidence, this was almost exactly 100 years after the enactment of the island's first company law in 1894. The new law received Royal Assent in December 1994 and came into force in May 1995.

Until the *Companies (Jersey) Law* 1991, the Channel Islands had made no serious attempt to modernise its company laws. For those wishing to incorporate well-regulated companies in the Channel Islands, the new Alderney law provides an alternative to incorporation in Jersey or Guernsey. Indeed, for those using Guernsey or Jersey as a location for trusts, there will be attractions in incorporating property holding companies in Alderney rather than in Guernsey or Jersey. While Guernsey has amended its companies law to provide for some important modernisation, it has yet to undertake a complete overhaul of legislation which in some respects requires updating.

The main features of the *Companies (Alderney) Law* 1994 are:

- A minimum membership of one person; incorporation by registration; distinction between public and private companies; abolition of the *ultra vires* rule; provision for companies limited by guarantee with or without a share capital;
- Provision for the adoption of pre-incorporation contracts; issue of fractional shares and shares of no par value; provision for purchase of own shares;
- Simplified accounting records for private companies without the need to appoint an auditor; private companies need only one director;
- Simplified annual returns for private companies, which include guarantee and hybrid companies;
- Directors to be fit and proper persons;
- Special resolutions to be passed by a three-quarters majority of those attending and voting at a general meeting in person or by proxy;
- Public companies to meet additional reporting requirements; and
- Modern provisions to protect members and creditors, including fraudulent and wrongful trading provisions; modern provisions for amalgamations, arrangements, investigations and winding up.

Alderney companies are under the general supervision of the Guernsey Financial Services Commission as well the Alderney Registrar of Companies. The main significance of this is that confidential disclosure of the beneficial ownership of any new company must be made to the Commission before incorporation can be completed.

The Confidential Disclosure Requirement

The reason for confidential disclosure is to exclude incorporation by those with track records involving fraud, money laundering or other dishonest dealing. Apart from that, the disclosure requirement is a formality which need not give rise to any cause for concern. Indeed, acceptance by the Guernsey Financial Services Commission of an incorporation in Alderney should be regarded as a hallmark of respectability.

The disclosure requirement can usually be completed in a matter of hours and need have no serious effect on the time taken to incorporate. As incorporation under the new law will be by registration and not by application to the Court, Alderney incorporations can usually be completed quickly and with minimal bureaucracy.

Costs

The cost of incorporation, inclusive of Government fees and taxes (£100) for a company with a share capital of £10,000 is usually about £600. The annual professional fee is about £350, exclusive of the yearly Government fee of £100. In addition to these annual costs, companies owned by nonresidents of Alderney and Guernsey can apply for exemption from Guernsey/Alderney Income Tax on payment of an annual fee of £500.

Unlike the position in Jersey, an Alderney (or Guernsey) company can change to exempt and back to non-exempt status as its income position changes.

Types of Companies

From a taxation point of view there are two basic types of Alderney companies to be considered – taxable and exempt. However, there is also a third category, the International Company, which can negotiate its tax rate with the authorities at any rate above 0 per cent up to a maximum 30 per cent. These companies are used for group financing, captive insurance, industrial and commercial activities, overseas investment and overcoming restrictions in controlled foreign corporation legislation.

From a companies law standpoint, there are four types of companies available:

- Public companies;
- Private companies;
- Guarantee companies; and
- Guarantee companies with a share capital.

The distinction between public and private companies is that a private company may not issue shares to the public. In general terms, the disclosure requirements for public companies are more onerous.

The provision of modern and flexible legislation to allow for guarantee and hybrid companies (ie guarantee companies with a share capital) is important and in this regard Alderney has been more advanced than Jersey. These companies can be useful for achieving tax savings in some jurisdictions, as alternatives to purpose trusts, such as those provided for in Bermuda, and as alternatives to conventional trusts where it is intended to give the settlor wide powers.

The Advisory Committee on Alderney Company Law

With the object of keeping Alderney's company law up-to-date, the Finance Committee of the Alderney States has appointed an Advisory Committee on Alderney Company Law. This Committee is made up of practitioners with international as well as local experience, the law draftsman and a representative of the Guernsey Financial Services Commission. Following reports made by the Committee in May 1996 and September 1997, a number of amendments are to be made to the *Companies (Alderney) Law* 1994. These include simplification of the distinction between public and private companies, greater flexibility for guarantee and hybrid companies, provision for the migration of companies and provision for cell companies. The other changes are largely technical, but designed to improve the efficiency and attractiveness of the law from the point of view of users of the registry.

Peter Willoughby OBE, JP, LL.B., LL.M., TEP, is a consultant with Deacons Graham & James. He is also a Visiting Professor of Law at the City University of Hong Kong, a Visiting Professorial Fellow at the University of London and an Honorary Lecturer at the Universities of Hong Kong and Macquarie. He is a regular contributor to various international journals on taxation and trust matters.

ANGUILLA

Don Mitchell

Introduction

Location and Time Zone

Anguilla is a small, 39 square mile, limestone and coral island in the northeast Caribbean. The Dutch/French island of St Maarten/St Martin is just 10 miles to the south. International airports most frequently used are St Maarten, San Juan in Puerto Rico and Antigua. Flights from Europe and North America to those airports include those run by American Airlines, Air France, BA and BWIA. Small airlines feed Anguilla from the international airports. These include LIAT, WINAIR and American Eagle. The island is five hours behind GMT (US Eastern Standard Time).

Political and Legal System

Anguilla is governed by a Governor appointed by the British Government and an Executive Council appointed from the political party holding a majority in the House of Assembly. The island is politically stable and its economy is sound, government accounts being in surplus each year. The standard of living is high and telecommunications are excellent. The language is English and the law is British common law supplemented by local statutes.

Professional Expertise

Professional infrastructure is weak, but growing. There are four banks, two of them internationally known, namely, Barclays Bank and Scotia Bank. There are also two indigenous banks regulated by the Eastern Caribbean Central Bank, namely Caribbean Commercial Bank and the National Bank of Anguilla. There are two small private trust companies and a local mortgage company. There are several management companies providing company formation and management company services, and there are also several law firms with experience in the international financial service industry. The Anguilla Financial Services Association (AFSA) publishes a directory of all members in good standing.

Business Incentives

The Anguilla Government actively discourages the inward flow of business and professional initiative to Anguilla on the basis that development in Anguilla is principally to be enjoyed by Anguillians. Work permits and permanent residence certificates are rationed, and are not treated on a liberal basis. In appropriate cases the Ministry of Finance has authorised the issue of multiple year work permits to nonbelongers of Anguilla who will contribute significantly to the development of Anguilla as an international financial centre. The development of tourism and international financial services on the island has been rapid, and the work force has been hard pressed to keep pace with developments. There is full employment, and the island enjoys one of the highest standards of living in the Caribbean.

Corporate Law

Legislation

Anguilla's corporate laws and other statutes relating to or affecting international financial services include:

- *Banking Ordinance* 1991
- *Companies Ordinance* 1994
- *Company Management Ordinance* 1994
- *Confidential Relationships Ordinance* 1981
- *Control of Employment Ordinance* 1980
- *Drugs Trafficking Offences Ordinance* 1988
- *Fraudulent Dispositions Ordinance* 1994
- *Insurance Act* 1968
- *International Business Companies Ordinance* 1994
- *Limited Liability Company Ordinance* 1994
- *Limited Partnership Ordinance* 1994
- *Mutual Legal Assistance (USA) Ordinance* 1990
- *Offshore Banks and Trust Companies Ordinance* 1991
- *Partnership Ordinance* 1994
- *Trust Ordinance* 1994

Most of the above Acts and Ordinances are supplemented by one or more statutory instruments and regulations which contain detailed provisions for the implementation of the main Ordinance.

The *Companies Ordinance* and the *IBC Ordinance* are the principal laws under which companies are formed in Anguilla. Except for public companies and ordinary companies, which are required to keep accounts and do various filings, companies formed under both the *Companies Ordinance* or the *IBC Ordinance* are similar. A simple Articles of Incorporation, about two pages in length, need to be filed; the detailed bylaws that a company or IBC adopts are not required to be filed. One shareholder and one director suffice in each case. For both IBCs and other companies, names may end in various UK, USA, French, Dutch, German and Spanish words and abbreviations such as 'Ltd', 'Inc', 'SA', etc. Companies are formed with an unlimited number of no-par-value share, while IBCs may be formed with capital of US$50,000.00 or less, over US$50,000.00, or an unlimited number of no-par-value shares. The only significant difference among these three types of IBCs is the amount of filing fee payable. Only IBCs may issue bearer shares.

Disclosure Requirements

In the case of a company, the names of the first directors are disclosed on registration. An IBC's shareholders and directors are never disclosed on registration or at any time thereafter. One year after incorporation, the annual return of a company listing its directors and shareholders must be filed. There is no annual return for an IBC. Nominee shareholders may be used.

There is a provision for the Governor of Anguilla to specify foreign regulatory authorities with whom the Registrar may exchange information in his possession. The Registrar may apply to the registered office for information and if refused may, in restricted circumstances, apply to the court, and the court may require any person acting on behalf of the beneficial owner of shares in either a company or an IBC to provide the information. The Ordinance specifically protects attorney-client privilege. Companies formed by a solicitor have the benefit of attorney-client privilege whenever the Registrar requests information from a solicitor's office.

The *Mutual Legal Assistance (USA) Ordinance* entitles the Attorney-General of Anguilla to issue subpoenas and search warrants, and to compel persons in Anguilla to testify and to provide information that would otherwise have been protected under the *Confidential Relationships Ordinance*. Attorney-client privilege is protected and US authorities will not be able to compel a breach of confidentiality in Anguilla under this law.

Types of Companies

The most commonly formed companies in Anguilla are:

Private company

A private company, may not have more than 11 shareholders. The right to transfer shares is restricted and it does not offer shares to the public. It is exempt from maintaining a stated capital account and from having to prepare, keep or file financial returns. The private company is exempt from having to appoint an auditor and is exempt from keeping minute books at the Registered Office.

Ordinary company

An ordinary company has to keep minutes and accounts, but is not a public company. As with all Anguillian companies a corporate seal is optional, the number of shares is unlimited and they are of no-par-value, or may be of different classes. A company may issue shares with pre-emptive rights, conversion privileges, and may acquire its own shares or cancel them. Except for a public company, which must have at least three directors, an Anguillian company may have one director. The directors may make, amend or repeal the bylaws. Electronic record keeping is permitted, meetings may be held by telephone, there is no requirement that any meeting be held in Anguilla or that there be a director resident in Anguilla. A unanimous shareholder's agreement binds the directors. Resolutions in writing take the place of minutes of meetings. Reconstruction, amalgamation and winding up are liberally provided for and companies may move in and out of Anguilla.

Public company

A public company must have three or more directors, produce financial returns for shareholders and publish a prospectus. As with ordinary companies, no restriction on the transfer of shares is permitted. Bearer shares are not permitted. Only an IBC may issue bearer shares.

Company limited by guarantee

A company limited by guarantee and not by shares has members, not shareholders. The Ordinance gives wide flexibility for the structuring of the bylaws.

Hybrid company

A hybrid company has both shareholders and guarantee members. There is no restriction on the bylaws that may be drafted, provided they do not conflict with the laws dealing with companies generally.

Not-for-profit company

A not-for-profit company has Articles that restrict the undertaking to one that is patriotic, religious, philanthropic, charitable, educational, scientific, sporting, athletic or of a similar nature.

International business company (IBC)

An IBC may be one that has capital of under US$50,000.00, over US$50,000.00, or an unlimited number of no-par-value shares. The identity of shareholders and directors are confidential. A two-page Articles of Incorporation is all that is filed in the Registry of Companies. No annual return is filed, but an annual fee is payable with penalties for late payment. An IBC has all the rights and powers of an individual except that it cannot be a bank, insurance company or trust company or carry on business in Anguilla. An IBC may issue fractional shares and increase or reduce its capital. When any foreign authority confiscates any shares or other interest in an IBC, the company, a creditor or any person holding an interest may apply to the court in Anguilla for an order that the company disregard the seizure. An IBC is formed by an incorporator, usually someone in a law office, and the first directors are appointed by the incorporator. There are provisions for merger and consolidation, redemption of minority shares, rights of dissenters, winding up and dissolution, and striking off the register. A company that has been struck off may easily be restored to the Register on payment of the appropriate filing fees.

Limited liability company

A limited liability company may be formed under the *LLC Ordinance*.

Offshore bank

An offshore bank may be formed under the *Companies Ordinance* and licensed under the *Offshore Banks and Trust Companies Ordinance*. In practice, only a subsidiary of an established bank in a well-regulated jurisdiction, whose home regulators agree to share supervisory information with the Superintendent of Offshore Banks in Anguilla, will be allowed to form an offshore bank in Anguilla.

Insurance company

An insurance company may be licensed under the *Insurance Act* to do one or more of three types of insurance business: life insurance, marine insurance or non-marine insurance. In practice, a captive insurance company will be licensed when qualified and experienced persons apply. A general insurance company is to be licensed only where it is a subsidiary, like a bank above, of an existing insurance company in a well-regulated jurisdiction.

Trust company

A company receives a general trust license under the *Offshore Banks and Trust Companies Ordinance* after the Superintendent of Offshore Banks is convinced of the expertise and capacity of the promoters. A restricted trust license is more easily granted.

Taxation

There are no direct taxes of any kind in Anguilla. There is no income tax or profit tax on individuals or companies. There are no death duties or gift or inheritance taxes. There are no currency exchange restrictions, value added taxes, capital gains taxes or withholding taxes. Government revenue is derived chiefly from custom duties and hotel bed taxes.

As Anguilla is a zero tax jurisdiction, all double taxation treaties inherited from its colonial relationship with Great Britain are inoperative.

Corporate Mobility

Both the *Companies Ordinance* and the *IBC Ordinance* liberally provide for the redomiciliation of a company into and out of Anguilla by a simple filing and the payment of the appropriate filing fees.

Merger Provisions

Two or more companies may merge by filing Articles of Amalgamation and a Certificate of Amalgamation is issued by the Registrar.

Fraud and Money Laundering

The *Fraudulent Dispositions Ordinance* amends the law relating to dispositions made with an intent to defraud. Every such disposition is made voidable at the instance of a creditor thereby prejudiced. The burden of proof is on the creditor, and the action must be commenced within three years of the relevant disposition. The disposition is set aside not entirely, but only to the extent necessary to satisfy the obligation to the petitioning creditor.

Money laundering is not a term in Anguilla law. There is no specific prohibition of money laundering. However, the *Drugs Trafficking Offences Ordinance* provides for the confiscation of the proceeds of drugs trafficking. The burden of proof is on the accused. Similarly, the *Mutual Legal Assistance (USA) Ordinance* empowers the Attorney General at the request of US authorities to compel witnesses to give evidence and produce evidence for US criminal proceedings in accordance with the terms of the 1986 US/UK Treaty.

Trust Law

Current Legal Framework

The *Trust Ordinance* 1994 (the Ordinance) is the principal statute in Anguilla governing the law of trusts. The English and other Commonwealth cases on trusts are of persuasive authority, while cases of Eastern Caribbean Supreme Court on the law of trusts are of binding authority. The 1994 Ordinance takes advantage of some of the most modern Commonwealth and US thinking on the law and structure of trusts. Some of the more interesting features are highlighted below. The *Fraudulent Dispositions Ordinance* 1994 and the *Offshore Banks and Trusts Companies Ordinance* 1991 also affect the provision of trust service from Anguilla as described.

Settlor

Any person, including a company, may be the settlor of an Anguillian trust. The settlor may also be a trustee, a beneficiary or a protector.

Beneficiaries

Beneficiaries must be identifiable, either by name or by reference to a relationship to some person or a class of persons; they need not be living at the time of the creation of the trust. The terms of the trust may provide for persons to be added or excluded as beneficiaries. The trust may impose obligations on beneficiaries. A beneficiary may disclaim part or all of his interest and this disclaimer may be temporary and may be revoked. Protective or spendthrift trusts are provided for.

Trustees

Any person other than a minor (under 21 years) may be a trustee. A trustee may also be the settlor, a beneficiary or the protector of the trust. If the settlor of an Anguillian trust is not resident in Anguilla then only a trust company licensed under the *Offshore Banks and Trust Companies Ordinance* 1991 may be appointed to act as an Anguillian trustee. There are small privately owned licensed trust companies established in Anguilla but no major trust company provides professional trust services in Anguilla. It is not unusual for a trust to be settled in Anguilla to take advantage of Anguilla's flexible modern trust legislation but to have the trustee reside in the Bahamas, Channel Islands or some other offshore jurisdictions with competent established trust companies. If the settlor of the trust is an Anguillian resident then the trustee need not be a licensed trust company.

Trust Companies

Trust companies are licensed under the *Offshore Banks and Trust Ordinance* 1991 to conduct trust business for trusts created by a settlor or guarantor who is not resident in Anguilla. Such a licence is granted only if the company has a principal office in Anguilla and has two authorised agents approved by the Governor of Anguilla. A licence may be either a general trust licence or a restricted trust licence to undertake business only with specified persons. The word 'trust' or any variation of it cannot be used in the name of a company that is not a licensed trust company. Trustees and trust companies providing fiduciary services to residents of Anguilla are not required to be licensed in any way.

Number of trustees
Subject to any other provision in the trust instrument the minimum number of trustees is one. The maximum number of trustees is four except in the case of a trust for a charitable purpose.

Creation of a trust
A trust other than a unit trust in respect of land situated in Anguilla, need not be created by an instrument in writing but may be created by an oral declaration, by conduct, by operation of law or in any other manner whatsoever.

Validity
A trust is invalid if it does anything contrary to the law of Anguilla or has no beneficiary identifiable, unless created for a valid charitable or non-charitable purpose, to the extent that a court declares that the trust was established by duress, fraud, mistake or is immoral or contrary to public policy, or that the terms of the trust are so uncertain as to render its performance impossible, or the settlor was incapable under the law of Anguilla of creating such a trust.

Appointment of new trustees
When the terms of the trust contain no provision for the appointment of new or additional trustees, then the protector, the remaining trustees, the personal representative or liquidator of the last remaining trustee or, if there is none of the above willing to act, the court may appoint a new or additional trustee. A trustee other than a sole trustee may resign by notice in writing to his co-trustees, or may be removed by the court, or by the protector, or upon the coming into effect of a provision of the trust under which he is removed from or otherwise ceases to hold his office.

Sham trusts
The concept of a sham trust is not recognised under the Ordinance. The court in Anguilla would be guided by the principles of law laid down by the courts of the Commonwealth to the extent that the principle of Anguillian trust law is similar to Commonwealth trust law.

Registration and Taxes
No registration is required or necessary, but an optional provision for registration exists in the Ordinance whereby the settlor or trustee may apply for registration of the trust. There are no taxes or duties payable in Anguilla by a trust. In addition, the Ordinance specifically exempts from any tax or duty that may be imposed in the future on a trust whose settlor and beneficiaries are not resident in Anguilla and where the trust property does not include land in Anguilla or shares in a company owning land in Anguilla.

Powers
In addition to the powers set out in the trust instrument and generally recognised in the Ordinance, the trustees are given extensive additional powers under Schedule 2 of the Ordinance.

Letters of wishes
A letter of wishes from the settlor or a beneficiary is specifically recognised by the Ordinance. A letter of wishes imposes no fiduciary duty on the trustee.

Delegation of powers

Delegation of powers is specifically provided for in the Ordinance. Essentially, a trustee is permitted to delegate powers not only according to the terms of the trust, but also to managers of trust property and investment managers; to appoint lawyers and accountants or other persons to act in relation to the affairs of the trust or to hold any of the trust property; and to authorise such persons to retain or receive any payment usually payable for the services rendered. The trustee is not liable for loss arising to the trust from such delegation provided the trustee exercised the standard of care of a prudent and reasonable man of business in selecting the delegate or appointee and in the supervision of the activities of that person.

Power of investment

The Ordinance gives the widest power of investment to the trustee. Where the terms of the trust call for 'authorised trustee investments' to be used then the Ordinance provides a wide and varied list of authorised trustee investments. These include, for example, securities of various governments and banks, shares and debentures in quoted companies, units in quoted unit trusts and shares in quoted mutual funds. Quoted means quoted on most of the major stock exchanges of the world.

Payment of Trustees

There is a liberal provision for the payment of trustees. Even when the terms of the trust are that a trustee shall not receive payment, payment may nevertheless be authorised by the court or by some or all of the beneficiaries.

Rule against Perpetuities

The Ordinance specifically state that the rule against perpetuities do not apply to a trust. No maximum duration of a trust is set.

Purpose Trusts

The Ordinance permits the creation of trusts for commercial or other non-charitable purposes provided the purpose is specific, reasonable and capable of fulfilment, not unlawful, and that there is a protector appointed who is capable of enforcing the trust.

Intervention by Court

The High Court may on the application of a beneficiary, trustee, settlor or his personal representative or protector, approve a variation of the terms of the trust on behalf of a minor beneficiary, a person unknown, an unknown member of a class, or any beneficiary under a protective or spendthrift trust.

Asset Protection Trusts

Provisions that encourage the use of an Anguillian trust for asset protection include:

- The three-year limitation period provided for in the *Fraudulent Dispositions Ordinance* 1994 within which an action must be brought after the date of the relevant disposition;
- The placing of the burden of establishing an intent to defraud upon the creditor seeking to set aside the disposition;

- The limiting of any eventual setting aside of a trust only to the extent necessary to satisfy the obligation to the creditor in question bringing the action;
- The exclusion of foreign law in determining the validity of an Anguillian trust; the capacity of a settlor; the powers, obligations, liabilities and rights of trustees; and the existence and extent of powers;
- The wide power conferred by the Ordinance, subject to the terms of the trust, for the governing law of the trust to be changed to or from the law of Anguilla;
- The wide power to vary the terms of the trust in any manner provided by its terms;
- The broad power to resign or remove trustees and appoint other trustees; and
- The wide power of investment.

Forced Heirship Rules

The Ordinance specifically defeats forced heirship rules.

Fees

There is no legal provision governing the payment of professional fees and there are no statutory fees for forming trusts. There is a registration fee of US$250.00 for an optional registration, US$150.00 for registering a variation, and US$100.00 for cancellation of a registration.

Migration

The Ordinance provides for a trust to migrate into or out of Anguilla either by the replacement of the trustees or by the changing of the governing law.

Foreign Trusts

A foreign trust is enforceable in the courts of Anguilla except to the extent that it purports to do something illegal under the law of Anguilla. Additionally, variant types of trust recognised by law or customs of any community may be created in Anguilla and may be written in a language other than English provided there is a certified translation appended.

Don Mitchell, QC, is a Barrister of the Eastern Caribbean Supreme Court. He has been practising law in the West Indies since being called at the Inner Temple in 1971. He is a member of several international financial institutions and has written and spoken widely on the laws of Anguilla and the use of its offshore legislation.

ANTIGUA & BARBUDA

Alice N Roberts

Introduction

Location

The twin island state of Antigua and Barbuda is located in the northern portion of the chain of islands in the Caribbean Sea. This geographical location places Antigua and Barbuda in a strategic position for international travel both by air and sea. Antigua boasts an international airport which can accommodate large jumbo jets and a deep water harbour which can accommodate the largest cruise ships. The island thus has direct air and sea links with North America and Europe as well as the other islands in the Caribbean. South American and the Far East are readily accessible via US and London.

Political

Antigua and Barbuda became independent in 1901 and is a common law country. It is a monarchical Caribbean state, sharing Queen Elizabeth II as its queen with the United Kingdom and many countries of the Commonwealth. In addition to being a member of the Commonwealth, Antigua and Barbuda is a member of the United Nations, the Caribbean Community (CARICOM) and the Organisation of Eastern Caribbean States (OECS). The country has enjoyed a long history of stable democratic government.

Language

Although Antigua and Barbuda is an English speaking country, its population is becoming more and more cosmopolitan. Thus it is possible to obtain translation or interpretation services for many foreign languages including German, Italian, Chinese, French and others.

Currency

The official currency of Antigua and Barbuda is the Eastern Caribbean (EC) Dollar which maintains a fixed exchange rate with the United States Dollar (US$1.00 = EC$2.60).

Economy

Antigua and Barbuda has traditionally been seen as a tourist destination and is well known for its beaches, carnival and cricket. However, it is now taking off as an offshore financial centre and this sector is contributing significantly to the economy. The growth of this sector has been due to the presence of the necessary legislative and institutional infrastructure, excellent telecommunication facilities as well as the availability of local professional expertise and modern banking facilities.

Corporate Law

The Legal Framework

The present laws which govern corporate structures in Antigua and Barbuda are the *Companies Act* and the *International Business Corporations Act* (*IBC Act*). The *IBC Act* deals with 'offshore companies' while the *Companies Act* deals with 'local companies'. Local companies are set up for conducting business locally within Antigua and Barbuda. A corporate tax rate of 40 per cent is imposed on income of local companies.

Administration

The administration of the *Companies Act* and the *IBC Act* are separate and distinct. The Director of International Business Corporations is responsible for the administration of the *IBC Act* and maintains a register of all companies registered or continued under the Act. This register is separate from the register of local companies.

In a move to further develop and promote Antigua and Barbuda as an offshore financial centre, the government set up the International Financial Services Board in 1994. This is an advisory body comprising persons from the private sector who are involved in the offshore business.

Permitted Activities

Corporations set up under the *IBC Act* (IBCs) are only permitted to carry on international trade or business, that is international banking, international trust business, international insurance, international manufacturing and other international trading or commercial activities. Thus IBCs are not permitted to carry on any business activity in Antigua and Barbuda except those activities which are solely in furtherance of their international business activities nor to trade within the CARICOM region. Corporations which are set up to conduct international banking activities cannot deal in any CARICOM currency.

Share Capital and Shareholders

There is no minimum share capital required for ordinary trading corporations. However the minimum share capital is US$1,000,000.00 for banks; US$500,000.00 for trust companies; and US$100,000.00 for insurance companies.

Shares may be issued in bearer or registered form, but companies engaged in international banking, trust or insurance are not allowed to issue bearer shares. Bearer shares must indicate that they are not transferable to a resident of Antigua and Barbuda. Several classes of shares are permitted and shares may be of no-par value. A corporation may have one shareholder and corporate shareholders are permitted.

Directors

An IBC must have at least one director, which can be a corporate entity. The directors can be citizens of any country except that in the case of banking, trusts and insurance corporations, at least one director must be a citizen and resident of Antigua and Barbuda or a corporation licensed under the *IBC Act* to carry on international trust business.

Management

Each IBC is required by law to have a resident agent in Antigua and Barbuda and to maintain a registered office in Antigua and Barbuda. The company must prepare and maintain at its registered office the usual corporate records, including the company's articles and bylaws, minutes and resolutions of shareholders' and directors' meetings and a register of shareholders and debenture holders. However access to these records is restricted to the directors and shareholders of the company and their agents and legal representatives. Creditors of the company can have access to records pertaining to the articles and bylaws of the company, the names of the directors and the register of debenture holders.

Meetings

Both annual shareholders and annual directors meetings are required to be held within Antigua and Barbuda. Special meetings can be held anywhere. However, the law does allow for telephone participation at directors' meetings. Thus a meeting of directors is deemed to have been held in Antigua and Barbuda so long as at least one director is present in Antigua and Barbuda during the meeting and all directors were able to hear each other. Shareholders can be represented by proxy holders, but if no shareholder is present in person, the resident agent must be present as a proxy holder for actions taken to be valid. In addition, resolutions in writing signed by all the directors or shareholders are valid and acceptable as if the resolutions were passed at an actual meeting.

Tax Considerations

Each corporation formed under the *IBC Act* enjoys a fifty-year tax holiday from the date of incorporation. Such companies do not fall within the tax regime of Antigua and Barbuda and are thus exempt from income tax, capital gains tax, asset transfer taxes, estate, inheritance or succession tax and other direct taxes. Furthermore, IBCs are not subject to the *Exchange Control Act* and are exempt from foreign currency levy or any taxes in respect of their dealings with currency. There is, therefore, no restriction on the movement of funds and corporations can maintain foreign currency accounts.

An IBC which is desirous of setting up physical presence in Antigua and Barbuda can be exempted from all or some of the duties payable under the *Customs Duties Act* in respect of goods (eg equipment and furniture) to be used solely for carrying on its international business from within Antigua and Barbuda.

Reporting and Disclosure

The reporting requirements are minimal for ordinary trading corporations. The only information which is filed with the Director is the names of the directors along with the name and address of the resident agent, the address of the registered office and the articles and bylaws including any amendments. Such corporations are not required to file annual returns. Corporations engaged in banking, trust or insurance business are subject to more stringent reporting and disclosure requirements. In addition to the information required to be filed by ordinary trading corporations, these corporations must also file the names and addresses of all the shareholders of the corporation as well as any changes. These corporations must also as a condition of their license file quarterly returns and annual audited financial statements. Confidentiality is recognised as a vital element of the formation of IBCs and the Act makes provisions for this. Thus, there are provisions governing the disclosure of information relating to the business affairs of the customers of banks and trust companies. There is a stiff penalty for persons found contravening these confidentiality provisions.

Disclosure of customer information is only allowed by an order of the court in matters involving alleged criminal offences.

Fees

The government initial registration and re-registration fees are not dependent on the capitalisation and is presently a flat fee of \$250.00 per annum. In addition, corporations engaged in international banking, trust or insurance must also obtain a license. The present license fees are US\$5,000.00 for banking and US\$2,500.00 for trusts and insurance companies. Professional fees vary, but the average for setting up an ordinary trading corporation is in the region of US\$1,000.00.

Corporate Mobility

The *IBC Act* allows for foreign corporations to be continued under the legislation of Antigua and Barbuda as well as for Antigua and Barbuda corporations to be continued in other countries. An Antiguan IBC which has been continued in another country ceases to come under the *IBC Act* of Antigua and Barbuda.

Amalgamations

Amalgamations of one or more IBCs are permitted under the *IBC Act*. There must be an agreement between the corporations involved specifying the terms and conditions of the amalgamation and this agreement must be approved by the shareholders of each of the corporation. The Director must be satisfied that no creditors will be prejudiced by the amalgamation and may require that adequate notice of a proposed amalgamation be given to all known creditors of the corporations involved.

Alice N Roberts, BSc has been involved in the offshore sector for the past ten years and is presently the Managing Director of Caribbean Management & Trust Company Limited. She is also a member of the International Financial Services Board and the Antigua Offshore Association.

THE BAHAMAS

Thomas A Evans

Introduction

Location and Time Zone

The Commonwealth of the Bahamas (the Bahamas) is a country consisting of a group of Coral Islands beginning 60 miles Southeast of the Coast of Florida and stretching to the Coast of Cuba and the Island of Hispaniola, home of the Republic of Haiti and the Dominican Republic. There are twenty-nine inhabited islands and in addition there are over 2,000 Cays or Islets and mere rocks in the ocean.

The Bahamas is in the same time zone as the East Coast of the United States and Canada, making business communication with major financial centres such as New York and Toronto quite convenient.

Political and Legal System

The Bahamas is a member of the Commonwealth of Nations. It is perhaps the most stable country politically in the Western Hemisphere apart from the United States and Canada. Its Parliamentary democracy has functioned without interruption and without any major upheavals for more than 275 years.

The legal system of the Bahamas is a Common Law System patterned after that of England. The Constitution is the Supreme Law. The Declaration of Human Rights and the United Nations Covenants on Social and Political Rights are protected.

Currency

The Bahamas is an independent monetary entity and the Bahamian Dollar is on par with the US Dollar.

Population and Language

The population of the Bahamas is approximately 275,000 people, roughly half of whom live on the Island of New Providence and most of the remainder live on the major Islands, namely Grand Bahama, Eleuthera, Abaco, Andros, Exuma, Long Island, Inagua, Cat Island, San Salvador and Bimini.

The official language of the Bahamas is English; its educational system is effective and modern, producing an adult literacy rate of 95 per cent. The work force is skilled and includes professionals in the fields of law, accountancy, banking and engineering.

Business Incentives

The environment for conducting offshore business that has been created by the Government of the Bahamas is perhaps the most flexible in the world, but at the same time contains a sufficiently strict regulatory regime to ensure that the system is not abused.

Tourism is the main engine of the economy of the Bahamas, but international banking and other financial services are also strong. The Bahamas is a tax haven. There is no taxation on income, profits, inheritance or estates. There is also no corporate tax charges payable in The Bahamas.

Corporate Law

International business companies (IBC)

The legal framework

The *International Business Companies Act* was passed in 1990 and upgraded with amendments in 1995. This Act provides for the incorporation of international business companies. These are companies that do not carry on business with persons resident in the Bahamas or own any interest in real estate situated in the Bahamas, other than the lease of property for use as an office. An IBC is also restricted from carrying on banking, trust, insurance or re-insurance business or providing a registered office for companies.

Incorporation

IBCs may be inexpensively incorporated. The incorporation process is very simple and may be completed within 24 hours. An IBC may be formed by two or more persons.

Shares

An IBC's shares may be issued with or without par value, in bearer form and as fractional shares.

Directors

An IBC needs only have one director, which may be either an individual or a company and need not be a resident of the Bahamas. Decisions are made by resolutions which may be passed by simple majority.

Registered office and registers

An IBC must keep a share register, minutes of all committee meetings, copies of all resolutions, a register of directors and officers, and accounts and records the directors feel necessary to reflect the financial position of the company. These documents are required to be kept at the company's registered office, which must be located in the Bahamas. It is also necessary for an imprint of the company's seal to be kept at the registered office.

Registry

The records which the company are required to keep do not have to be lodged with the Registrar of Companies but may be kept at the registered office. As a result, they are not available for public inspection.

Annual return

The annual filing requirements are minimal. It is not necessary to file an annual return with the Registrar of Companies and consequently, the names of directors and shareholders are not available for public inspection. Thus, the members of an IBC are afforded a very high degree of confidentiality.

Domestic Companies

Incorporation

The incorporation of domestic companies in the Bahamas is governed by the *Companies Act* 1992. Provision is made for the incorporation of a company by filing a Memorandum of Association and Articles of Association with the Registrar of Companies, resulting in the issuance of a Certificate of Incorporation.

The Memorandum of Association is the constitution of the company containing the objects for which the company is created. These objects are usually drafted in such a way as to enable the company to conduct a wide variety of businesses. A minimum of two shareholders must subscribe to the Memorandum of Association.

Directors

The officers and directors of the company need not be Bahamian citizens or residents and the minimum number of directors is one.

Registered office and registers

The registered office of the company must be located in the Bahamas and files must be kept at that office.

Foreign currency account

A domestic company may be designated nonresident for the purposes of exchange control if the beneficial owners of the shares are persons who are not residents of the Bahamas and the business of the company is conducted entirely outside the Bahamas. The major significance of this designation is to enable the company to hold foreign currency.

Annual returns

The company is required to make annual returns to the Registrar of Companies showing the names and addresses together with the occupation of its members, officers and directors. It must also set out the share capital and the number of shares issued to each member.

Investment Incentives

There are a number of incentives available to companies that are engaged in investment in the Bahamas. Once a proposal for investment is approved by the National Economic Council, the company is exempted from the payment of customs duties on building materials, equipment and approved raw materials, business licensing fees and real property taxes for up to twenty years. Statutes providing for incentives are the

- *Export Manufacturing Encouragement Act*;
- *Industries Encouragement Act*;

- *Agricultural Manufacturing Act*;
- *Tariff Act*,
- *Free Trade Zone Act*;
- *Hotel Encouragement Act*; and
- *Spirits and Beer Manufacturing Act*.

Miscellaneous

Merger provisions
There is no prohibition on the merger of companies and this may be easily done by acquisition of shares.

Fraudulent transfer provisions
Fraudulent transfer of shares will attract criminal liability pursuant to the Penal Code of the Bahamas and those responsible may be charged with conspiracy to defraud or fraudulent breach of trust, depending on the circumstances.

Trust Law

Legal Framework
As mentioned earlier, the Bahamas inherited the Common Law of England during the period of colonialism. The main legislation on the subject of trusts is the *Trustees Act* 1893, which is based on the English Act passed in the same year. English decisions interpreting English Statute are of persuasive authority in the Bahamas.

The main provisions of the *Trustees Act* govern the following matters:

- Investment of trust monies;
- The appointment of replacement trustees;
- The vesting of trust properties;
- The appointment of agents;
- Insurance of buildings; and
- Indemnity of trustees.

The *Trust (Choice of Governing Laws) Act* 1989, was the beginning of the modern legal framework for the positioning of the Bahamas as the leading offshore jurisdiction in this region.

In addition to a number of other matters, The *Trustee (Choice of Governing Law) Act* 1989 makes provision for the following matters:

- Where the trust deed provides that the Laws of the Bahamas shall govern the trust, such a clause is effective and conclusive on this point;

- If the trust deed declares that the laws of the Bahamas shall govern a particular section of a trust, in that the trust shall be administered in the Bahamas, then that is conclusive evidence of the settlor's intention that Bahamian Law is to be the governing law of the trust;
- In seeking to determine the governing law of the trust, reference must be made to the terms of the trust deed firstly and then to any other evidence of the intention of the parties. If no such intention is evident, then consideration may be given to other circumstances; and
- It is only when the trust deed so provides that the governing law of the trust may be changed from Bahamian Law to some other or vice versa, and all questions as to the capacity of the seller or donor, the validity of the trust, the administration of the trust, the powers of trustees; and any other questions respecting the trust with limited exceptions shall be governed by Bahamian Law.

Settlor

In Bahamian Law, any individual who is 18 years old or over and of sound mind, capable of freely disposing of property including bodies corporate who are so authorised by their Memoranda of Association may be a settlor. There are no restrictions in Bahamian Law as to who may be an international trustee.

Trustee

Persons 18 years and above and a company that is authorised by its Memorandum of Association in this regard may be a trustee. These companies are the most common corporate entities to act as trustee. The settlor may be a trustee of a trust of which he is not the sole beneficiary.

Trust companies are subject to the regulations provided for by the *Bank and Trust Companies Regulation Act* of the Bahamas which contain elaborate provisions regulating the conduct of business by such entities.

With respect to the number of trustees, the general principle is that any number of persons may be trustees, depending on the nature of the trust, consideration being given to the practicalities of having enough trustees to take advantage of various skills and experience but not too many to make the administration of the trust cumbersome. The minimum number of trustees is one.

Beneficiary

Anyone may be named as beneficiary under a trust including minors, unborn persons, the settlor or a body corporate as well as a nonresident. The Bahamas is not a party to the Hague Convention.

The Trust

Writing is not necessary to create a trust, but there must be written evidence of the trust for it to be effective and enforceable.

It is a necessary ingredient to the effectual creation of a trust that there should be some beneficiary capable of enforcing it. In other words, there must be someone in whose favour the court can order performance. This requirement is not applicable to charitable trusts, which are enforced by the Attorney General.

The exceptions to this rule, which have to be recognized by the courts, are trusts for the erection of monuments or graves, trusts for the saying of masses, trusts for the maintenance of animals and trusts for the benefit of unincorporated associations.

Transfer of trustees

When a settlor creates a trust *inter vivos* he will usually appoint the first trustees of the settlement. He may and usually does in the trust instrument give someone the power to appoint future trustees of the settlement. If the trust instrument does not make provisions for the appointment of new trustees, such appointment will be made by the court, except in cases where the beneficiary are all *sui juris* and among them they are entitled to the whole of the beneficial interest in the trust and to make the appointment.

One of the first acts that a new trustee should do upon his appointment is to ensure that all trust properties are vested in himself and his co-trustees since he becomes responsible with his co-trustees for the trust property as soon as he is appointed.

The properties may be vested in the new trustee and his co-trustees by way of the mode of transfer applicable to the type of the relevant property. For example, if the trust property is a simple title in land, a conveyance is required. If it is a leasehold title in land, then an assignment is necessary. Shares in a company must be transferred and the transfer registered. In the case of debts, there must be an assignment in addition to notice to the other party in order to ensure priority.

If the property is a negotiable instrument, there should be delivery and endorsement. For personal chattel, physical delivery and/or assignment is necessary. There is no requirement in Bahamian Law for registration of a trust, although a trust deed may be recorded if the settlor or trustees so desires. Trust funds for the provisions of superannuation allowances, pensions and for death benefits may be registered under the *Superannuation and Other Trust Fund (Validation) Act* Ch 167 of the Statute Laws of the Bahamas.

Duties

There are no duties payable in respect of a trust, but if a trust deed is to be recorded, stamp duty must first be paid.

Letters of wishes

Letters of wishes are not used in the Bahamas.

Power of trustees

The source of the trustees' powers is firstly the trust instrument and the general laws of the Bahamas, particularly the *Trustees Act* 1893. There are no variations on the bona fide principle.

The authority of trustees with respect to investments are contained in the *Trustees Act* 1893, Ch 164 of the Statute Laws of the Bahamas, which gives wide powers of investment to trustees unless forbidden by the trust instrument. The trustee may invest any trust funds in investments.

Fees

It is usual for the trust instrument to contain a charging clause authorising the trustee to charge for his professional services and reimbursement for out-of-pocket expenses out of the trust fund.

Perpetuity period

The English Common Law rule against perpetuities applies to trusts in the Bahamas. The Bahamas has no legislation similar to the *Perpetuities and Accumulation Act* 1964, but lawyers who draft trust documents usually refer therein to the eighty-year period as the trust period.

Variations of Trusts

The *Variation of Trusts Act* (Ch 166) provide that the Supreme Court may, if it thinks fit, by order approve on behalf of:

- Any person having directly or indirectly an interest whether vested or contingent, under the trusts who by reason of injury or other incapacity is incapable of asserting; or
- Any person (whether ascertained or not) who may become entitled directly or indirectly to an interest under the trust (whether ascertained or otherwise) as being at a future date or on the happening of a future event, a person or any specified class of persons (however, this paragraph shall not include any person who would be of that description, or a member of that class, as the case may be if the said date had fallen or the said event had happened at the date of the application to the Supreme Court); or
- Any person unborn; or
- Any arrangement by any person proposed and whether or not there is any other person beneficially interested who is capable of assenting thereto or varying or revoking all or any of the trusts, or enlarging the powers of the trustees of managing or administrating any of the property subject to the trusts.

There is a provision that the court shall not approve an arrangement on behalf of any person unless the carrying out thereof would be for the benefit of that person.

Asset Protection Trusts

In 1991 the government enacted the *Fraudulent Disposition Act*, which governs asset protection trusts. By virtue of this Act, 'every disposition of property made with intent to defraud and at an undervalue shall be voidable at the instance of a creditor thereby prejudiced' (s 1). The burden of proof of a fraudulent intent is on the creditor who challenges the disposition (s 4(2)). A creditor is defined in the Act as 'a person to whom an obligation is owed' (s 2). The Act further provides that any challenge to a disposition must be made within two years of such disposition.

Money Laundering

The Bahamas has recently enacted the Money Laundering (*Proceeds of Crime Act* 1995) Legislation, making money laundering in relation to the proceeds of all crimes a criminal offence. It is said to be the first and only offshore jurisdiction to do this.

The rationale of this legislation is to meet the need for people to feel safe and comfortable in the offshore environment and also to protect and safeguard the financial system in keeping with the highest standards of international banking.

According to s 1 of the Act, money laundering is committed by a person who 'uses, transfers, transports, transmits, alters, disposes of or otherwise deals with in any manner and by any means any property or any proceeds of any property with intent to conceal or convert that property or those proceeds and knowing that all or part of that property or of those proceeds was obtained or derived directly as a result of:

- The commission in the Bahamas of any offence under the *Dangerous Drugs Act*;
- The commission in the Bahamas of any offence which is punishable by a term of imprisonment of not less than five years;
- An act or omission anywhere that would have constituted an offence in the Bahamas under the *Dangerous Drugs Act*; and
- Any act or omission anywhere that would have been punishable in the Bahamas by a term of imprisonment of not less than five years.'

Facilitators

Persons who may be considered facilitators are set out in s 3 of the Act and include bankers, lawyers and trustees. The Act also gives the Governor General the authority to add to the list of facilitators upon the advice of the Central Bank of the Bahamas.

It is mandatory that all persons who facilitate financial transactions keep and retain records relating to financial activities in accordance with regulations. It also provides in s 22(1) that:

> 'A person is guilty of an offence if:
> - he knows or reasonably suspects that another person is engaged in money laundering;
> - the information or other matter on which that knowledge or suspicion is based came to his attention in the course of his trade, profession, business or employment; and
> - he does not disclose that information or other matter to a police officer as soon as is reasonably practicable after it comes to his attention.'

Bank Secrecy

The *Bank and Trust Companies* Act established a regime of bank secrecy regarding confidentiality of all information which bank officers, employees and agents come to know in the course of their employment and made it a criminal offence for any such person to disclose such information without the expressed consent of the customer or an order of the court in the Bahamas.

Other Legislation

Amendments were made to the *Limited Partnerships Act* and the *Companies Act* in 1995. During this period, the *Mutual Funds Act* and the *Securities Board Act* were passed. In addition to establishing the regulatory regime for the registration of mutual funds, the *Securities Board Act* also set the foundation for the implementation of a stock exchange for the Bahamas.

Thomas AE Evans, QC, LLb, (Hons), is a Barrister and Attorney-At-Law practising in Nassau, Bahamas as Senior Partner in the firm of Evans & Co. He served as a Director of the Central Bank of the Bahamas from 1982 to 1992 and as Chairman of the Industrial Relations Tribunal for the Bahamas from 1982 to 1993.

BARBADOS

Citco Barbados Ltd

Introduction

Location
Barbados is the most easterly of the Caribbean islands.

Political and Legal System
It was formerly a colony of Great Britain and, consequently, the country has a legal system based primarily on English law. Since its independence in 1966, Barbados has remained politically and economically stable, with its own independent government, legislature and judiciary. Barbados remains a member of the Commonwealth and is also a member of the Caribbean Community (CARICOM).

Infrastructure
The infrastructure of the country is well developed, with an efficient phone system and regular flights to many international destinations.

Currency
The currency of Barbados is the Barbados Dollar (BDS).

Corporate Law

Barbados Resident Companies

The legal framework
The corporate law of Barbados is governed by the *Companies Act*, Cap 308, which came into force on January 1 1985.

Incorporation
To incorporate a Barbados company, Articles of Incorporation and notices of directors and the registered office must be filed with the Registrar of Companies. The Registrar will then issue a certificate of incorporation.

Shares and shareholders

Shares issued by a Barbados company have no nominal or par value and must be fully paid up. Although a company has no stated authorised capital, the articles of incorporation should specify the classes of shares and the maximum number of shares which can be issued. The company is also required to maintain a stated capital account for each class of shares.

The law permits a Barbados company to have a single shareholder. A register of shareholders must be kept by the company in Barbados and bearer shares are not permitted. The first annual general meeting of shareholders must be held not later than 18 months after the date of incorporation. Meetings of shareholders thereafter must be held at intervals of no longer than 15 months, although it is possible for such meetings to be held by written consent in lieu of meeting.

Company management and administration

The directors of a Barbados company are appointed by the shareholders. It is permissible for a single director to be appointed and directors are not required to be resident in Barbados. Directors' meetings can be held either in or out of the jurisdiction and may be held by written consent in lieu of meeting. Minutes of all meetings must however be kept in Barbados.

Registered office

The registered office of a Barbados company must be in Barbados.

Residence

A company will be determined to be a resident of Barbados for tax purposes if it is incorporated in Barbados or, if incorporated outside Barbados, if it is managed and controlled there.

Corporate mobility

A Barbados company may be re-domiciled in another jurisdiction by filing articles of continuance provided that the other jurisdiction has the requisite enabling legislation.

A foreign company may become resident in Barbados by transferring its management and control to Barbados and registering with the Registrar of Companies. The foreign company can subsequently re-transfer its residence from Barbados by the removal of the management and control.

International Business Company

An International Business Company (IBC) has the same corporate structure as a Barbados resident company but differs from a resident company in its tax treatment. It is governed by the *International Business Companies (Exemption from Income Tax) Act* 1965.

To qualify as an international business company, a company must hold a valid licence and comply with the following conditions:

- The company must either be incorporated in Barbados or be a foreign company registered under the laws of Barbados;

- At least 90% of the company shares must be owned by Barbados nonresidents;
- The company must not carry on business as an offshore bank, an exempt insurance company or a foreign sales corporation; and
- The company must not trade in goods to be consumed in Barbados, provide services to residents in CARICOM or manufacture products in Barbados for sale in CARICOM.

Taxation

An IBC is subject to tax on income at the following rates:

Income	Rate
Up to US$5,000,000	2.5%
Over US$5,000,000 to US$10,000,000	2.0%
Over US$10,000,000 to US$15,000,000	1.5%
Over US$15,000,000	1.0%

However, if the shares of an IBC are part of the assets of a Barbados offshore trust, the IBC is exempt from tax.

There are no withholding taxes on payments by the IBC of dividends, interest, royalties, rents or management fees to nonresidents of Barbados.

Exempt Insurance Company

Exempt insurance companies are governed by the *Exempt Insurance Act* 1983 and when established as captive insurance companies allow an effective means for providing insurance cover.

In order to obtain a licence, a company must:

- Be incorporated under the laws of Barbados;
- Limit its activities to the insurance of risks originating outside of Barbados;
- Have no shareholders resident in Barbados or CARICOM;
- Have a paid-up capital of US$125,000; and
- Have at least one Barbados resident director who is also a citizen of Barbados.

Once established as an exempt insurance company, the company must:

- Maintain its office, books and records in Barbados;
- File audited financial statements and an auditor's certificate with the Supervisor of Insurance; and
- Pay an annual licence fee of US$2,500.

Taxation

Exempt insurance companies are exempt from all income tax, capital gains tax and other direct taxes. No withholding taxes are paid on dividends or interest to shareholders.

The Offshore Bank

Offshore banks are regulated by the *Offshore Banking Act* 1979 and obtain exemption from all exchange control provisions. To qualify for a banking licence, a company must:

- Be incorporated in Barbados or be a qualified foreign bank;
- Maintain a minimum issued capital of up to US$500,000;
- Have at least one resident citizen director;
- Pay an annual licence fee of US$12,500; and
- Maintain a reserve fund equal to issued capital.

Offshore banks are required to file quarterly statements with the regulators and annual audited financial statements.

Taxation

Tax is levied at the following rates:

Income	Rate
Up to US$5,000,000	2.5%
Over US$5,000,000 to US$10,000,000	2.0%
Over US$10,000,000 to US$15,000,000	1.5%
Over US$15,000,000	1.0%

Withholding tax is not paid on dividends and interest paid to nonresidents.

Societies with Restricted Liability

The *Societies with Restricted Liability Act* 1995 provides for the formation of societies with restricted liability (SRLs) by filing prescribed articles of organisation. These entities have characteristics of both a company and a partnership.

The Foreign Sales Corporation

The foreign sales corporation is a company incorporated in Barbados and recognised as such by the laws of the country of its parent company. Only the United States of America has so far implemented such legislation. Foreign sales corporations are governed by the *Foreign Sales Corporation Act* 1984.

Tax Treaty Arrangements

Barbados has entered into tax treaties with the following countries and with the following withholding tax rates:

		Interest	Dividends	Royalties
Non-treaty countries		15%	15%	15%
Treaty countries:	Canada	15%	15%	10%
	Finland	5%	15%	5%
	Norway	5%	15%	5%
	Sweden	5%	15%	5%
	Switzerland	0	0	0
	United Kingdom	15%	0	15%
	United States	5%	15%	5%

Trust Law

Legal Framework

Barbados trusts are governed by the following legislation together with equitable principles derived from English law:

- The *Barbados Trustee Act;* and
- The *International Trusts Act.*

Classification

Barbados trusts may be fixed, where one or more beneficiaries are given a specific beneficial share in the trust fund, or discretionary, where the trustee decides beneficial entitlement by selection from a nominated class of beneficiary.

Creation

A Barbados trust is one whose proper law is that of Barbados and this is usually stated in the trust instrument. Assets can be settled on trust by any person regardless of whether they are a resident of Barbados. A trust is established by the execution of a trust instrument and the transfer of the property to a trustee.

The trust instrument may also specify the appointment of a protector of the trust. There are no requirements as to minimum capital which must be held on trust and it is usual to settle only a nominal sum when the trust is established with further money or assets subsequently settled as an accretion to the fund. Registration of a trust is not required.

Trustees

Trust assets are managed by the trustees in accordance with the terms of the trust instrument and applicable laws. Both resident and nonresident individuals and corporations can act as trustees of a Barbados trust although it is usual for at least one trustee to be resident in Barbados. There are a number of banks, trust companies and professional advisers performing these services in Barbados. Barbados corporations acting as trustees must hold a licence to carry on offshore banking business in Barbados.

Beneficiaries

The only requirement as to beneficiaries is in connection with international trusts, ie the beneficiaries of such trusts must be persons resident outside of Barbados.

Accounts and Auditing

A trustee must keep accounts and records of the administration of the trust assets, although there are no statutory audit requirements.

Confidentiality

Since there is no requirement to register a Barbados trust or file a copy of the trust deed, all information relating to a trust will remain confidential.

Migration

Provided that provision is made in the trust instrument, it is possible to migrate a trust by appointing a trustee in another jurisdiction and nominating the law of that jurisdiction to be the proper law of the trust.

The International Trust

The *International Trusts Act* was enacted in 1995 for the creation and regulation of international trusts.

In order to qualify as an international trust, the following conditions must be complied with:

- The settlor is a nonresident of Barbados;
- At least one of the trustees is a resident of Barbados;
- Trust assets must not include immovable property situated in Barbados;
- The beneficiaries of the trust must not be residents of Barbados; and
- The trust will terminate 100 years after date of creation or sooner. The rule against perpetuities is not applicable.

Under the 1995 legislation, disposition of property made with the intent to defraud or undervalue will be deemed voidable with respect to a prejudiced creditor. However, any action by such a creditor must be commenced within three years from the date of the disposition.

Taxation

Resident trust

A Barbados trust will be subject to income tax if:

- The settlor and/or beneficiaries are resident in Barbados;
- The trust assets are located in Barbados; and
- The trust derives income outside Barbados which is subsequently remitted to Barbados.

International trust

In the case of an international trust, no income tax is due in respect of the distribution of income or capital to any eligible beneficiary and the trust is exempt from income tax in Barbados.

Citco Barbados is part of the Citco Group, an independent international financial services group offering trustee, fiduciary company management services, mutual fund administration and fund advisory services, and banking and custody.

BELIZE

Howard Bilton

Introduction

Location and Time Zone

Belize, formerly British Honduras, is located on the Caribbean seaboard of Central America.

Political and Legal System

Since independence from Britain in 1981, Belize has enjoyed a stable and democratic government. The cabinet, under the leadership of a prime minister, directs government policy. The prime minister chooses ministers from an elected house of representatives and an appointed senate. The political system is a parliamentary democracy based on the Westminster system. Her Majesty, Queen Elizabeth II is the constitutional head of state who is represented in Belize by a Governor General.

Population and Language

The population of Belize is 205,000. English is the official language, though Spanish is widely spoken.

Currency

Its currency is the Belize Dollar, which is fixed at Bz\$2 to US\$1.

Economy

The economy is still dominated by agriculture and in particular forestry.

Infrastructure and Communications

Belize has a developing system of highways linking the main two cities, Belmopan and Belize City. Belize also has an international airport with the ability to accommodate wide-bodied aircraft and there are regular international services to USA, Central America and Mexico. There is a state-of-the art satellite earth station providing quality telecommunications to the outside world.

Corporate Law

Belize Companies

Although there are high tax rates for Belize companies and residents, the country now offers tax-free International Business Companies (IBCs) under the *IBC Act* of 1990. This legislation is modelled on

British Virgin Island (BVI) legislation. However, in Belize, the annual government fees are only US$100, whereas the equivalent fee payable in BVI is US$300.

International Business Company

A Belize IBC has the following characteristics:

Taxation

A Belize IBC pays no taxes in Belize.

Shareholders

A minimum of one shareholder is required and either registered or bearer shares may be issued. No shareholder details appear in the public file, but a register of shareholders must be kept at the registered office of the company in Belize.

Directors

A minimum of one director is required and corporate directors are permitted. Details of the directors do not appear in the public file.

Annual Reporting

No annual return or accounts need be filed. It should be noted that penalty fees of up to 50% of the annual government fee will be incurred if the licence fee is not paid when due.

Timescale

Incorporation can be achieved within a matter of hours, but it does take approximately one week for documents to arrive from Belize. Ready-made companies are widely available for immediate purchase.

Restrictions on name and activity

Names must end with one of the following words, or their abbreviations: Limited, Corporation, Incorporated, Societe Anonyme or Sociedad Anonima. The following words, and their associated activities, are not permitted: Assurance, Bank, Building Society, Chamber of Commerce, Chartered, Cooperative, Imperial, Insurance, Municipal and Royal.

Local requirements

The company must maintain a registered office address within Belize and must also appoint a Belize resident as a registered agent.

Secrecy

There are no specific statutory provisions governing secrecy in relation to companies, but English Law, which applies within the jurisdiction, does impose a common law duty on professionals to keep the affairs of their clients confidential.

Trust Law

Legislation

Trust law exists in Belize's English common law system. This was further enhanced by the enactment of the *Trusts Act* in 1992, which specifically outlines the purpose of a trust.

Settlor

There are no restrictions on whom can be the settlor, so a settlor may be an individual or a corporation. The settlor can be a beneficiary, trustee and/or protector.

Beneficiaries

The trusts law also allows for unborn individuals and minors to be beneficiaries, as well as corporations, be they resident or not.

Confidentiality

Confidentiality is a key part of the *Trust Act*. The trustees are not obliged to disclose information on the state and the amount of the trust. They are also not required to reveal details of the deliberations that led to the agreement on exercising their functions as trustees or how any decision was reached. The law on confidentiality which protects information held by trusts was proved effective in the case of the *Securities and Exchange Commission v Swiss Trade and Commerce Trust Ltd, Banner Fund International, Lloyd Winburne et alia* held in the Supreme Court of Belize. In this 1994 case, the USA Securities & Exchange Commission was attempting to obtain files from the offices of Swiss Trade & Commerce Trust Ltd. The court held that, because of the Belize confidentiality provisions, documents belonging to the Swiss Trade and Commerce Trust Ltd could not be released. This overturned a previous ruling by a lower Belize court and upheld the confidentiality accorded to trust companies.

There is an all encompassing asset protection clause (Part 7, sub-s 6) which reads as follows:

> 'Where a trust is created under the law of Belize, the Court shall not vary it or set it aside or recognise the validity of any claim against the trust property pursuant to the law of another jurisdiction or the order of a court of another jurisdiction in respect of :
>
> - The personal and propriety consequences of marriage;
> - Succession rights (whether testate or intestate) including the fixed shares of spouses or relatives; or
> - The claims of creditors in an insolvency.'

The above section appears to remove any possibility of foreign judgements being used to attack a Belize trust, although there is little precedent to refer to giving guidance as to how the courts of Belize will actually apply this relatively new legislation.

Trustees

There is no requirement to be licensed as a trustee. The maximum number of trustees for a non-charitable trust is four. Trusts can be formed orally or in writing. There is an optional procedure whereby trusts can be registered, but the register is not open to public inspection. A registration fee of US$200 is payable.

Trustees are entitled to full reimbursement for expenses and are allowed to charge for any professional fees that were previously agreed to in writing. The trustees may invest money at their own discretion as long as the investments are within the terms of the trust and authorised under the *Trust Act*.

Taxation

A trust is considered to be exempt from tax if the settlor and beneficiaries are nonresident and the trust property does not include land in Belize. This exemption includes estate duties, capital gains tax, income tax or stamp duty.

Howard Bilton is a Barrister at Law of the UK and Gibraltar, Chairman of The International Company Services Ltd Group and Managing Director of Sovereign Trust International, Suites 1601-1603 Kinwick Centre, 32 Hollywood Road, Central, Hong Kong, Tel: (852) 2542 1177, Fax: (852) 2545 0550, E-mail: hk@icsl.com.

BERMUDA

Monica Jones & Francis Woo

Introduction

Located in the Atlantic Ocean, off the coast of North America and just a two-hour flight from most major cities on the east coast of the US, Bermuda is the world's largest offshore domicile for captive insurance companies and one of the largest reinsurance centres in the world.

Bermuda's significance in Hong Kong and Asia for the past decade has been its use as a jurisdiction for the redomiciliation of public companies and for the formation of holding companies, the shares of which are then listed on stock exchanges around the world. To date, approximately 50 per cent of the companies listed on the Stock Exchange of Hong Kong are companies incorporated in Bermuda as the holding company of substantial Hong Kong, Chinese and Asian companies.

Bermuda received an 'AA' rating from Standard & Poor's in May 1995 which is the highest rating a small-sized economy such as Bermuda can achieve. With its affluent and highly-educated population, sophisticated infrastructure and strong economy, Bermuda has long been established as a financial centre, having sanctioned the incorporation of its first 'exempted company' in the 1930s. It remains a British Dependent Territory with internal self-government, having had its own elected Parliament since 1622 and enjoys multi-party politics. In common with many of the other offshore centres, it is a common law jurisdiction with ultimate right of appeal to the Privy Council in the UK. In particular, its company laws are essentially based upon English statutes.

As a general philosophy, endeavours are made to exercise control over the quality of business carried out by Bermuda companies and other entities and those associating themselves with the jurisdiction, by reviewing the reputation and quality of those incorporating companies and forming other entities in Bermuda. The overall focus of the jurisdiction has therefore been towards the quality of business rather than volume. Bermuda also has an established code on fraud and money laundering.

Bermuda's role has additionally focused on the establishment of collective investment vehicles such as mutual funds, securitisation of asset exercises using the Bermuda purpose trust vehicle and numerous other forms of commercial activity. For example, a Bermuda structure was used in connection with the Mitsubishi Bank US$2bn Yankee Bond Issue in 1995, a trend which continues.

With the advent of easily-accessible computer communications via the Internet and the presence of Bermuda's professionals in Asia, any previously encountered hurdles to communication across several time zones have been removed. Organisations with a base in Asia can have their matters dealt with by the many representatives of Bermuda (including banks and law firms) also based in Asia.

Corporate Law

Incorporation

Incorporation in Bermuda requires the prior written consent of the Minister of Finance. Companies in Bermuda are incorporated by registration upon the filing of the Minister's consent. These procedures are designed to maintain Bermuda's high standards by scrutinising both the proposed ultimate beneficial ownership and control of a Bermuda company and the intended business activity of the company. This review procedure is carried out by the Bermuda Monetary Authority (BMA) on behalf of the Minister of Finance and the information reviewed is required by law to be maintained on a confidential basis (except as governed by the US-Bermuda Tax Convention of 1986).

The incorporation of companies in Bermuda is governed essentially by the *Companies Act* and supplemented by governmental policy.

Types of Companies

A clear distinction is made between exempted companies, which carry on business outside Bermuda from a principal place of business in Bermuda, and local companies, which carry on business in Bermuda.

A permit company may also be established. These overseas companies obtain a permit to 'carry on business outside Bermuda from a place of business in Bermuda'. However, good reason has to be shown why the company wants to operate from Bermuda and why it could not incorporate a Bermuda company.

The following types of companies are also permitted:

- A company limited by shares – a company having the liability of its shareholders limited to the amount if any, unpaid on the shares held by them;
- A company limited by guarantee – a company having the liability of its shareholders limited to such an amount as the shareholders may respectively undertake to contribute to the assets of the company in the event of it being wound up;
- An unlimited liability company – a company not having any limit on the liability of its shareholders; and
- A mutual company – being a company (other than a company limited by shares or having a share capital) which is authorised to engage in or carry on as a principal object insurance or reinsurance on the mutual principle.

Constituent Documents

The business activities of a company are governed by the provisions of its memorandum of association, which sets out its specific business objects and the powers that may be exercised in support of its principal business objects.

The bylaws of the company govern its administration and the relationship between its members and the board of directors. The bylaws are required to make provision for a certain limited number of matters. The members of the company are entitled to receive copies of the Memorandum of Association and its bylaws upon request.

Additional Requirements of Bermuda Law and Policy

The minimum authorised and issued capital of a Bermuda company is US$12,000 or its equivalent in any currency other than Bermuda dollars, which must be fully subscribed and issued, but need not be fully paid. Bearer shares are not permitted.

The annual fee ranges on a sliding scale from US$1,680 to US$25,000 depending on share capital and share premium account as shown in Table 1.

Table 1. Government Fee Scale

Assessable Capital (USD)	Fee (BMD)	Approximate HK$ Equivalent
12,000	1,680	13,104
12,001 - 120,000	3,360	26,208
120,001 - 1,200,000	5,040	39,312
1,200,001 - 12,000,000	6,720	52,416
12,000,001 - 100,000,000	8,400	65,520
100,000,001 - 500,000,000	15,000	117,000
500,000,001 or more	25,000	195,000

USD1 = BMD1 = HKD7.8

Where the capital is expressed in HKD and provided that the BMD equivalent is less than BMD15,000, then the lowest fee of BMD1,680 is payable, ie capital is HKD100,000 or circa BMD12,820 equivalent, then, notwithstanding the fact that it exceeds the USD12,000 base, the lower fee of BMD1,680 is payable.

Assessable Capital = Authorised Share Capital + Share Premium

Taxation

In Bermuda there are no taxes on profits, income or dividends, nor is there any capital gains taxes, estate duties or death duties. Profits can be accumulated and it is not obligatory for a company to pay dividends. The company is required to pay an annual government fee, which is determined on a sliding scale by reference to a company's authorised share capital and share premium account, with the minimum fee being BD$1,680 and the maximum BD$25,000 (the Bermuda dollar is equal to the US dollar).

The Bermuda Government has enacted legislation under which the Minister of Finance is authorised to give an assurance to an exempted company or a partnership that, in the event of there being enacted in

Bermuda any legislation imposing tax computed on profits or income or computed on any capital asset, gain or appreciation, then the imposition will not be applicable to such entities or any of their operations. In addition, there may be included an assurance that any such tax or any tax in the nature of estate duty or inheritance tax, shall not be applicable to the shares, debentures or other obligations of such entities.

Stamp duty

A stamp duty is not chargeable for incorporation, registration or licensing of an exempted company, nor, subject to certain minor exceptions, on their transactions. Accordingly, no stamp duty will be payable on the increase in or the issue or transfer of the share capital of the company.

Other taxes

There is no probate tax in Bermuda. On filing for probate in Bermuda, there are filing fees of circa BD$300. There is a stamp duty imposed on death in relation to BMD denominated assets only, ie Bermuda real estate and chattels owned by the deceased which are in Bermuda. Basically, therefore, there will be no duty payable in respect of any person who is not resident in Bermuda, and it really only applies to Bermuda residents who have purchased real property in Bermuda. The stamp duty rates which apply to Bermuda dollar denominated assets (real estate, chattels, and BMD bank accounts and shares in local companies) are as follows:

BMD denominated assets	Rates
First BD$50,000	nil
$50,000 to $200,000	5%
$200,000 to $1 million	10%
$1 million and up	15%

Gifts to spouses and charities are exempt. Shares in exempted companies and vessels are exempt. In addition, non-Bermudian employees of exempt companies, and non-Bermudian retired residents are designated nonresident for exchange control purposes and are not therefore entitled to hold BMD and as a result unlikely to hold dutiable assets in Bermuda, other than real estate and chattels.

Management and Administration

The management and administration of a Bermuda company is essentially governed by the *Companies Act*. The management and administration of a Bermuda company is in the hands of not less than two directors elected by the members. It should be noted that the general provisions of law require the annual election of directors or the election of directors in such other manner and for such term as may be provided in the bylaws of the company.

The *Companies Act* requires that a Bermuda company maintain either

- A Bermuda Resident Secretary and a Bermuda Resident Representative;

- A Bermuda Resident Secretary and a Bermuda Resident Director; or
- Two Bermuda Resident Directors,

all of whom must be individuals.

Exempted companies, the shares of which are listed on an appointed stock exchange, may appoint a Resident Representative in Bermuda in place of the other Bermuda resident officers, who or which may be either an individual or a corporate entity, whose statutory rights, duties and obligations are established by the *Companies Act*.

The *Companies Act* contains no specific restrictions on the power of the Directors to dispose of assets of a company, although it specifically requires that every officer (which includes a director and managing director and secretary) of a company shall act honestly and in good faith with a view to the best interests of the company and exercise the care, diligence and skill that a reasonably prudent person would exercise in comparable circumstances. Every officer should also comply with the *Companies Act*, regulations passed pursuant to the *Companies Act* and the bylaws of the company.

Continuation or Discontinuation and Amalgamation

A company incorporated overseas in a jurisdiction with reciprocal legislation may be discontinued in that jurisdiction and continued in Bermuda. Similarly, a Bermuda company may be discontinued in Bermuda and continued in another jurisdiction on the same basis. This involves a transfer of legal domicile of the company without any change in corporate personality.

The amalgamation of two or more Bermuda companies or one or more exempted companies with one or more foreign corporations is permitted subject to the consent of the Minister of Finance. However, this also requires reciprocal legislation in the jurisdiction of the foreign corporation.

This route is not often followed by Hong Kong or Asia-based clients in relation to companies incorporated in the area since most jurisdictions do not possess reciprocal legislation permitting continuation or amalgamation. However, the procedure has been used to 'continue' companies incorporated in the Cook Islands, the British Virgin Islands and certain provinces in Canada into Bermuda in preparation for a listing on a major stock exchange.

Investigation of the Affairs of a Company and the Protection of Minorities

The *Companies Act* makes specific provision with regard to the foregoing and provides that the Minister of Finance may appoint inspectors to investigate the affairs of an exempted company.

Class actions and derivative actions are generally not available to members under the laws of Bermuda; however, the Bermuda courts ordinarily would expect to follow English case law precedent. Furthermore, consideration would be given by the court to acts that are alleged to constitute a fraud against the minority members.

Members may be able to bring claims against a company; such claims must, however, be based on the general laws of contract or tort applicable in Bermuda.

Trust Law

Sources of Trust Law

Bermuda's trust law is based on statute supplemented by English common law. The statutory sources of trust law in this jurisdiction (which specifically pertain to trusts) are the *Trustee Act* 1975, the *Pension Trust Funds Act* 1966, the *Trust Companies Act* 1991, the *Trusts (Special Provisions) Act* 1989 and the *Perpetuities and Accumulations Act*, 1989. There are, however, many other Acts which although do not specifically pertain to trusts are applicable such as the *Conveyancing Amendment Act* 1983 and the *Bankruptcy Act* 1989.

Parties to a Trust

Settlor

The settlor of a trust may be any person (over the age of majority and of sound mind) or a corporation which has the corporate power to create a trust.

Beneficiary

Any person may be a beneficiary of a Bermuda trust, for example, minors, unborn persons, the settlors, companies and charities, and there is no requirement for beneficiaries to be resident in Bermuda. At any given time during the life of the trust, it must be possible to ascertain who the beneficiaries may be. It is not uncommon for the trust deed to give power to add and remove beneficiaries. The beneficiaries must all be born within the perpetuity period.

Trustees

Trustees may be either individuals or trust companies licensed to offer services to the public, by virtue of the enactment of the *Trust Companies Act* 1991. Alternatively, a private trust company may act as a trustee. A settlor may be a trustee. There are currently more than 36 licensed trust companies in Bermuda which are owned by international banks and also by local banks, firms, attorneys or accountants.

Regulations Applicable to some Trust Companies

Under the *Trust Companies Act* 1991, trust companies offering services to the public are subject to special vetting on incorporation and special regulations after incorporation. They must have audited financial statements and are regulated by the Bermuda Monetary Authority. They are also subject to the Code of Conduct on Money Laundering (as a condition of a grant of licence to carry on trust business). The *Trust Companies Act* 1991 also provides guidelines for investigation into the affairs of a licensed trust company in the event that its activities are in question and appropriate punitive measures.

The Code of Conduct applies to all financial institutions (eg banks and trust companies). Licensed trust companies in Bermuda are subject to the Code of Conduct which is designed to encourage the implementation of systems and procedures to assist in the prevention and detection of money laundering.

Under the Code of Conduct, licensed trust companies are expected to take particular vigilance in relation to obtaining information such as identification and references of the settlor (or any person who funds the trust) and also to know the source of the funds held in the trust. Furthermore, the Code of Conduct expects the maintenance of comprehensive records in relation to funds administered by licensed trust companies, the education of new employees within licensed trust companies with respect to the Code of Conduct and, in general, that licensed trust companies should have procedures in place to ensure that all unusual transactions are reported to senior management.

Formation of a Trust

Most trusts are created by deed; however, it is possible to create a trust for individuals orally. Constructive and resulting trusts are recognised under common law rules. The trust deed would normally be signed by the settlor and the trustee and the deed would usually detail the initial trust fund, the identity of the beneficiaries, the terms of the trusts and would also deal with administrative matters, such as removal of trustees, change of law and also give the trustees powers, for example, investment, voting of shares in companies and others. It is essential that the trust is validly created, that there is certainty of intention to create trust beneficiaries and assets. In order to meet the evidential requirements to create a valid trust, trusts should be created in writing.

Purpose Trusts

Non-charitable purpose trusts are permitted and have a life of up to 100 years. The *Trusts (Special Provisions) Act* 1989 introduces the concept of the non-charitable purpose trust and also sets out the particular requirements. A purpose trust is created for a specific purpose, such as holding the shares in a company, and can have no ascertainable beneficiary, although the trust deed must state what happens to any surplus at termination. The purpose of the trust must be specific, reasonable and possible and the purpose must not be immoral, contrary to public policy or unlawful. One of the trustees must be a designated person, such as an attorney, an accountant or a licensed trust company. The Minister of Finance has the power to 'designate' other persons as trustees of a specific purpose trust. In Bermuda, purpose trusts are often used as an alternative to charitable trusts in commercial transactions, such as in securitisations, capital asset financing and holding the shares in a private trust company.

Asset Protection Trusts

In relation to asset protection trusts, in 1994 Bermuda passed an amendment to the *Conveyancing Act* 1983 which allows creditors a reasonable opportunity to set aside a gift to a trust but, thereafter, protects transfers from being set aside.

In relation to gifts to trusts, if the settlor has the dominant intention to defeat claims of creditors in making the transfer, then a creditor who either exists at the time of the transfer or who comes into being within two years from the date of the transfer has six years in addition to the two year period to initiate proceedings to set aside a transfer to a trust. The onus of proof to prove dominant intention to defeat claims must be proved by the creditor on the balance of probabilities and the court must be satisfied that the creditor was someone who would be reasonable foreseeable to the settlor. If the settlor does not have the dominant intention to defeat claims, then the transfer may not be set aside (except in relation to bankruptcy).

Perpetuities and Accumulations Rule

By virtue of the *Perpetuities and Accumulations Act* 1989, it is now possible for the perpetuity period of a Bermuda trust to be a specified number of years not exceeding 100 years. It is still possible to define the perpetuity period by reference to a period commencing on the date of the creation of the trust and expiring 21 years after the death of the last survivor of a class or persons living at such date. There is no limit to the number of 'lives in being' which may be named for the purpose of determining the perpetuity period provided that they are easily ascertainable; nor need the persons named as lives in being have any connection with the trust deed. Income may be accumulated during the perpetuity period.

Trustees

There are no restrictions on the number of trustees in Bermuda. However, for practical reasons, most trust deeds provide for either a trust company or at least two individuals up to a limit of four trustees. Usually, the individual trustees who are chosen are either professionals, such as lawyers and accountants, or a relative or trusted friend of the settlor. A trustee may also be a beneficiary.

The source of trustee powers is the common law, the trust deed and the *Trustee Act* 1975. Trustee powers found in the *Trusts (Special Provisions) Act* 1989 may be incorporated by a specific reference in the trust deed.

The trustees' powers of investment are defined primarily in the trust deed itself. If these powers are not contained in the trust deed, then the trustees will be limited to investments allowed under the provisions of the *Trustee Act* 1975. Trustees generally have a common law duty to diversify investments. The trust deed will usually negate the need for diversity as trusts are often created to hold a particular asset which the settlor does not wish sold.

The delegation of powers is recognised under the statutory authority pursuant to s 15 and 17 of the *Trustee Act* 1975.

Where a discretionary trust is created, a letter of wishes is frequently used. The letter guides the trustees by indicating to them what the settlor's wishes are in relation to the beneficiaries and the trust fund. While letters of wishes are not enforceable against the trustees, trustees invariably give the letter of wishes the utmost respect in exercising their discretion. Most trust deeds provide for removal of the trustees by either the settlor or another person named in the trust deed and, therefore, the trustees can be removed if it is felt that the trustees are not carrying out their duties responsibly or properly, or in accordance with the letter of wishes.

There have been no developments in the light of the Rahman case. There have been no cases pre or post Rahman in Bermuda.

Trustees are not permitted to charge for their services unless the trust deed allows them to receive remuneration. Professional trustees act based on a scale fee (or as negotiated). Nonprofessional trustees are not usually paid. The rules pertaining to the resignation, removal and appointment of trustees are located in the trust deed itself. If there are no rules in the trust deed then the *Trustee Act* 1975 sets out the applicable rules.

Variation of Trusts

Section 48 of the *Trustee Act* 1975 gives the court jurisdiction to vary trusts. A court may vary the terms of a trust created by will or deed and may enlarge the administrative powers of the trustees. The court may also authorise particular transactions in respect of trust property. The court must be satisfied that the variation is for the benefit of the beneficiaries (born or unborn).

Section 11 of the *Trust (Special Provisions) Act* provides protections from forced heirship provisions which may apply in the country of the domicile of the settlor.

Fees

Annual fees for professional trustees vary and may be charged either on a scale fee or by reference to professional fees and would vary amongst the professionals. The annual fee payable to a trust corporation varies and could be either a fixed fee or a percentage fee, or as negotiated.

There are no statutory, registration or annual Government fees in relation to trusts in Bermuda. In fact, registration or filing of trust deeds or details is not required in Bermuda.

Protectorships and enforcerships usually require a minimum fee of US$1,000. Attorney fees for trust formation are minimum US$2,950 or based on time spent.

In relation to the incorporation of a private trust company, professional fees in the order of US$2,000 apply as a minimum. It is conventional for an initial deposit of US$4,600 to be charged, which is inclusive of annual government fees of US$1,680. Professional fees to incorporate a licensed public trust company would usually be in the region of US$10,000 plus disbursements (subject to time).

Migration and Recognition of Foreign Law

There are no particular rules on migration in Bermuda; however, trusts can be migrated easily. The migration (or flee) provisions are usually outlined in the trust deed. The Bermuda courts are able to assert jurisdiction where Bermuda law is the proper law of the trust, or where a trustee is resident in Bermuda, or any trust property is situated in Bermuda (but only in respect of that property), the administration is carried out in Bermuda or otherwise where the court thinks it appropriate. Where Bermuda law is not the proper law of the trust, then under Bermuda law the court has the ability to apply 'closer connection' rules as set out in Section 6 of the *Trusts (Special Provisions) Act* 1989.

The *Trusts (Special Provisions) Act* contains provisions similar to those of the Hague Convention on the law applicable to trusts and on their recognition.

Monica Jones is a partner in the Trusts & Estates department of Appleby, Spurling & Kempe. Frances Woo is a resident associate at the Hong Kong branch office of Appleby Spurling & Kempe.

BRITISH VIRGIN ISLANDS

Barry Mitchell

Introduction

Location and time zone

The British Virgin Islands is a group of more than forty islands situated in the Caribbean approximately 60 miles east of Puerto Rico. British Virgin Islands is one hour behind New York time. The territory is connected by numerous daily flights to San Juan in Puerto Rico. San Juan has direct flights to the United States, South America and Europe.

Political and Legal System

The British Virgin Islands is British territory, self-governing since 1967. Lying sixty miles east of Puerto Rico in the Caribbean, the 40 islands have a democratically elected legislature with thirteen members and an executive council whose members are the governor, four ministers plus an attorney general drawn from the legislature. The head of state is Queen Elizabeth II, represented in the territory by the governor.

The legal system is based on the English Courts of Equity. The judiciary are appointed by the governor. The highest court is the Privy Council in London.

Corporate Law

International Business Companies

The *International Business Companies Act* 1984 governs the incorporation, maintenance and termination of International Business Companies (IBCs) in the British Virgin Islands. An IBC must have a registered office and a registered agent in the British Virgin Islands.

IBCs are exempt from income tax and benefit from flexible legislation. Further advantages of using an IBC include:

- Availability of Chinese and English names, memorandum and articles of association and certificates of incorporation;
- The identity of shareholders and directors is not a matter of public record. The only documents which must be filed with the Companies Registry are the Memorandum and Articles of Association and amendments thereto;

- Only one director is required. The first director is appointed by the subscriber and that director may be a corporate director and may or may not be resident in the British Virgin Islands;
- The right of the IBC to finance or repurchase its shares out of surplus. Repurchased shares can be cancelled;
- No minimum capital requirement. Share capital may be denominated in any currency and in any number of currencies. Shares may be issued with or without a par value;
- Only one shareholder is required. The memorandum and articles of association are subscribed to by the registered agent;
- No requirement for a resident British Virgin Islands director;
- No requirement to file annual returns or financial statements;
- No requirement to hold annual meetings of directors or shareholders;
- A straightforward procedure for capital increase and capital reduction;
- A straightforward procedure for voluntary liquidation;
- Books and records can be held at such place as the directors determine; and
- The *IBC Act* provides a straightforward procedure to facilitate redomiciliation into and out of the British Virgin Islands.

Types of Companies

IBCs can only be companies limited by shares. However companies can also be established under the *Companies Act*, Chapter 285 of the Laws of the Virgin Islands. The *Companies Act* includes provision for companies limited by shares, unlimited liability companies, companies limited by guarantee and companies without a share capital and hybrid companies.

Although companies incorporated under the *Companies Act* are not as extensively used as IBCs, they can be a useful tax planning vehicle if structured so that they are nonresident companies.

The British Virgin Islands has over sixty companies licensed as registered agents which provide offshore financial services. These are a mix of multinational and private companies. The registered agents are all members of the Registered Agents Association which consults with the Financial Services Department, the government's body which regulates the offshore financial services industry on matters affecting the industry.

Confidentiality

The British Virgin Islands is not party to any treaty with a foreign government concerning disclosure of tax or other fiscal information. There is still in place relief of double taxation treaties with Japan and Switzerland and a double tax treaty is being negotiated with Canada. There is also a Mutual Legal Assistance Treaty with the United States which allows exchange of information in relation to drug and other bona fide criminal investigations. The treaty is drafted in such a way as to prevent 'fishing expeditions' and specifically excludes exchange of tax information.

Mutual Funds

It is believed that there are several billion dollars worth of mutual funds held or managed by IBCs in the British Virgin Islands but until recently the industry had relied on self-regulation. The *Mutual Funds Act* was enacted on June 6, 1996.

Trust Law

The Legal Framework

The general law relating to trusts in the British Virgin Islands is derived from English common law principles. The *Trustee Ordinance* 1961 was based on the *English Trustee Act* 1925. The *Trustee Amendment Act* 1993 has modernised trust law in the British Virgin Islands.

The *Recognition of Trusts Act* 1987 (England) has been extended to the British Virgin Islands so that the provisions of the Hague Convention on recognition of trusts applies in the British Virgin Islands.

Settlors

The settlor of a trust can be any person, including a corporate body, who transfers property by way of gift or testamentary disposition on trust or to a trust. The reservation of powers by a settlor and the fact that the trustee may be a beneficiary is expressly deemed not to be inconsistent with the existence of a trust.

Beneficiaries

A beneficiary of a trust can be any person whether resident or nonresident in the British Virgin Islands. British Virgin Islands trusts are not subject to tax in respect of nonresident beneficiaries and offshore income and property.

Trustees

A trust may have one or more trustees. They can be individuals or corporate trustees. There is no requirement for the trust to have a resident British Virgin Islands trustee. The settlor or a beneficiary may also be a trustee.

Protectors

The law specifically provides for the conferment on any person various powers including appointment and removal of trustees and consenting to specified actions of the trustees in relation to the trust. Such person can be named as protector, nominator committee or any other name and that person shall not by virtue of the exercise of these powers be deemed a trustee or be liable to the beneficiaries of the trust for the bona fide exercise of those powers.

Trustee Company Regulations

British Virgin Islands Registered Agents are governed by the *Banks and Trust Companies Act* 1990. For a British Virgin Islands company to act as a trustee it must be licensed under this Act or fall within one of the exceptions contained in the *Banks and Trust Companies (Application Procedures) Directions* 1991. The most utilised exception is a British Virgin Islands company owned by family members which is a trustee of a trust for the benefit of members of the family.

Types of Trusts

A British Virgin Islands trust is a trust where the laws of the British Virgin Islands are stated to be the proper law of the trust or where, if no law is stated, there is some other connection with the British Virgin

Islands. For example, the administration of the trust takes place in the British Virgin Islands. Trusts can be express or implied, discretionary or fixed, revocable or irrevocable, constructive, resulting, *inter vivos* or testamentary.

The Act also provides for purpose trusts, that is trusts established for a purpose rather than particular beneficiaries. These can be settled for any purpose provided the purpose is specific, reasonable and possible and not immoral, contrary to public policy or unlawful.

The settlor may provide the trustees with a letter of wishes in respect of a discretionary trust. The trustee will generally follow the requests detailed in the letter of wishes if these fall within the provisions of the trust instrument. However, the trustee is not bound to do so.

Powers and Duties of Trustees

The powers and duties of a trustee will be governed by the trust document and the general law. The Act specifically permits trustees to invest trust funds in any investment they choose provided they exercise reasonable diligence and prudence.

The Act also includes a schedule of powers which can be specifically incorporated into the trust instrument by reference. These powers include a power to engage and delegate to an investment adviser. There is also a specific provision dealing with trustees' responsibilities in relation to the management of companies in which the trust has invested. A trustee is not required to interfere in such management unless the trustee has notice of 'wilful negligence, wilful default or fraud or dishonesty on the part of the directors having the management of such company'.

The trust deed should include a provision authorising charging remuneration of trustees given the general law position that a trustee must not profit from his position.

Registration, Fees and Filing

The trust instrument is exempt from registration under the *Registration and Records Act* but all trusts which provide British Virgin Islands law as the proper law are liable for US$50.00 trust duty. Professional and trustee's fees are not fixed by law.

Tax

British Virgin Islands trusts are exempt from tax in the British Virgin Islands except where the trust owns land or carries on business in the British Virgin Islands or the trust has resident beneficiaries, in which case such beneficiaries will be liable for tax on distributions to them.

Migration of trusts

British Virgin Islands law allows, subject to the provisions of the trust instrument, a change of proper law to another jurisdiction provided that jurisdiction recognises the trust and the rights of the beneficiaries. If the trust is migrating to the British Virgin Islands, it is not necessary for the previous jurisdiction to recognise the change. There is also the ability to allow for an automatic transfer of trust assets from one trustee to another on the happening of certain specified events such as the introduction of exchange control.

Other Features

The *Trustee Ordinance* includes statutory provision for

- A perpetuity period not exceeding 100 years as well as a 'wait-and-see' period;
- Protection of a settlor's dispositions to the trust from forced heirship laws of the settlor's home jurisdiction. Under the provision the settlor is deemed to have capacity to make such dispositions and provides that the laws relating to inheritance or succession in the settlor's place of domicile do not affect the validity of the trust;
- Amendment by the trustee of the trust provided such power is expressly contained in the trust instrument;
- Inclusion of protector provisions to provide a 'watchdog' in respect of trust assets and trustee decisions;
- Accumulation of income for the duration of the trust;
- Power for the courts to vary trusts in limited circumstances;
- Trustees to act by majority decision; and
- Creation of trusts by declaration affording greater confidentiality.

Barry Mitchell is managing director of TrustNet (British Virgin Islands) Limited. Mr Mitchell was educated in New Zealand and gained law and accounting degrees from Auckland University in 1981. He was admitted to the New Zealand bar in 1982.

THE CAYMAN ISLANDS

Michael L Alberga

Introduction

The Cayman Islands are a British Crown Colony located approximately 590 miles or one hour and ten minutes flying time from Florida. It is one of the world's leading financial centres with a population of approximately 30,000 persons, the majority of whom live on Grand Cayman. The capital is George Town. Grand Cayman is serviced by major airlines from various points in the US and by Cayman Airways.

The Cayman Islands are surrounded by powder-white sand beaches and pristine aquamarine water; tourism is a major industry.

Financial Services

The financial industry is serviced by professionals from the Caymans, Europe, Canada and the US. All major accounting firms have a presence at Grand Cayman. More than 500 registered banks, 450 captive insurance companies, 1,500 mutual funds and 30,000 corporations do business from or within the Cayman Islands.

Political and Legal System

The legal system of the Cayman Islands has been developed from the British model, with the common law forming the backbone together with local statutes. The final Court of Appeal is the Judicial Committee of the Privy Council in London.

The Cayman Islands remain one of the few British Crown Colonies left in existence. The Cayman Islands have internal self-government, with a governor appointed as the Queen's. Elections are held every four years and a local parliament is appointed.

Taxation and Exchange Control

The Cayman Islands impose no insurance, capital gains, estate or inheritance tax. There is no exchange control and currency is freely convertible. The Cayman Islands have no central bank. The local currency – the Cayman Islands dollar – is pegged to the United States dollar at a fixed rate CI\$1.00 = US\$1.25 and is controlled by a currency control board.

Regulation of the Financial Industry

Over the last 20 years, the Cayman Islands have passed legislation which has served as a model for the world's leading financial centres in the areas of banking, trusts, corporations and insurance. These laws have been carefully modelled to provide a degree of regulation which has proved to be effective by providing internationally acceptable standards while avoiding a large bureaucracy. This careful balancing act has led to unprecedented growth and has contributed to the Cayman Islands' reputation as a financial centre.

Recent Legislative Changes

The Cayman Islands have recently established a monetary authority, which is a statutory body that replaces the office of the Inspector of Financial Services. This authority will bring under one body the licensing and regulation of all banks and trust companies, mutual funds, insurance companies and service providers, and regulate and operate the Cayman Islands' currency board. Plans for a stock exchange are in the works.

On 20 September 1996, the Proceeds of Criminal Conduct Bill was passed. This anti-money laundering legislation gives statutory effect to a regulatory regime which has been in place for many years and introduces mechanisms which allow the courts to restrain and confiscate assets. The law applies to all serious offences except tax and fiscal offences, which are excluded from the provisions. The law sends a clear message that the financial service industry of the Cayman Islands is not available to unscrupulous persons.

Confidentiality

The Cayman Islands have led the world in legislation which essentially codifies the common law position in the United Kingdom regarding confidentiality between a bank and its customers and has enlarged and extended that confidentiality to all business and professional people. The Cayman Islands have also entered into agreements and passed laws to ensure that the confidentiality laws do not protect criminal activity.

Corporate Law

The words 'corporation' and 'company' are synonymous for the purposes of Cayman Islands law and may be defined as 'an entity invested by law with most of the powers and responsibilities of a natural person'. Companies are classified into:

- Companies limited by shares;
- Companies limited by guarantee, with or without share capital;
- Unlimited companies (ie those not limiting the liability of their members); and
- Hybrid companies.

Types of Companies

Ordinary companies

An ordinary company is any Cayman company which is not an ordinary nonresident company, an exempted company or an exempted limited duration company. It may, upon obtaining the necessary licenses, carry on business in the Cayman Islands.

Ordinary nonresident company

An ordinary nonresident company is a Cayman company with perpetual succession which does not intend to carry on business in the Cayman Islands and, in respect of which the Financial Secretary has issued a certificate designating it to be a nonresident.

Exempted company

An exempted company is a Cayman company with perpetual succession which may not operate in the Cayman Islands except in furtherance of its business carried on outside of the Cayman Islands and, for this purpose, it may effect and conclude contracts in the Cayman Islands and exercise in the Cayman Islands all of its powers necessary for carrying on its business outside the Cayman Islands. For example, it may maintain and operate bank accounts in the Cayman Islands. An exempted company is not subject to certain provisions of the Companies Law, and there are certain provisions peculiar to it. In particular:

- The register of members need not be kept at the registered office and is not open to inspection by the public nor is it necessary to file an annual return of members, though the directors must file annually (in January) a declaration that the company has complied with the relevant provisions of the Companies Law;
- Shares may have a par value or no par value, but a company cannot have both types of shares;
- Bearer shares (only if fully paid) may be issued, but any company with the power to issue bearer shares cannot own land in the Cayman Islands;
- At least one meeting of the board of directors must be held each year in the Cayman Islands (Meetings can be attended by proxies or alternates);
- The name need not include the word 'Limited' or the abbreviation 'Ltd' and the words or letters used in other countries to designate limited liability (eg Inc, BV, NV, SA and Corporation) may be used. Unless it is a Limited Duration Company, LDC may not be used;
- No annual general meeting need be held;
- It must not make any invitation to the public in the Cayman Islands to subscribe for any of its shares or debentures;
- It can obtain an exemption from future Caymanian taxes under the Tax Concessions Law for a specific period, the present practice being for twenty years. The exemption takes the form of an undertaking from the Governor-in-Council and applies to any tax which may in the future be levied on profits, gains, income or appreciation. The undertaking also states that neither the above taxes nor any tax in the nature of estate duty or inheritance tax will be payable on the shares, debentures or obligations of the company in question;

- It can, if it meets certain requirements, be de-registered in the Cayman Islands and register by way of continuation in another qualifying jurisdiction; and
- It can be incorporated as or changed into an exempted limited duration company.

Exempted limited duration companies

An exempted limited duration company is an exempted company with a limited duration of thirty years or less with certain specific provisions applicable to it. These are:

- It must have at least two members;
- Its name must include 'Limited Duration Company' or 'LDC';
- Its Articles of Association may provide:
  i. that the transfer of any share or other interest of a member requires a unanimous resolution of all other members; and
  ii. that the management of the company is vested in the members in proportion to their share or other ownership interests, in which case the members will be considered directors but with power to delegate the management to a board of directors;
- It is deemed to commence voluntary winding up:
  i. unless otherwise provided in its Memorandum, within ninety days of death, insanity, bankruptcy, dissolution, withdrawal, retirement or resignation of a member; or the redemption, repurchase or cancellation of all of a member's shares; or the occurrence of an event which terminates the membership of a member; unless at least two members remain who unanimously resolve to continue the company within the ninety-day period, or
  ii. if so provided by its Articles, on the termination of a period or the happening of an event.

Properly structured, these can qualify to be treated as a partnership for United States tax purposes.

Limited life companies

Where a company with a fixed life is required, but the maximum thirty years of a limited duration company (LDC) is inappropriate, what is often called a limited life company can be formed. This can be an ordinary, ordinary nonresident or exempted company. It differs from an LDC in that:

- It need only have one shareholder;
- There is no statutory limitation on its duration; and
- It may not use the words 'limited duration company' or the abbreviation 'LDC' in its name.

It may include in its Articles of Association any of the four partnership elements, at least two of which the US Internal Revenue Service requires for tax transparency. These are:

- Management and control is reserved to the members (it should be noted that this element is not available to an exempted company – other than an LDC – since exempted companies must have directors);
- Issue of two or more classes of shares carrying either limited or unlimited liability;
- Restriction on transfers of shares; and

- Mandatory commencement of winding-up and dissolution when the fixed period expires or a specified event happens.

The US Internal Revenue Service may not treat a company with only one shareholder as a partnership.

Companies limited by guarantee

Companies limited by guarantee may be formed with or without share capital. They may be ordinary, ordinary nonresident or exempted companies or LDCs. Every member agrees to pay a sum fixed by the Memorandum of Association if it is wound up and is insolvent.

Guarantee companies without a share capital are often used for clubs, eg golf or tennis clubs. Membership normally ceases on death or resignation. It is possible to provide for transferability of members' rights, but this is more easily dealt with by issuing shares. Where such a company has more than one class of member, the Memorandum of Association may provide that in a winding up the liability of the members of a particular class will be unlimited.

Where a guarantee company has share capital, not all members need be shareholders and not all shareholders need be members. Guarantee companies with a share capital can be used:

- For retaining limited liability, but if properly structured, be treated as partnerships for US tax purposes;
- For confidentiality – no public record exists as to members who have agreed to guarantee a fixed sum;
- For setting up and running charities or other non-profit organisations;
- For owning and operating time share resorts; and
- As an alternative to a trust, with a trustee as shareholder, having administrative and voting powers, and the beneficiaries being members, and having income and capital rights.

Foreign companies

Any company incorporated outside the Cayman Islands which establishes a place of business in the Cayman Islands or commences carrying on business in the Cayman Islands must deliver to the Registrar for registration:

- A copy certified and authenticated under the public seal of the country, city or place under the laws of which the company was incorporated of its Charter, Bylaws, Memorandum and Articles of Association or other instrument constituting or defining its constitution and, if the instruments are not in the English language, certified translations of them;
- A list of its directors and officers, their addresses and nationalities; and
- The name and address of a person resident in the Cayman Islands who is authorised to accept service of notices and documents on the company's behalf.

Every foreign company must exhibit at its place of business in the Cayman Islands and state on all letterheads, notices, bills, advertisements and other publications, its name and country of incorporation and that the liability of the members is limited, if such is the case.

Formation of a Company

A company may be formed by one or more persons (two for an LDC) executing the Memorandum and Articles of Association and registering those documents with the Registrar of Companies. The initial subscriber is not necessarily the beneficial owner of the shares in the company but may become a shareholder for and on behalf of others who wish to remain anonymous. The Memorandum and Articles, when registered, bind the company and its members to the same extent as if each member had subscribed his name and affixed his seal to them and as if there were in them contained on the part of the member or subscriber, his heirs, executors and administrators a covenant to observe all the conditions of the Memorandum and Articles.

Memorandum of Association

The Memorandum of Association sets out, among other things, the purposes and objects of the company, ie the activities which the company may pursue. Historically, a company was unable to undertake any activity which it was not empowered to do by this document, but recent amendments to the Companies Law have effectively abolished the concept of *ultra vires*, save to the extent that it is specifically stated that the company is restricted from doing any particular business. Memoranda of Association are normally all encompassing, allowing the company to do anything which an individual of full age and mental capacity can do. The document must be signed by each subscriber in the presence of, and be attested by, at least one witness.

The Memorandum must make provision for the following matters:

- The name of the company;
- The registered office;
- The objects, purposes or powers of the company (a company may do anything an individual is able to do);
- Unless it is an unlimited company, a statement of limitation of the liability of the members or, if such is the case, that in a winding up the liability of members holding shares of a particular class will be unlimited;
- The share capital of the company if limited by shares and the limit of liability of members if limited by guarantee.

Names cannot be reserved and certain words may not be used in the name without the Registrar's consent. These words include 'Royal', 'Imperial', 'Empire', 'Municipal', 'Chartered' and 'Co-operative'. In addition:

- The words 'Bank' or 'Trust' may not be used unless the company in question is licensed under the Banks and Trust Companies Law;
- The words 'insurance', 'assurance', 'indemnity', 'guarantee', 'underwriting', 'reinsurance', 'surety' or 'casualty' or any derivative, in any language, may not be used unless the company is licensed under the Insurance Law;
- No name may contain the words 'building society'.

A company may change its name by special resolution.

Articles of Association

The Articles of Association regulates the manner in which the affairs of the company will be managed and determines in what manner the powers of the company will be exercised. These are commonly known as bylaws in jurisdictions such as United States and Panama. This document must be stamped as though it were a deed, even though the persons affixing their signatures to it (called the subscribers) do not execute it under seal. The signatures of the subscribers must be attested by at least one witness.

Certificate of Incorporation

On registration with the Registrar of Companies and payment of the necessary fees, the company obtains a Certificate of Incorporation, which is the equivalent of a birth certificate. The issue of this certificate brings the company into existence and enables it to commence business (subject to obtaining the necessary licenses if it proposes to carry on business locally). It should be noted that a contract entered into on behalf of a company before its incorporation does not bind it, although it may afterwards ratify it and thereby accept it. But the person who purported to sign it on the company's behalf will be personally liable until the company ratifies it.

Share Capital

The share capital of the company may be divided into different classes of shares and a company may have fractional shares. The following classes of shares may be issued by a company:

- Ordinary shares, voting or nonvoting;
- Cumulative preference shares, voting or nonvoting;
- Non-cumulative preference shares, voting or nonvoting;
- Redeemable ordinary or preference shares, cumulative or non-cumulative and voting or nonvoting (subject to restrictions);
- Deferred shares; and
- No-par-value shares (exempted companies only).

A company may also raise money by the issue of notes, debentures or debenture stock. There is no requirement in Cayman law for shares to be fully paid up on issue except for shares issued to bearer, but the holder of registered shares is liable to be called upon to pay all unpaid amounts on his shares. A company is permitted to have an authorised capital in any amount or currency which the incorporators may wish, but need not issue more than one registered share which can be paid in full or in part, or one bearer share which must be paid in full.

Share Certificates (Registered Shares)

A share certificate is a document issued by a company stating that the person named in it is registered as the holder of the specified number of shares of a certain class (if more than one class of shares has been issued) and that the shares have been paid for in full or up to a certain amount.

Share Warrants (Exempted Companies Only)

An exempted company which is so authorised by its Articles may issue fully paid share warrants under its common seal. The warrant (or bearer share certificate) certifies that the bearer is entitled to the shares represented by it which are transferable by delivery. Warrants are negotiable instruments so that any person who purchases a share warrant or advances his money on the security of it will be entitled to it free from all defects in the title of the person who delivered it to him provided he was unaware of the defects (if any) at the date of delivery.

Appointment of Directors and Officers

It is usual for the subscribers to the Memorandum of Association to appoint the first directors of the company. The subscribers may appoint themselves or persons of their own choosing as directors who, in turn, appoint the officers of the company. It is usual to have at least two or three directors and a secretary. It is possible, however, to have one person who is the sole director and officer of the company, if the Articles so provide.

There are only three statutory requirements in the Companies Law concerning public issues.

- Section 34(3) – Every prospectus relating to the issue of shares must contain particulars of the discount allowed on the issue of shares or of so much of that discount as had not been written off at the date of the issue of the prospectus.
- Section 194 – An exempted company is prohibited from making any invitation to the public in the Cayman Islands to subscribe for any of its shares or debentures.
- Section 206 – Every foreign company must in every prospectus inviting subscriptions for its shares or debentures in the Cayman Islands state the country in which it is incorporated.

Note that for the purposes of Cayman law, there is no difference between a 'member' and a 'shareholder'.

Statutory Meetings

Every company in Cayman (other than an exempted company) is required by law to have one general meeting per year (known as the Annual General Meeting). The business of an Annual General Meeting is usually to:

- Receive and consider the accounts and balance sheet of the company, if any;
- Elect directors in place of those retiring;
- Elect auditors, if applicable; and
- Declare a dividend if any.

All meetings other than the Annual General Meeting of the shareholders are called Extraordinary General Meetings.

Reporting Requirements

Annual

All companies in the Cayman Islands having a capital divided into shares (but not companies limited by guarantee having no share capital, nor unlimited companies) must file an annual return. Ordinary companies and ordinary nonresident companies must set out *inter alia* the names of directors, officers and shareholders, and changes in shareholdings since the date of the last return. Exempted companies have to file an annual return in the form of a declaration, which does not require any of the above information but states *inter alia* that the operations of the company since the last return (or since registration) have been mainly outside the Cayman Islands. Printed forms for annual returns may be obtained from the Registrar of Companies. Foreign companies are exempted from this requirement; they simply pay the annual fee to the government.

Other

Other reporting requirements are:

- All Caymanian companies must send to the Registrar a list of directors and officers, their addresses and occupations and notify him of any changes within fifteen days of the appointment or change. Foreign companies are allowed twenty-one days;
- A copy of all special resolutions must be sent to the Registrar within fifteen days of their being passed; and
- Notice of any resolution passed for winding up a company voluntarily must be published in the Gazette.

Registers

All companies are required to keep the following statutory registers:

- Members (Shareholders);
- Directors and officers; and
- Charges (Mortgages).

Corporate Mobility and Merger

Corporations incorporated under the laws of other jurisdictions may be transferred to the Cayman Islands 'by continuation', allowing it to obtain the benefits of incorporation in the Cayman Islands without losing its established identity (including its incorporation date) or having to transfer its assets or liabilities to a new entity. Adequate merger and restructuring provisions are provided for by the laws.

Fees

The fees payable to the Registrar of Companies on formation and annually vary depending on the type of company. For companies with an authorised capital of $50,000 or less, the fees are as follows:

Type of companies	Incorporation fee	Annual fee
Exempted company	US$500.00	US$500.00
Ordinary nonresident	US$427.00	US$427.00

Trusts Law

Regulation of Trusts in the Cayman Islands

The creation and operation of settlements and trusts is governed by the *Trusts Law* 1967 and by English Common Law principles. The Law is based on the *English Trustee Act* 1925 and contains provisions based on the *English Variation of Trusts Act* 1958. Special legislation has been passed to enhance Cayman as a jurisdiction for international trusts and forms part of the overall trust legislation. The Laws are:

- The *Trusts (Foreign Element) Law* 1987 (Law 17 of 1987)
- The *Fraudulent Dispositions Law* 1989 (Law 15 of 1989)
- The *Perpetuities Law* 1995 (Law 7 of 1995)
- The *Trusts (Foreign Element) (Amendment) Law* 1995 (Law 6 of 1995)

Advantages of Trusts

The trustee can be given power to invest the trust funds with complete flexibility and all income and gains can be accumulated tax free in the Cayman Islands until such time as it is expedient to make a distribution to the beneficiaries. Often, persons setting up trusts will also set up a company to hold the cash or other property that it is intended to settle so that the sole asset of the trust is the issued capital of, and possibly loans by, the trustee to the company.

Classification of Trusts

Trusts can be broadly classified in the following categories:

- Those created by statute;
- Those created intentionally by the act of parties;
- Those implied arising from the presumed intention of parties; and
- Those arising by operation of law, eg constructive trusts.

Trusts are either inter *vivos* (ie created during the settlor's lifetime) or testamentary (created by will).

Creation of Trusts

In the Cayman Islands, trusts are usually created by a deed made by the settlor and the trustee or by a declaration made by the trustee only.

These trusts may be discretionary in nature, ie giving the trustee a discretion as to which beneficiaries and the amounts by which such beneficiaries or any of them will benefit under the trust. Trusts may also be fixed in nature, allowing the trustee no discretion as to which beneficiaries may so benefit or the amount of the benefit each is to receive

A Declaration of Trust provides complete anonymity as to the source providing the trust with its assets.

There are no restrictions on who may be a trustee and a settlor may also be a trustee. Professional trustees including corporations who provide trust services as a business must be licensed under the *Banks and Trust Companies Law*. This trust instrument usually sets out the powers and duties of the trustee and may expand or limit the investment powers allowed by the law. The payment of fees to trustees whether an individual or corporation must be specifically provided for in the instrument.

Letters of Wishes

Letters of Wishes are used in conjunction with some discretionary trusts and allow settlors to leave trustees an indication of their desires. These have no binding legal effect on the trustees and may be used by the trustee or trustees in exercising their discretion.

Shams

Settlors should be careful not to maintain excessive control over a trust and to ensure that the trust is properly constituted to avoid an attack on the basis of a sham. Recent cases in other jurisdictions have demonstrated that the failure to take adequate advice and the following of the advice can have unfortunate repercussions for the settlors and others.

Beneficiaries

There are no restrictions on who may be appointed the beneficiary of a trust and it is possible to name the settlor, minors, unborn persons, bodies corporate, charities to be the beneficiary or beneficiaries of a trust. In certain instruments, powers of appointment are given to named persons who may appoint beneficiaries under the power.

Protectors

It is possible for the trust instrument to provide for the appointment of persons who are called protectors and who will give investment and other advice to trustees.

These persons may or may not be considered to be co-trustees, depending on the particular circumstances. It is possible to provide that certain powers set out in a trust document cannot be exercised by the trustee without the consent of the protector.

Perpetuity Period

The common law rule against perpetuities was abolished with effect from 1 August 1995 in respect of instruments coming into effect after that date. There is a statutory limit of 150 years on the perpetuity period applicable to a disposition of property and on the power to accumulate income. The maximum period that a trust may last is therefore 150 years.

Wait-and-see Rule

Generally, there is now a 'wait-and-see' rule; a disposition is not void merely because it can take effect outside of the perpetuity period. Until the end of that period, a disposition is treated as if it is not subject to the rule against perpetuity, nothing done previously in relation to it by way of advancement, application of intermediate income or otherwise is invalid.

Forced Heirship Rules

Under the *Trusts (Foreign Element) Law* 1987:

- A term in a trust expressly selecting Cayman Islands law to govern the trust, or a particular aspect of the trust, or selecting the courts of the Cayman Islands to be the forum for administering the trust is valid, effective and conclusive;
- If a trust so provides, its governing law may be changed to or from the laws of the Cayman Islands;
- Subject to certain provisos, all questions arising in regard to a trust governed by Cayman Islands law or in regard to dispositions of property under that trust, including:
  i. the settlor's capacity;
  ii. any aspect of its validity, interpretation or effect; and
  iii. questions as to rights, liabilities, powers and obligation of trustees and their appointment and removal;

  are to be determined by Cayman Islands law;
- Subject to the same provisos as in above, no trust governed by Cayman Islands law is void, voidable or liable to be set aside, nor the settlor to be questioned, nor is any person subjected to any liability or deprived of any right because
  i. the laws of a foreign jurisdiction prohibit or do not recognise the concept of a trust; and
  ii. the trust avoids or defeats foreign heirship rights; and
- The law does not validate a testamentary trust of property which is invalid under the law of the testator's domicile.

Foreign Judgment not Recognised

A foreign judgment is not recognised and will not be enforced in so far as it is inconsistent with the provisions of the law dealing with exclusion of foreign law and heirship rights.

The Cayman courts will apply the statute to property over which it has jurisdiction, but if property which is the subject of a dispute is situated outside of the Cayman Islands, the courts of the country in which they are located may apply its own conflict of laws rules and disregard Cayman law. Before putting property into a trust, it would be best to move it where possible (eg money, jewellery, art work) to the Cayman Islands or transfer it (eg shares, land) to a Cayman company and settle the shares of that company on trust.

Exempted Trusts

The Trusts Law of the Cayman Islands provides for the creation of a type of trust known as an 'Exempted Trust'. Such a trust may obtain from the Governor of the Cayman Islands an undertaking that, should tax of an income or capital nature ever be introduced in the Cayman Islands, the exempted trust will not be subject to such tax for 50 years from the date of its creation.

Requirements for the establishment of an exempted trust are:

- The trust must be discretionary in nature;
- Beneficiaries must not include Cayman residents, except charities; and
- The form of the trust deed must first be approved by the Registrar of Trusts.

It is possible to create an exempted trust by first having a draft of the deed approved, or by applying to register an already existing trust.

The Fraudulent Dispositions Law

The *Fraudulent Dispositions Law* applies in place of the law in effect previously, s 107 of the *Bankruptcy Law* and the English Statute of Elizabeth. A creditor who is prejudiced may set aside a disposition made at an undervalue and with an intent to defraud. Both characteristics are essential.

The property disposed of may be Caymanian or foreign property. The creditor must bring his action within six years of the date of the disposition. 'Intent to defraud' means an intention of a transferor wilfully to defeat an obligation owed to a creditor, and 'obligation' means an obligation or liability (including a contingent liability) which existed on or before the date of a relevant disposition and of which the transferor had notice. The Law does not require notice to be 'actual', so presumably constructive notice suffices. A creditor must therefore exist at the time of the disposition and the transferor must have notice of his claim. The burden of proving intent to defraud is on the creditor seeking to set the disposition aside.

If a disposition is set aside:

- A transferee (eg trustee) who has acted in good faith has a first charge over the property for his entire costs properly incurred in defence of the action (not limited to costs which might otherwise have been allowed by the Court); and
- A beneficiary who has acted in good faith may retain any distribution properly made to him before the disposition is set aside.

Mobility

Trusts usually have flight clauses which allow a change of domicile in the event of certain specified events. These should be carefully drafted as they may have unintended results.

Recognition of Foreign Trusts

The Hague Convention on Recognition of Trust has not been extended to the Cayman Islands, primarily because of Art 13, which allows a convention party jurisdiction not to recognise a trust the significant elements of which, except for the choice of applicable law, the place of administration and the habitual residence of the trustee are more closely connected with states which do not have the institution of the trust or category of trust involved. In relation to foreign trusts, general common law conflicts or laws principles apply, as supplemented by the *Trusts (Foreign Element) Law*.

Tax Planning

Tax legislation in metropolitan countries is often aimed at reducing or eliminating the tax advantages of foreign trusts, for example, the United Kingdom, Canada and the United States all have anti-avoidance legislation that is directed at trusts created in tax-free jurisdictions. Competent tax advice should always be an integral part of the creation of a trust.

Fees

The stamp duty on trusts and the registration and annual fees payable on Exempted Trusts are fixed and are not based on the asset value of the trusts. These are minimal.

Michael L Alberga has practised law in the Cayman Islands for over 18 years and is a partner of the firm Myers & Alberga. Myers & Alberga is a full service law firm with a large corporate department which provides various management functions for numerous corporations.

THE COOK ISLANDS

Alan Taylor

Introduction

Location and Time Zone

The Cook Islands are situated in the middle of the South Pacific, south of Hawaii and northeast of New Zealand. The Islands are ten hours behind Greenwich Mean time.

Population and Economy

The Cook Islands have a population of approximately 15,000 people, 10,000 of whom live on Rarotonga, the largest of the 15 islands that make up the Cook Islands. The business language of the Cook Islands is English and its official currency is the New Zealand dollar. The largest sources of income for the Cook Islands Government are tourism and the offshore industry.

Political System

The Cook Islands have been an independent country since 1965. Its parliamentary and legal systems are similar to those in most common law jurisdictions. Elections are held every five years under a system of universal suffrage. Since independence only two political parties have formed a government, both fully supportive of the offshore industry.

Corporate Law

International Companies

The *International Companies Act* 1981-82 (the Act) governs the incorporation, maintenance and termination of Cook Islands International Companies (IC). The advantages of using an IC include:

- The availability of Chinese and English names, memorandum and articles association, certificates of incorporation and renewal certificates;
- Bearer shares and bearer share warrants are available;
- The IC's articles of association may provide that on the happening of a specified event, the membership interest of any member of the IC affected by that event shall automatically be vested in a person specified in the articles of association;
- The IC has the right to finance the purchase of its own shares as well as repurchase and cancel its own shares;

- Only one director is required. That director may be a corporate director and may or may not be resident in the Cook Islands;
- Only one shareholder is required;
- Share capital can be expressed in any currency and can be more than one currency; and
- Shares of no par value are permitted.

Confidentiality

Comprehensive confidentiality provisions limit access to the Registrar of International Companies' records and the use of any information about a Cook Islands International Company. It is an offence for any person to divulge, attempt to or threaten to divulge any information about an International Company. The company's records held by the Registrar are not a matter of public record. They can only be searched by an officer, member, debenture holder, director or liquidator of the company or a person who has the written consent of a director or liquidator.

Types of Companies

The *International Companies Act* provides for the incorporation of

- Companies limited by shares;
- No liability companies;
- Unlimited liability companies;
- Companies limited by guarantee; and
- Companies limited by shares and guarantee.

Taxation

No Cook Islands tax, duty or levy whatsoever is imposed on an International Company.

Administrative Requirements

International Companies are required to file annual returns. This will generally be done upon renewal of the company's registration. There is no requirement for the company to have its accounts audited or to file those accounts. Members of the company are able to dispense with calling annual general meetings if they wish.

The law provides a procedure to facilitate corporate redomiciliation into and out of the Cook Islands.

Trust Law

The Legal Framework

The general trust law of the Cook Islands is derived from the English Courts of Equity. In 1984 the Cook Islands enacted its own international trust legislation, the *International Trusts Act*. It provides a simple registration procedure whereby the general trust law will only apply to a registered trust to the extent that such law has not been modified by the *International Trusts Act*.

For a Cook Islands international trust to obtain the benefits of the *International Trusts Act* (ITA) it must be registered in accordance with the provisions of the Act. There are no provisions preventing an oral trust constituting a trust.

An international trust may be governed by the law of any jurisdiction, but the choice of governing law must be specified in the trust instrument.

Settlor

The settlor may be any person who assigns or disposes property to that trust or declares or otherwise creates such a trust. The settlor may be a corporate body. The *International Trusts Act* provides that a trust is not invalid by reason that the settlor retains control over the trust or the trust property. Such control can include possession and distribution of trust assets, amendment of the trust instrument and appointment and removal of trustees and protectors.

Beneficiaries

A beneficiary may be any person who is not domiciled or ordinarily resident in the Cook Islands.

Trustees

The trust may have one or more trustees. However, at least one of the trustees must be a Cook Islands international company, a Cook Islands registered foreign company or a company registered as a trustee company under the provisions of the *Trustee Companies Act* 1981-82. The settlor or a beneficiary can be a trustee.

Protector

A protector can be appointed by the settlor to give the settlor a degree of comfort in respect of the trustees' administration of the trust. The Act provides a simple definition of who is protector but does not give any indication of the protector's powers, duties or functions. The position of the protector is therefore governed by the common law which provides that the protector owes fiduciary duties to the beneficiaries of a trust and not to the settlor who appointed him or her. The trust instrument will prescribe the duties and functions of the protector.

Types of Trusts

The trusts can be classified similarly to trusts in most common law jurisdictions. Trusts can be express or implied, discretionary or fixed, revocable or irrevocable, constructive, resulting, *inter vivos* or testamentary.

A trustee's discretion, pursuant to a discretionary trust, will often be limited by the settlors providing the trustee with a letter of wishes indicating how they want their trust property to be managed and distributed. The letter of wishes is not legally binding on the trustee, but its terms will usually be followed by the trustee, subject to the terms of the trust instrument. A protector may also be appointed by the settlor to oversee certain actions of the trustee, further limiting the trustee's discretion.

Purpose trusts are also possible, ie trusts established for a purpose rather than particular beneficiaries. Historically, purpose trusts were created for charitable purposes, however, the line between what is charitable and what is not charitable has become increasingly blurred. It is often difficult therefore to determine whether a trust would be valid and enforceable because it was for a charitable purpose, or invalid and unenforceable because it was otherwise. The blurred line has been clearly redrawn under the ITA. The Act says that an International Trust shall not be void or voidable where the trust fund is held for anything other than a charitable purpose.

Powers and Duties of a Trustee

The powers and duties of a trustee of an International Trust are determined by the trust instrument and the general law. The trust instrument prescribes the powers given to the trustee and any limitations. The duties of the trustee are provided for by the general law. It says the trustee must act as a prudent person managing the affairs of others; act in the best interests of beneficiaries; observe the utmost good-faith; and preserve and enhance the value of the trust property so far as is reasonable.

The Act does not provide any limitation of liability provision for a trustee. Any such limitation or exculpation of a trustee from liability will be contained in the trust instrument. The degree of exculpation is therefore a matter between the settlor and the trustee. The common law does not allow the trustee to limit its liability to its own actual fraud.

Features of an International Trust

International trusts have the following features:

- A trustee and the trust will not incur any form of tax, levy or duty in the Cook Islands;
- A perpetuity period not exceeding 100 years may be specified with a statutory wait-and-see period of a further 21 years;
- General law rules against accumulations and double possibilities do not apply; and
- The rule in *Saunders v Vautier* does not apply.

In 1989, a major review of the Act was undertaken with the specific intention of enhancing the asset protection provided by a trust. Specific features are:

- The overriding of the Statute of Elizabeth;
- A creditor seeking to set aside a transfer to a trust must prove beyond reasonable doubt that the transfer was made with the principal intent of defrauding him;
- Foreign judgements against a Cook Island International Trust are unenforceable if inconsistent with Cook Islands law;
- Foreign bankruptcy rules are specifically excluded as are foreign rules regarding forced heirship and spendthrift beneficiaries;
- Community property laws of the settlor's home jurisdiction are preserved. Where community property is transferred to a trust by a husband and wife, the property shall continue to be community property after the transfer;
- An existing domestic or international trust from another jurisdiction can obtain the protection of the fraudulent conveyance provisions from the date that the assets in the trust were originally transferred to the trust;

- A settlement or transfer will not be fraudulent against a creditor where
  i. it occurs prior to that creditor's cause of action accruing;
  ii. it occurs more than two years after that creditor's cause of action accrued; or
  iii. it occurs within two years of that creditor's cause of action accruing if that creditor fails to bring an action before one year from the date of the settlement or transfer;
- Where a creditor is not precluded by the above provisions, it must make a claim in the High Court of the Cook Islands within two years of the date of the settlement or transfer of the property in question to the trust.

Confidentiality

The Cook Islands is not a party to the Hague Convention or any information sharing treaties with any other countries. It is an offence for any person to divulge or communicate any information to any person relating to the establishment, constitution, business undertaking or affairs of an International Trust.

Alan Taylor graduated from Auckland University, New Zealand in 1987 with degrees in Law and Economics. He was admitted as a barrister and solicitor of the High Court of New Zealand in 1988. He joined the TrustNet Group in early 1996.

COSTA RICA

Juan Carlos Chavarría

Introduction

Location and Time Zone

Costa Rica is located in Central America, south of Nicaragua and north of Panama. The Atlantic Ocean is on one side and the Pacific Ocean is on the other. The country covers an area of approximately 51,100 square kilometres (19,730 square miles). Costa Rica is divided into seven provinces: San José, Heredia, Alajuela, Cartago, Puntarenas, Guanacaste and Limón. The capital city is San José, located in a valley in the centre of the country.

Political and Legal System

Costa Rica is an independent Democratic Republic. It is one of the most stable and peaceful countries in Latin America. The army was abolished in 1949 and permanent neutrality in international conflicts was established in 1983. Costa Rica is a civil law jurisdiction based on the Spanish legal system. However, there is also a strong influence from the French and Italian legal traditions.

Currency

The Costa Rican monetary unit is the colón, which is divided into 100 céntimos. Under the current foreign currency exchange system, free possession and convertibility of foreign currency to local currency and vice-versa is allowed, except for export proceeds. The 'crawling peg' system has been eliminated and the exchange rate is currently determined by a 'managed floating system', whereby the Central Bank of Costa Rica intercedes in the market to maintain stability.

Infrastructure and Communications

Costa Rica enjoys highly developed communications, electricity and transportation infrastructure. Costa Rican telecommunications provide direct international dialling telephones, as well as telex, telegram, facsimile and data transmission services.

Population and Language

By July 1995 the population had reached approximately 3,333,223. Although Spanish is the official language in Costa Rica, a significant percentage of the population speaks English.

Corporate Law

Types of Companies

Businesses are regulated by the Commerce Code. They must be registered in the Registry of Commercial Concerns, where copies of the articles of incorporation and the confirmation of the Board of Directors are publicly available.

Corporations

Given their structural flexibility, corporations are the most common business entity. Since local laws define a corporation as a bilateral agreement, they must be formed by at least two parties. However, immediately after formation, all the shares of stock may be legally owned by a single party. Founding parties (and any shareholders thereafter) may be physical individuals, registered business concerns of any nature or a combination of people and companies, regardless of citizenship and domicile. Since formation takes place according to local laws, the company or corporation is legally Costa Rican-based and thus domiciled there.

The company name must be in Spanish and consist of a word or a number of words with or without a meaning, as long as it is not deemed generic and provided it has not been previously registered. There is no minimum share capital requirement. Shares must be registered; local regulations do not allow bearer or non-par value shares. However, shares may be endorsed openly and therefore perform, for all practical purposes, as bearer shares. Corporations are required to assign yearly 5 per cent of net earnings to form a legal reserve up to 20 per cent of its share capital.

Limited liability companies (Ltds)

Incorporation procedures and costs for limited liability companies (Ltds) are very similar to those of corporations. The Ltds divide their share capital in what local regulations call 'quotas', as opposed to shares. Unless specially provided otherwise in the articles of incorporation, transfer of 'quotas' may only be performed with the unanimous consent of all partners. The legal structure of Ltds is in accordance with the United States' concept of 'Partnerships' and thus they qualify as such for US tax purposes.

Limited partnerships and general partnerships

Limited partnerships and general partnerships are seldom used, mainly because of the strong personal involvement of the parties regarding liabilities, management and direct exposure, among other disadvantages. Formation procedures are basically the same as in corporations, although much simpler. Foreign companies may transfer their legal domicile to Costa Rica provided their articles of incorporation allow such a transfer. Transfer of the legal domicile does not imply dissolution of the parent company and jurisdiction of its original legal domicile. However, with regards to all acts and actions performed within the Costa Rican territory, the foreign company shall be subject to the local legal system, including income tax regulations, but only with respect to those activities performed in Costa Rica.

According to Costa Rican law, there is a merger of corporations when one or more corporations merge to form one corporation. A merger agreement must be submitted to the shareholders of each corporation in an extraordinary shareholders meeting and must be approved according to the rules established in their articles of incorporation or by a statute approved by the majority of all outstanding shares. The minutes of each of these shareholders meetings must be notarised and submitted as one public deed to the Registry of Commercial Concerns. A summary of this instrument must be published in the official gazette.

Taxation

The Costa Rican tax system is based on the territorial principle. Costa Rican residents and corporations are subject to taxes only on income earned within Costa Rica. Deductions to taxable income, in general, include all expenses necessary to produce taxable income. Income tax is applied to all income obtained in Costa Rica, without consideration of citizenship, domicile or residence of the taxpayer. Applicable rates range from 10 per cent to 30 per cent depending on the size of the company. Companies with gross income of more than US$80,000 are subject to a 30 per cent rate.

Dividends paid or credited by companies to individuals (both local and foreign) or foreign entities are subject to a 15 per cent withholding tax. If the shares of the paying company are registered at a local stock exchange and the shares were bought through such exchange, the withholding is reduced to 5 per cent. Dividends paid or credited to another Costa Rican company are exempt from this withholding. This withholding does not apply to stock dividends.

Payments for dividends and any other distribution of earnings made from Costa Rican source income to individuals or companies residing abroad are subject to a 15 per cent withholding tax. Any remittance of Costa Rica source income not expressly established by statute is subject to a 30 per cent withholding tax. Tax Authorities may authorize a waiver of such withholding tax provided that the beneficiary can prove that he or she is not allowed a foreign tax credit for the withholding assessed in Costa Rica.

Trust Law

Trusts in Costa Rica are governed by the Commercial Code, drafted in 1964. According to these local regulations, any individual capable of freely disposing property or a corporation duly authorized in its articles of incorporation may be a settlor. A trust may be created for the benefit of anyone, with the exception of unborn children, regardless of age, nationality or residence, as well as corporations. There are no statutory provisions protecting trusts from forced heirship provisions of domicile and settlor. The settlor may also be a beneficiary. However, if the trust is questioned, the burden of proof is on the settlor to show that it was not instituted as a fraud to creditors.

The settlor may not act as trustee. Only one trustee is required by statute. There are no special regulations or registration requirements for trust companies. Aside from when authorized in specific instructions, the trustee must always act with the diligence of a *bonus pater familiae*. A trustee may delegate its powers to a third party through a power of attorney.

A trust must necessarily be set forth in writing, therefore oral and constructive trusts are not recognized. Letter of wishes are neither recognized nor used in Costa Rica. This trust instrument along with the general law constitutes the source of the trustees' authority. Courts have no authority to vary the trust deed. In case remuneration to the trustee is agreed on, it must be expressly authorized in the trust deed. Trustee fees vary according to the nature of the trust and the services required from the trustees. The maximum allowed duration of a trust is thirty years.

Although local regulations establish no general purposes for trusts, trust deed may establish specific purposes. Secret trusts, however, are prohibited. There are no particular provisions encouraging or restricting use of asset protection trusts. However, if questioned, a trust in which the settlor is also the beneficiary is presumed to be in fraud of creditors. Nevertheless, this presumption may be defeated by the settlor if he or she shows that the trust was not designed to defraud.

There are no specific registration or filing requirements for legally constituted trusts. Consequently, there are no registration fees for the formation of trusts. In the case of real estate property transfers, however, the property must be registered in the name of the trustee as fiduciary owner. This transfer is exempt from all legal duties. On the other hand, professional fees for the constitution of a trust may vary greatly.

Juan Carlos Chavarría is an attorney and a Notary Public and holds the post of managing partner at KPMG in Costa Rica. His main practice areas are foreign investment, corporate law, mergers and acquisitions, trust services, estate planning and international trade.

CYPRUS

Howard Bilton

Introduction

Location and Time Zone

Cyprus is an island situated in the north eastern Mediterranean Sea at the crossroads of Europe, Asia and Africa. It is the third largest island in the Mediterranean, with an area of 99,251 square kilometres. Cyprus is two hours ahead of Greenwich Mean Time (+2 GMT).

Political and Legal System

Cyprus gained independence from Britain in 1960 and adopted a presidential system of government. Elections are held every five years. In 1974 Turkey invaded Cyprus and has since occupied the northern 40 per cent of the island. Discussions are currently taking place with a view to reunification of the island.

Laws are based on the English legal system and company law is modelled on the UK *Companies Act* 1948. In addition, Cyprus has signed an associate agreement with the European Union.

Currency

The currency of Cyprus is the Cyprus pound (CP), which is divided into 100 cents.

Population and Language

The capital city of Nicosia has a population of about 200,000 people. The official languages are Greek and Turkish, but English is widely spoken and is the language most used in business, government and the courts.

Infrastructure and Communications

The Island's two international airports, situated near Larnaca and Paphos, provide a network of air-routes to Europe, Africa and Asia. Larnaca and Limasol are multipurpose shipping ports whereas Vassiliko is the industrial port of Cyprus.

Corporate Law

Offshore Company

A Cyprus 'offshore' company is similar to a normal Cyprus company but is owned by nonresident of Cyprus and does business mainly outside the islands. Such a company has the following characteristics:

Taxation

Tax is levied on worldwide income at a rate of 4.25 per cent on profit. As such, Cyprus is a low tax country rather than a no tax country. However, one of the benefits of Cyprus companies is that the country has signed a range of tax treaties which provide for reduced or zero withholding taxes on dividends, interest and royalties paid to a Cyprus company. Treaties have been concluded with Austria, Bulgaria, Canada, China, Czechoslovakia, Denmark, France, Germany, Greece, Hungary, India, Ireland, Italy, Kuwait, Norway, Poland, Romania, Russia, Sweden, United Kingdom, the United States and Yugoslavia.

Shareholders

A minimum of two shareholders are required and while their details appear in the public file, anonymity can be retained by the use of nominee shareholders. Bank references on the beneficial owners must be submitted to the Central Bank of Cyprus, but the information is protected by secrecy laws. Bearer shares are not permitted.

Directors

A minimum of one individual director is required. Details appear on the public file, but anonymity is possible by using third party directors. There is no legal requirement that the directors be Cyprus residents, but in order to obtain relief under the taxation treaties signed by Cyprus it is likely that the company would need to be seen to be Cyprus resident and therefore have a majority of the directors based in Cyprus.

Annual reporting

An annual return which gives details of all those who have held shares throughout the year and the current directors must be filed. In addition, every Cyprus company must prepare audited accounts and submit these to the Central Bank and the income tax office.

Time scale

Normally it will take approximately 10 days from the receipt of bank references on the beneficial owners for incorporation to be achieved. However, in special circumstances an accelerated process is available which allows incorporation one day after receipt of those references. Pre-incorporated companies are available, but the requirement to provide bank references on the beneficial owners means that such companies cannot be activated until references have been received in Cyprus.

Restrictions of name and activity

Names must end with the word 'Limited'. The following words and their associated activities are prohibited: Assurance, Bank, Building Society or any words deemed sensitive or offensive.

Local requirements

As a matter of local company law, the company must maintain a registered office address within Cyprus and must also appoint a company secretary who, for practical reasons, must be resident in Cyprus.

Tax Treaties

In practice, not all the tax treaty partners will extend tax treaty benefits to Cyprus offshore companies. Benefits are limited by discriminatory clauses within the tax treaties or by practices of the relevant revenue departments of the country in question:

- Canada completely excludes Cyprus resident offshore companies from the benefits of the treaty;
- France applies the benefits to the 'active' income of Cyprus offshore branches, but does not extend beneficial withholding tax rates on dividends, royalties or interest when paid to a Cyprus offshore company;
- Germany does not extend tax exemptions to income derived from international shipping by foreign-owned Cyprus resident companies;
- Swedish tax exemptions are not applicable on income derived from international shipping by foreign owned (by 25 per cent or more) Cyprus resident companies. Also, dividends received in Sweden from a Cyprus offshore resident company is excluded;
- United Kingdom excludes Cyprus offshore resident companies from the benefits of the treaty for foreign source dividends, interest or royalties. It also excludes the treaty benefits of reduced withholding tax on interest if the loan was made mainly for the purpose of taking advantage of the treaty. The latter exclusion applies to all persons (not only to offshore companies); and
- United States completely excludes Cyprus resident offshore companies from the treaty benefits and limits benefits in the case of a company (either offshore or onshore) under foreign ownership. The treaties with Eastern Europe are particularly advantageous and Cyprus is the favoured route for investment into the former Soviet Bloc.

Trust Law

The Legal Framework

Cyprus is an English Common Law jurisdiction and the trust law is based on the *Trustee Law* of 1955, which closely follows the *English Trustee Act* of 1925. Section 29 of the Cyprus *Courts of Justice Law* of 1960 states that UK statute and common law applies except when inconsistent with the constitution. Therefore pre-1960 English law and cases apply, but post-1960 English case law has no direct application.

International Trusts Law

The *International Trusts Law* (ITL) of July 1992 creates a new form of trust known as the International Trust. The *Trustee Law* of 1955 applies except to the extent that ITL overrides it.

Settlor

An International Trust must be settled by a Cyprus nonresident for the benefit of nonresident beneficiaries (except where the beneficiary is a Cyprus charity or Cyprus offshore company). The settlor may be an individual or a company.

Trustee

One trustee must be a permanent resident of Cyprus, but a Cyprus offshore company qualifies in this regard. There is no requirement to register the trust. There is a fee of CY£250 payable as a stamp duty on the creation of a Cyprus trust, but no other government fees are payable initially or annually.

Perpetuity period

The perpetuity period is 100 years and there is no restriction on the time during which income can be accumulated. Charitable or purpose trusts, which can be created by virtue of Section 7 of ITL, can have unlimited duration.

Asset protection

Cyprus has been particularly aggressive in the matter of asset protection. Its international trusts are not void or voidable in the event of the settlor's bankruptcy, notwithstanding any rule of law which applies either in Cyprus or in any other country, except where it is proved that the trust was made with the intent to defraud the creditors of the settlor at the time of the transfer of his assets into the International Trust. The onus of proof of intent is upon the person alleging such intent.

In addition, no law relating to inheritance or succession in force in Cyprus or elsewhere shall affect the transfer or disposition into an International Trust or its validity. This section also states that the settlor shall be deemed to have the capacity to dispose of assets to a trust as long as he is of full age and sound mind under the law of the country of which he is a permanent resident.

The law prohibits trustees from disclosing information about the trust without an order from a competent Cyprus authority. This section covers all documents and information received in relation to the setting up of the International Trusts as well as that regarding the trust itself.

Taxation

The income and gains of a trust derived or deemed to be derived from sources outside the country shall be exempt from all taxes. A Cyprus trust is completely exempt from tax on income and capital gains, although the profits derived by the trustees from acting in that capacity would be taxable. By making a Cyprus offshore company the trustee of its own assets and trading activities, the 4.25 per cent tax rate normally payable by a Cyprus offshore company may be reduced to zero.

Howard Bilton is a Barrister of Law in the UK and Gibraltar, Chairman of The International Company Services Ltd Group and Managing Director of Sovereign Trust International, Suites 1601-1603 Kinwick Centre, 32 Hollywood Road, Central, Hong Kong, Tel: (852) 2542 1177, Fax: (852) 2545 0550, E-mail: hk@icsl.com

GIBRALTAR

Robert M Vasquez

Introduction

Location and Time Zone

Gibraltar is located on the northern shore of the Straits of Gibraltar which is a busy shipping lane connecting the Mediterranean and the Atlantic. Gibraltar has Central European Time (+1 GMT in winter, +2 GMT in summer). The climate is temperate with an average temperature of 15.6°C in winter and 21.1°C in summer.

Political and Legal System

Gibraltar obtained self-government from Britain under the Gibraltar Constitution Order 1968. Gibraltar has a locally elected House of Assembly modelled on a Westminster style of democratic government. The House of Assembly governs on internal matters. The United Kingdom retains control of foreign affairs, defence and internal security through the Governor. Its legal and court system is modelled on that of England. English Common Law and principles of Equity apply save as amended by statute, locally called ordinances. European Union law, with some exceptions, applies by operation of Article 227(4) of the Treaty of Rome.

Currency

Gibraltar's currency is denominated in Gibraltar pounds (GBP) and pence and is freely convertible. 100 pence is equal to 1 pound. Gibraltar pounds are on a par with sterling pounds.

Economy

Gibraltar's economy is in the process of successful transition from a defence based economy to a private sector economy. Its success is based on finance centre activities (fuelled by concessionary tax legislation), tourism, port-related activities and a nascent satellite telecommunications park.

Infrastructure and Communications

Gibraltar has a modern international telecommunications and road system. It is easily accessible via London, or alternatively from many destinations via Malaga airport in Spain. It has well-developed educational and medical facilities and housing, and office and business accommodation is readily available.

Population and Language

The local Gibraltarian population (approximately 24,000) has developed from UK, Italian, Maltese, Portuguese, Jewish and Spanish origins. There are approximately 6,000 expatriate residents from various nationalities. Business is generally transacted in English and fluent Spanish is spoken. The population comprises a well-educated work force and professional managerial and supervisory personnel are locally available.

Corporate Law

Company Law

Company law is governed by the Companies Ordinance which substantially re-enacts the *Companies Act* 1929 of England.

There has been some statutory amendment in recent years. The rule that a company cannot acquire its own shares applies in Gibraltar. The law allows flexibility in regard to the creation of various kinds of shares to which different rights attach, and generally accommodates the most varied requirements of structure, in relation to investment and participation in a company.

Formation

Formation requires the preparation of a Memorandum and Articles of Association and the filing of returns stating the nominal capital, the situation of the registered office (which must be in Gibraltar), directors' details and a Declaration of Compliance.

Subscribers appoint the first directors and directors allot shares as required. A Return of Allotment must be filed. An Annual Return must be filed every calendar year containing particulars of the share capital, details of shareholders and directors. An Annual General Meeting of shareholders should also be held.

Private companies are not presently required to file accounts. The directors must present accounts at the Annual General Meeting. Accounts need to be submitted to the Commissioner of Income Tax; exempt and qualifying companies are exempted.

Private companies may be formed with a single shareholder, if permitted by the Articles of Association. Private companies may not have bearer shares but public companies may. Some lawyers opine that exempt private companies are permitted to do so by the *Companies (Taxation and Concessions) Ordinance.*

Types of Companies

Companies may be private or public and may be:

- Limited by shares;
- Limited by guarantee;
- Limited by guarantee and have a share capital; or
- Unlimited.

The most common type of company is that limited by shares. Companies limited by guarantee are usually incorporated for non-profit making objects only.

Redomiciliation

Redomiciliation is permitted to Gibraltar from any Commonwealth country, British dependent territory, member of the European Union or the European Economic Area, Hong Kong, Panama and Liberia. Redomiciliation of Gibraltar companies is permitted to any member of the European Union or European Economic Area.

Provisions for Fraudulent Transactions

The *Companies Ordinance*, the *Bankruptcy Ordinance* and the *Fraudulent Conveyances Act* 1571 provide provisions for setting aside fraudulent transactions and transactions which amount to a fraudulent preference.

Legislation has been enacted in Gibraltar to prevent both drugs money laundering and money laundering of proceeds of all other crimes. It essentially criminalises dealing with moneys knowing or suspecting the same to be the proceeds of any crime.

Taxation

Ordinarily resident companies are liable to tax on their taxable profits at 35 per cent. Rules govern the withholding of tax at the rate of 30 per cent on certain payments of interest to nonresidents (exempt and qualifying companies are exempted) and payments to subcontractors.

Tax Concessions

Exempt companies

The *Companies (Taxation and Concessions) Ordinance* has as its main object the exemption of:

- Income tax on profits not arising from local trade;
- Estate duties on the value of assets held through or in exempt companies; and
- Stamp duties on many transactions.

The privileges of an exempt company are available only to non-Gibraltarians and nonresidents.

An exempt company can carry on business from Gibraltar in any part of the world, but it cannot:

- Engage in local trade or business; or
- Conduct business with Gibraltarians or residents without permission from the Financial and Development Secretary unless it is another exempt company.

The Exemption Certificate defines the actual business the company is authorised to conduct.

Details and references of shareholders must be submitted and the law allows the acquisition of shares by trustees.

Annual Tax is payable at the rate of £225 per annum if it is ordinarily resident, or at the rate of £200 per annum if it is not ordinarily resident.

A foreign incorporated company registered in Gibraltar may be granted an Exemption Certificate.

Qualifying companies

Like an exempt company, a qualifying company can be either a company incorporated in Gibraltar or a foreign company registered in Gibraltar.

The requirements which have to be met by a qualifying company are the same as those of an exempt company. A deposit of £1,000.00 must be kept with the Government as security for the payment of future taxes. A fee of £250.00 is also payable to the Government on application for a Qualifying Certificate.

Qualifying companies enjoy the same advantages as those enjoyed by exempt companies except that they are taxed on taxable profits. A percentage rate must be agreed with the Government at between 2 and 35 per cent. At present the minimum accepted rate seems to be 5 per cent.

Trusts Law

The Legal Framework

The English concept of trust is fully recognised and the courts will enforce the same. Gibraltar has the certainty resulting from many years of English case law to support its trusts which is not available in other jurisdictions where a *Statutory Trust Law* has been implemented. Not all English statutory law relating to trusts applies in Gibraltar. The *Trustee Ordinance* substantially re-enacts the *Trustee Act* 1893, the *Trustee Investment Act* 1961 and introduces parts of the *Trustee Act* 1925. The *Variation of Trust Act* 1958 applies to Gibraltar.

The *Perpetuities and Accumulations Ordinance* 1986 extends the perpetuity period to 100 years and also increases the accumulations period to 100 years.

Settlor and Trustees

Any individual capable of freely disposing of property and any corporate body with suitable power by their constitutions (subject to commercial benefit considerations) may be settlors. There is generally no restriction as to who can be either a beneficiary or a trustee. In Gibraltar property may be held in common or jointly, but there is no law by which community of property is obligatory. However, in matrimonial situations care must be taken that a constructive or resulting trust does not arise.

Individuals or companies who offer trust services to the public in or from Gibraltar must be licensed under the *Financial Services Ordinance*. Trusts which own real property should have a minimum of two trustees (unless the trustee is a Trust Corporation), otherwise one suffices.

Beneficiaries

A trust must have beneficiaries except for a charitable trust which may be for charitable purposes. Non-charitable purpose trusts are not permitted. An incomplete transfer to trustees results in the assets, the subject matter of such transfer not forming part of the trust fund.

Creation

Trusts may be created orally, but this causes evidential problems and is not recommended. Trusts should be created in writing. The concept of constructive and resulting trusts is recognised.

Registration Requirements

There are no registration or filing requirements on the creation of a trust. There are stamp duty considerations on transfer of property depending on circumstances.

Powers

The trustees' powers are usually contained in the trust instrument, but some are conferred under principles of equity and the *Trustee Ordinance*. A trust deed would normally provide for the resignation, removal and appointment of trustees. In the absence of specific provision, the *Trustee Ordinance* provides for the person nominated, or, if none, the surviving or continuing trustees, to appoint a trustee or trustees in place of a trustee who is dead, remains out of Gibraltar for more than 12 months, desires to be discharged, refuses to act as such or is unfit to act or incapable of acting. The Supreme Court also has power to appoint new trustees if it is found inexpedient, difficult or impractical to do so without the assistance of the court. The power to delegate by power of attorney for a period not exceeding 12 months is recognised under the *Trustee Ordinance*.

Powers of investment are normally expressed in the trust instrument, but in the absence of specific powers they are contained in the *Trustees Ordinance*. If the trustees intend to charge remuneration, then this power must be specifically included.

Letters of Wishes

Letters of Wishes are commonly used in conjunction with trusts which contain discretionary powers. They are not legally enforceable.

Asset Protection

Gibraltar has amended its *Bankruptcy Ordinance* to provide for 'Asset Protection Trusts' which can be registered on meeting statutory requirements. There are no statutory provisions protecting trusts from forced heirship provisions. However, there are no forced heirship provisions in Gibraltar. Applications for maintenance may be made by dependants under the *Inheritance (Provision for Family and Dependants) Ordinance*. The concept of resulting and constructive trusts could also apply.

There are no specific statutory provisions relating to the migration of trusts. The trust instrument will need to provide for these.

Taxation

The *Income Tax (Allowances, Deductions and Exemptions) Rules* 1992 exempt the income received by any trust or beneficiary under the trust in the following circumstances:

- The trust is created by or on behalf of a nonresident person;
- The income either accrues or is derived outside Gibraltar, or in the case of income received by a trust would, if it had been received directly by the beneficiary, be not liable to tax under the *Income Tax Ordinance*; and
- Except in the case of a trust created before the 1st July 1983, the terms of the trust expressly exclude residents of Gibraltar (as defined in the Companies (*Taxation and Concessions) Ordinance*) as persons who either are, or may be, under any discretionary power of the trustee under the terms of the trust, a beneficiary or any class or classes of beneficiary.

Taxation of Individuals

Tax is charged on any income which is derived from, accrued in or is received in Gibraltar. However, no income tax is charged on income arising from moneys deposited with a bank or building society in Gibraltar if the depositor is nonresident.

A nonresident will not have income received from exempt or qualifying companies taxed. There are other concessions for certain exempted individuals as outlined below. Resident individuals are liable to pay income tax on worldwide income. There is unilateral tax relief given in respect of any investment income which is taxed in the United Kingdom and is not remitted to Gibraltar. If the income is remitted then credit is given for the tax paid in the United Kingdom.

Residents benefit from certain allowances, for example:

- The first £600 of interest paid on a building society deposit is tax free;
- An allowance of £10,000 against the taxable income of a first time purchaser of a residence for his own occupation which can be deducted over a period of five years; and
- All mortgage interest is allowed as are life insurance premiums to a maximum one sixth of taxable income and certain pension premiums up to a maximum of 17 per cent of taxable income.

Tax is payable at the following rates:

Taxable income	Rate
First £1,450 or in the case of a married couple the first £2,800	Tax free
First £1,500	20%
Next £5,500	30%
Next £5,500	35%
Next £3,500	40%
Next £3,500	45%
Balance	50%

Tax concessions for individuals

The *Qualifying (High Net Worth) Individuals Rules* 1992 makes concessions for certain individuals.

To qualify the individual must have available for his exclusive use for a minimum period of seven months approved residential accommodation. He must also reside in this accommodation for a minimum of thirty days. The individual cannot otherwise be resident and must not have been so resident in any of the previous five assessment years.

If the individual meets these requirements then he may apply to the Financial and Development Secretary for the issue of a certificate designating him as a High Net Worth individual. A fee of £500 is payable on making the application. This fee is not refundable.

Once issued with a certificate such individual's taxable income becomes chargeable to tax in accordance with the provisions of the *Income Tax Ordinance*. However, there are limitations to the amount of tax for which he is liable. Liability is limited to a maximum taxable income of £45,000 (the maximum liability is therefore £19,750 at present tax rates). There is a minimum liability to pay £10,000 in each year of assessment.

Other Tax Matters and Exchange Control

Estate duty

Real property situated in Gibraltar and personal property wherever situated of any person domiciled in Gibraltar is chargeable to estate duty.

The estate of a person dying who is not domiciled in Gibraltar is chargeable to estate duty to the extent that the estate consists of any property situated in Gibraltar except if it is a bank or building society deposit.

Estate duty is chargeable at the following rates:

Estate value	Rate
Estate value exceeding £20,000 but not exceeding £40,000	5%
Next £20,000	10%
Next £40,000	15%
Next £100,000	20%
Any amount exceeding £200,000	25%

The first £100,000 of the deceased's primary residence in Gibraltar is not chargeable to estate duty. Exemptions to this charge exist if the property consists of shares in or loans to exempt or qualifying companies as outlined above.

Stamp duty

Stamp duty is levied on certain documents listed and at the rates set out in the schedule to the *Stamp Duties Ordinance*. There are concessions in respect of exempt and qualifying companies as explained above.

Development aid

The *Development Aid Ordinance* relieves income of development projects in Gibraltar from income tax if a development aid licence has been issued to the project by the Minister responsible for economic development as advised by the Development Aid Advisory Committee.

Double taxation treaties

There are no such treaties with any other jurisdiction.

Exchange controls

Exchange controls were abolished in Gibraltar as in the United Kingdom. A company incorporated in Gibraltar may express its share capital in any currency except Swiss Francs.

Costs

Professional fees charged vary from adviser to adviser. On registration of a company, nominal capital duty is payable at the rate of 0.5 per cent on the authorised share capital as is a registration fee amounting to £50.00. Stamp duty is payable on a deed of settlement at the rate of 0.25 per cent of the amount or value of the property settled or agreed to be settled.

Robert M Vasquez is a senior partner of Triay&Triay, Gibraltar. Triay&Triay is engaged on a daily basis in both common law and chancery matters. Its particular experience extends over the fields of banking, insurance and company law, shipping and admiralty, conveyancing and property, trusts, fiscal matters and administrative law. Tel: 350-72020, Telex: 2219 TRIBAR GK, TELEFAX: 350-72270.

GUERNSEY

Nigel Robins

Introduction

Geography

The Bailiwick of Guernsey includes all the Channel Islands except Jersey. Of the eight islands in the Bailiwick, the best known are Guernsey, Alderney and Sark. Guernsey is the second largest of the Channel Islands and lies 30 miles from the French coast in the Bay of St Malo. Guernsey has an area of 24 square miles (62 square kilometres). The Island adopts the same time as London. Although the climate is similar to that of southern England, it does not suffer the extremes of continental temperatures, with milder winters and cooler summers. The average summer and winter temperatures are 16°C and 6°C.

Political and Legal System

The Islands were formerly part of the Duchy of Normandy but when Normandy was lost to the English Crown in 1204 the Islands remained loyal to the English. Today the Islands remain crown dependencies. However, Guernsey is self-governing with its own Parliament, the States of Guernsey, which run on non-political party lines. The legal system is based on common law with early Norman French law having substantial influence, particularly in relation to real property and inheritance. Guernsey has a Royal Court with both civil and criminal jurisdiction. Appeals from the Royal Court are heard by a Channel Islands Court of Appeal and ultimately the Privy Council.

Currency

The pound sterling is the unit of currency. Notes are issued by the States of Guernsey, but Bank of England notes are also in general circulation.

Infrastructure and Communications

Guernsey has over 300 miles of tarmac roads. The Island is 40 minutes by air from London. The airport has daily services to many cities in the UK and, particularly in the summer months, direct flights to many European cities, including Paris, Zurich, Amsterdam and Frankfurt. There are up to 12 flights per day to London airports. Guernsey has direct dial telephone and telex links with the UK and the rest of the world with back up links via France. Medical and educational facilities are also first class. Housing on the Island is expensive particularly for non-islanders, where the supply of houses is controlled. The financial services infrastructure is excellent, with over thirty accountancy practices and more than fifty lawyers. There are over seventy banks incorporated in Guernsey.

Population and Language

English is the main language, but strong French influences are apparent in many aspects of island life. Guernsey Patois (a form of Norman French) is still spoken by a number of islanders. The finance industry employs approximately one third of the working population.

International Treaties

Guernsey is not a member of the European Union (EU), but has a special relationship with the EU. The Channel Islands are subject to a protocol attached to the United Kingdom's Treaty of Accession to the EU. The arrangements provide for the free movement of industrial and agricultural goods between the Islands and the EU.

However local rules may restrict the entry of some goods. The protocol effectively excludes taxation and therefore the EU policy of harmonizing taxation within the EU does not apply to Guernsey.

Exchange Control

Guernsey forms part of the United Kingdom for exchange control purposes. However, all exchange controls were suspended in October 1979 and the UK *Exchange Control Act* 1947 was repealed in 1987. No local exchange control consents are required to set up companies or trusts in Guernsey.

Corporate Law

Company Law

The *Companies (Guernsey) Law* 1994 consolidated the previous laws dating from 1908 and simplified practitioners' task. Criticism by the industry of the lengthy legislative process has resulted in a law which will allow the States to make changes to the law by Ordinance. Draft ordinances have been published to permit the creation of companies limited by guarantee and hybrid companies; to incorporate protected cell companies; to create provisions for the immigration and emigration of companies; for the issue of shares of no par value; and for company amalgamations.

Incorporation and Registration

The 1994 law permits the incorporation by registration of companies with their liability limited by shares for a fixed or indefinite period. Bearer shares and shares of no par value are not permitted. The law requires at least two shareholder, who need not be resident. The fiduciary or law firm normally provides two nominee subscribers.

The application for registration is completed by the advocate and reviewed by the Attorney General and by the Guernsey Financial Services Commission, which requires the disclosure of full details of the ultimate beneficial owners of the company. If the company is to be owned by a trust, the full name of the settlor, whether named in the deed or not, must be disclosed. For this reason it is not possible to form shelf companies in Guernsey and incorporation takes seven to ten days. The company must have a registered office in Guernsey.

Share Capital

There are no minimum capital requirements, but as there is a minimum and maximum document duty payable most companies are formed with an authorised capital of at least £10,000 (or equivalent). Shares must be issued at least 5 per cent of par value paid.

Annual Return

All Guernsey companies have to file an annual return which discloses details of the directors and registered shareholders and is open to public scrutiny. For this reason most shares are registered in nominee names.

Disclosure Requirements

It is worth mentioning that there are no disclosure requirements relating to non-Guernsey companies administered in the Island even if the board is made up of Guernsey residents.

Taxation

Corporate tax

Guernsey is a low tax financial centre so a company may be treated for tax purposes in one of three ways: as a resident Guernsey company paying 20 per cent tax on profits, adjusted for tax purposes; as an exempt company paying a flat exempt company licence fee of £500 and effectively exempt from all Guernsey tax; or as an International Company (IC) under the *Income Tax (International Bodies) (Guernsey) Law* 1993. The IC will pay a rate of tax above zero but not more than 30 per cent.

Double tax treaties

Guernsey has double tax treaties with the UK and Jersey. The treaty with the UK does not follow the OECD model and has been tailored to the needs of the Island. Dividends and debenture interest from the UK do not attract double tax relief. The benefits of the double tax agreement are not available to Guernsey exempt companies.

Tax concessions

There are no taxes on wealth or capital (except on short term property gains) or on inheritance or gifts. Nonresident companies are liable to income tax only on income arising in the Island, but local bank deposit interest is excluded by concession. Guernsey resident companies may deduct income tax from dividend payments, but are under no duty to do so. Nonresident and exempt companies are not required to deduct tax at source from any dividend payments made to nonresidents. A further concession, formalised by the Administrator of Income Tax in 1996, is the ability of a non-Guernsey investment company to appoint Guernsey resident directors without the company being deemed resident in Guernsey for tax purposes. This concession makes Guernsey an ideal location for the administration of offshore companies generally.

Trust Law

The Legal Framework

The enactment of the *Trusts (Guernsey) Law* 1989 strengthened Guernsey as a trust jurisdiction. Prior to 1989 some practitioners saw the lack of a statute as a negative factor for Guernsey particularly as relatively few modern trust cases had come to court. However there are references to trusts in Guernsey jurisprudence dating from the 16th century. The Law distinguishes between a Guernsey trust and a foreign trust which has a Guernsey resident trustee or any property which is situated or administered in Guernsey. A Guernsey trust may be created by any person whether natural or juridical.

Trustee

Section 13 of the *Trust Law* requires that the number of trustees shall not be less than two unless only one trustee was originally appointed; a corporate trustee resident in Guernsey is acting; or the terms of the trust provide otherwise. In the absence of specific provisions in the deed, the Law provides that new or additional trustees may be appointed by the existing or last remaining trustee, his personal representative or the court. A co-trustee may resign by written notice to his co-trustee. If the number of trustees falls below the number required by s 13, the continuing trustee shall act only to preserve trust property until additional trustees are appointed. Again, subject to the provisions of the deed, only the court may remove a trustee. There is no bar to the settlor acting as a trustee.

Creation of Trust

The *Trust Law* provides that a trust may be created by oral declaration, by an instrument in writing, by conduct or in any other manner whatsoever. However, a unit trust may be created only by an instrument in writing. The wording of the Law clearly contemplates the existence of constructive trusts and s 38 of the *Trust Law* deals specifically with one example of a constructive trust. However, the equitable principle of a constructive trust has been recognised in Guernsey for centuries.

Guernsey trusts do not have to be registered and there are no filing fees or government duties payable at any time. There is no disclosure to any regulatory authority of the name of the settlor or principal beneficiary of a trust created or administered in Guernsey. If a trust creates a Guernsey company, disclosure would be required under the company formation procedure described above.

There is no legislation for the regulation of fiduciaries at present. However, this is being debated and a discussion paper was circulated amongst interested organisations some time ago. It is not possible to form a trust company in Guernsey without regulatory consent. Regulations are being considered which may include a set of standards for trust companies and other fiduciaries.

Beneficiary

Any person, company or another trust, wherever they are resident, may be a beneficiary of a Guernsey trust. The beneficiary must be identifiable either by name, or be ascertainable by reference to a description or relationship to the settlor. A settlor or trustee of a Guernsey trust may be a beneficiary of it.

There has been much discussion in the past years over whether a valid noncharitable purpose trust can be created in Guernsey. The *Trust Law* contains some ambiguity for it states that a trust can be established for a purpose but it must have a beneficiary. To remedy this, an amending law, likely to introduce enforcer-type provisions, is under consideration by the Guernsey Financial Services Commission.

Powers of Trustees

Many of the provisions of the *Trust Law* particularly in relation to the powers of trustees are similar to UK law. However, under the *Trust Law*, directors of corporate trustees are personally liable for breaches of trust, although the court (but not the terms of the deed) may excuse them from liability. The principle of the prudent man of business acting in good faith is given a local twist. Section 18(1) provides that a trustee shall act *en bon pere de famille*, literally as a good father of his family. A Guernsey trust may exist for 100 years and there are no restrictions on accumulating income. The Law also permits the trust deed to override many of its provisions including the requirement to provide information to a beneficiary, which may be a significant advantage in certain circumstances.

Asset Protection

Guernsey has taken no steps to encourage the creation of Asset Protection Trusts and has no intention of doing so. The Statute of Elizabeth has no application in Guernsey and any further legislation on creditor protection has been shelved pending a more comprehensive review of local insolvency law. The latter is still largely based on early French law, with actual and contingent future liabilities being the determining factors when looking at a transfer at undervalue. The Island did, however, amend the *Trust Law* in 1990 to protect trust assets from challenges under the forced heirship provisions of a settlor's country of domicile.

Costs

The costs of setting up a Guernsey trust and its proper administration vary widely depending on the service provider. However a high net worth individual contemplating setting up a trust should not make a choice based on price alone. If a trust structure is going to provide the advantages and protections the settlor is seeking, it must be run properly by experienced fiduciaries.

Financial Regulation

The finance industry in Guernsey is regulated by the Guernsey Financial Services Commission, a statutory body established in 1987. The commission's principal duty is to protect and enhance the Island's reputation as an international finance centre. Only institutions of the highest quality are granted a licence to operate from Guernsey. Regulatory legislation in Guernsey keeps pace with developments in other major financial centres and the local anti money laundering provisions follow UK rules very closely.

Nigel Robins is a director of Kleinwort Benson (Guernsey) Limited, Head of the Bank's Trustee Division and a Director of Kleinwort Benson (Guernsey) Trustees Limited.

ISLE OF MAN

Paul M Brennock

Introduction

Location and Time Zone

The Isle of Man is a British dependency lying in the Irish Sea between Britain and Ireland. It occupies an area of 588 sq km (277 sq miles) and is in the same time zone as United Kingdom.

Political and Legal System

Constitutionally the Isle of Man has never been part of the UK, but is rather a self-governing territory within the Commonwealth of Nations. Tynwald, the Isle of Man parliament (the oldest in the world), is responsible for the Island's domestic affairs, including taxation. Britain is responsible for the Island's defence and foreign affairs. The Island has a special relationship with the European Union; whilst associated with the EC, it is excluded from the EC's fiscal harmonisation policy.

The Isle of Man is in customs union with the UK and accordingly imposes value added tax (VAT) at UK rates on goods and services. As such, an Isle of Man company may be registered for VAT and may therefore prove a suitable vehicle for international trade with other member states of the European Union. Isle of Man law is closely based on English common law and the decisions of the UK courts are regarded as persuasive in the Manx courts.

Currency

The currency of the Isle of Man is pounds sterling, but the Isle of Man issues its own notes and coins bearing the same names and denominations as those issued by the UK. UK notes and coins circulate alongside Isle of Man notes and coins.

Economy

The mainstay of the Isle of Man economy is the finance industry, a consequence of the Island's policy of low direct taxation. The continued expansion of the Isle of Man economy is dependent upon it been seen as a reputable offshore finance centre.

Infrastructure and Communications

The Isle of Man's airport serves various cities in the UK and Ireland and there are direct services to Belfast, Birmingham, Blackpool, Cardiff, Dublin, Glasgow, Jersey, Leeds, Liverpool, London (Heathrow),

London (Luton), Manchester, Newcastle and Southampton. Ferry services operate from Douglas to Heysham and Liverpool, with summer-only services to Ardrossan, Belfast, Dublin and Fleetwood.

The Island's state-of-the-art telephone and communications systems are operated by Manx Telecom.

Population and Language

The Isle of Man has a population of about 70,000 persons and the official language is English.

Corporate Law

Types of Companies

The Isle of Man offers three types of non-income tax paying company.

Nonresident companies

A nonresident company is beneficially owned, managed and controlled by persons a majority of whom reside outside of the Isle of Man. Upon the filing of a nonresident declaration and payment of the nonresident company duty of £660, the company ceases to be subject to Isle of Man taxation. The duty is payable annually thereafter on the filing of the company's annual return. A nonresident company may not trade or have a source of income (apart from approved bank deposit interest) on the Island.

Exempt companies

An exempt company must be owned by nonresidents and have at least one Manx resident director and a professionally qualified company secretary. Exempt status can be obtained provided that the company's business and trading (apart from the receipt of approved bank deposit interest) is carried on outside the Isle of Man. The company's activities may nonetheless be controlled from within the Island and any income and profit derived therefrom will not be subject to Isle of Man taxation. The exempt company fee is £300, payable in the first year upon application and annually thereafter before 30th June.

In practice an exempt company should have only Manx directors to demonstrate for the purposes of taxation that central management and control of the company is based on the Island. This is not possible with a nonresident company.

International companies

An international company is similar to the exempt company but it may negotiate a rate of tax of its choice with the Assessor of Income Tax subject to the proviso that this may be not less than one per cent or more than 35 per cent. The minimum amount of tax payable in any one tax year may not be less than £300. This type of company can be useful when it is necessary to show that tax has been paid at certain minimum rate in order to obtain tax relief in another jurisdiction.

Statutory Requirements

Taxation

Isle of Man exempt and nonresident companies are not subject to any form of tax on profits in the Isle of Man but do pay a flat rate annual fee to the Isle of Man Government which is £660 for the nonresident company or £300 for the exempt company. An international company may negotiate a rate of tax of its choice, which may not be less than one per cent or more than 35 per cent, with a minimum annual amount of £300.

Shareholders

A minimum of one shareholder is required for Isle of Man private companies. The shareholders may be individuals or corporations. Details of the shareholders are shown on public file, but anonymity can be preserved by the use of nominee shareholders. There is no requirement to reveal beneficial ownership to the Island authorities.

Bearer shares and nil paid shares are not permitted

Directors

Isle of Man company law stipulates a minimum of two directors. Corporate directors are not permitted. Details of the directors are shown on public file. It is important to note that an exempt company must have at least one Isle of Man resident director and would usually have all its directors resident to clearly demonstrate that the control and management of the company takes place on the Isle of Man. This is not a requirement for a nonresident company, which may have nonresident directors.

Annual reporting

An annual return must be filed each year showing, *inter alia*, details of shareholders and directors. There is no requirement to file accounts with the Registrar, but note that companies which are resident on the island do need to produce annual audited accounts for the Assessor of Income Tax.

Time scale

Companies can be incorporated within one week (including the time taken to obtain name approval), but pre-incorporated 'shelf' companies are available for immediate purchase.

Restrictions on name and activity

Many finance-related words may not be used without Government approval. Other grandiose-sounding words (such as 'international' or 'global') require specific paid-up capitalisation. A comprehensive list of 'sensitive' words is available from the Registry.

Local requirements

All companies incorporated in the Isle of Man must maintain a registered office address within the jurisdiction. Exempt Isle of Man companies must appoint an Isle of Man resident professionally qualified company secretary as well as a local director. For resident and nonresident Isle of Man companies it is a practical but not a legal requirement to appoint an Isle of Man based company secretary.

Trust Law

Current Legal Framework

Trust law on the Isle of Man has developed parallel to that of English equitable principles, which govern the regulation of trusts and form Isle of Man law provided that they are not contrary to any local rules or customs. Trusts can be in either oral or written form and are not required to be registered.

The Trustee Act

The main act is the *Trustees Act* 1961, which states that the number of trustees must be between two to four individuals. Alternatively, a trust corporation may act as sole trustee.

A trust corporation may either be a public trustee appointed under the UK's *Public Trustee Act* 1906 or a company that has been approved by the High Court. At present, a trustee is not subject to any special regulations, though this may change in the future. Unless stated to the contrary in the trust document, the trustees are permitted only to invest in such securities as are set out in the *Trustees Act* 1961. The trustees are permitted to delegate all or any of the trust powers and discretion that they may have to any person or persons by power of attorney for up to 12 months at a time. In addition, they will not be responsible for the default of any such agent provided that he was employed and acted in good faith.

In addition to their equitable powers, the courts have extensive powers under the *Variation of Trusts Act* 1961 to vary or revoke a trust or enlarge the powers of the trustees to manage or administer any of the trust property.

In recent years there have been a number of statutes which deviate from English trust law. A Manx trust may last up to 80 years, as is the case with a UK trust. However, unlike a UK trust, a Manx trust is allowed to accumulate income throughout the period of its existence.

In 1988 the Isle of Man followed the United Kingdom and applied the Hague Convention in respect of the conflict of laws relating to the jurisdiction of trusts. The *Recognition of Trusts Act* 1988 states that the Manx Courts will uphold private international law principles applying to local trust law.

The Trusts Act 1995

However, the 1995 *Trusts Act* modifies this position. It allows for the change of jurisdiction of a trust to and from the island. The significance of this is that it states that trusts governed by the law of the Isle of Man will be determined 'according to the laws of the island without reference to the laws of any other jurisdictions with which the trust ... may be connected'. In particular it states that a trust will not be affected by forced heirship rules or by the fact that any jurisdiction to which it was connected did not recognise the concept of a trust. The two exceptions to this rule involve immovable property and testamentary dispositions, such as wills.

The Purpose Trust

The most important deviation from UK equitable principles is the *Purpose Trusts Act* 1996, which enables a trust which is not a charity to be set up for a purpose rather than for the benefit of beneficiaries. In order to safeguard the purpose an enforcer must be appointed whose sole purpose is to ensure that the trustees adhere to the purposes of the trust. In effect, the enforcer's position is similar to that of the Attorney General in relation to charitable trusts.

A purpose trust is an extremely useful financing vehicle as it enables a company to place assets off balance sheet whilst retaining effective control of them. It also enables a company's assets to be held by a nominally independent offshore entity in a tax neutral jurisdiction.

A purpose trust can be structured so that it protects a lender from the insolvency of the parent company that wishes to borrow the assets. A lender can take security over the assets which are owned by a trust, or by a company owned by a trust. These assets are insulated from the potential problems of the parent as the lender will enforce its rights against the trust rather than attempt to liquidate the parent company.

Miscellaneous

Aside from the introduction of the purpose trust, which has been designed to facilitate asset financing on the Isle of Man, trust law has kept within traditional equitable principles. There has been recent debate on whether asset protection trusts can be formed in the Isle of Man. The question centres around whether the applicability of the Statute of Elizabeth, which prevents a person from organising his affairs so as to avoid his creditors. The argument rests upon the generally held principle that English statutes do not apply to the Island unless there is specific reference. Whilst this is the case in this instance the legal principle is upheld by the 1737 *Fraudulent Assignments Act*. It is not envisaged that the Island will introduce any specific asset protection measures.

Registration and fees

An Isle of Man trust can cost as little as £500 to establish and £500 for the annual trustee's fees. Provided that neither the settlor nor the beneficiary is Manx resident the trust will not be liable to Isle of Man taxation.

Paul Brennock is a Chartered Secretary and a consultant to International Company Services Limited, Sovereign House, Station Road, St Johns, Isle of Man, IM4 3AJ, Tel: +44 (0) 1624 801801, Fax: +44 (0) 1624 801800, E-mail: paul.brennock@icsl.com.

JERSEY

Edmund Bendelow

Introduction

Geography

The British Channel Islands are located 15 miles off the North West coast of France in the English Channel. The islands are divided into two administrative areas, or Bailiwicks, of Jersey and Guernsey. The island of Jersey, together with two seasonally inhabited islets of the Minqiers and the Echrehous forms the larger Bailiwick. The topography of Jersey is basically a north to south sloping plateau some 45 square miles in area, while the population is approximately 85,000 permanent residents. The Island operates on the same time as London.

Political and Legal System

The earliest associations of the peoples of the Channel Islands were with France, their nearest neighbour. In the year 911 the Channel Islands were annexed by Duke Rollo of Normandy and from that period Jersey became culturally and constitutionally part of Normandy. Rollo's descendant, Duke William, conquered England after the Battle of Hastings in 1066 and thereafter he and his successors were simultaneously Kings of England and Dukes of Normandy. When, however, William's descendant King John lost the greater part of his possessions on the mainland of France to the French King in 1204, the Channel Islands were left as virtually the last remnant of the once extensive continental possessions of the Crown.

Though it has thus owed allegiance to the Crown for almost a thousand years, Jersey is neither a part of the United Kingdom nor a British colony. Whilst it is ultimately the responsibility of the British Crown to ensure good government in the Island and although the United Kingdom is responsible for its defence and foreign affairs, Jersey is in all other respects self-governing. The rights and privilege of the Islanders, including that of freedom from British taxation, have been enshrined in successive Royal Charters, the first of which was granted by King John in 1210, from which the Island's own elected Parliament, the States of Jersey, derives its authority and autonomy.

Currency

The pound sterling is the unit of currency. The States of Jersey issues its own notes and coinage, but notes issued by the Bank of England and other United Kingdom banks are also in general circulation.

Infrastructure and Communications

Jersey has one airport which is approximately 20 minutes drive away from the financial centre, St. Helier. The Island is easily accessible by air from London, has daily services to many UK cities and frequent direct flights to many European cities, including Paris, Amsterdam, Geneva, Munich, Hamburg and Frankfurt. It should be noted that some direct European flights are reduced in the winter months. The Island has an excellent telecommunications infrastructure with easy global connections. The Island's financial services infrastructure is well developed, with over 76 registered deposit taking institutions owned by parent institutions most of which appear in the top 500 of the world's banks. In June 1997 there were 324 funds registered in the Island which together administered funds worth £35.2 billion. In addition some 50 accountancy, 25 legal and over 20 insurance companies have offices in the Island.

Population and Language

English is the main language although French is also spoken. Over 50 per cent of the Island's national income comes from the finance industry which employs some 20 per cent of the Island's work force.

International Treaties

Through the United Kingdom, Jersey successfully sought a special relationship with the European Union under which the Island is included in the Treaty of Rome solely in respect of those provisions relating to free trade and for no other purposes. It should be noted however that as a matter of law Jersey is not a member of the European Union.

Exchange Controls

There are no exchange controls limiting the movement of funds to and from the island.

Corporate Law

Company Law

The *Companies (Jersey) Law* 1991 came into force in 1992. The new law included several major changes the most significant of which were the abolition of the *ultra vires* rule, the introduction of a Standard Table of Articles of Association and the introduction of provisions relating to directors, a register of director, amalgamations and acquisitions. It is possible to create limited partnerships under Jersey Law and administer from Jersey dual resident companies, offshore hybrid companies and international business companies.

Share Capital

There is a minimum requirement to issue two shares of £1 or currency equivalent. However there is a minimum duty fee payable and companies are therefore usually formed with an authorised share capital of £10,000. Shares may be issued on a partly paid up basis and at a premium.

Annual Returns

Before the end of February in each calendar year every company must deliver an annual return to the registrar of companies. The annual return must set out details of the company's share capital, its registered shareholders which are often nominees, and, if it is a public company, its directors. Failure to deliver an annual return by the end of February will result in a late filing fee becoming payable. If no annual return has been delivered by the end of June, the company will be guilty of an offence and liable to a daily default fine.

Disclosure Requirements

There are no disclosure requirements relating to non-Jersey companies administered in the Island.

Taxation

Corporate Tax

In accordance with the Jersey *Income Tax Law* of 1961 (as amended) all Jersey companies are liable to income tax at the rate of 20 per cent on taxable profits. However, companies beneficially owned outside Jersey may chose how they wish to be taxed. By default they will be treated as income tax companies but they may elect to be treated as an exempt company or an international business company (IBC). Exempt companies pay a flat annual fee of £600 which at present is not pro-rated in the year of incorporation. IBCs are liable to tax on a sliding scale at a rate ranging from a minimum of 0.5p to a maximum of 2.0p in the £ with a minimum of £1,200 payable annually.

Double Tax Treaties

Jersey has double tax treaties with the United Kingdom and Guernsey and a limited treaty with France relating to the avoidance of double taxation on aircraft and shipping profits. The treaty with the United Kingdom has been specially tailored to meet the needs of the Island. Dividends and debenture income from the United Kingdom do not attract double tax relief however, such income being assessed on its net value for Jersey residents.

Tax Concessions

The Jersey Taxation Authorities do not levy a charge on wealth, capital gains, gifts or inheritance. Nonresident or taxation exempt companies, and trusts created on behalf of nonresidents, pay tax only on income arising in the Island, but local bank deposit interest is excluded. Nonresident and exempt companies are not required to deduct tax at source from any dividend payments made to nonresidents.

Trust Law

The Legal Framework

Trusts created in Jersey are subject to the *Trusts (Jersey) Law* 1984. The trust document is a purely private arrangement between the settlor and the trustee. There is no requirement to register a trust with any public body.

Trustee

The *Trusts (Jersey) Law* 1984 requires that the number of trustees shall not be less than two unless the trust deed provides to the contrary. Corporate trustees are also permitted and in practice most offshore trusts are created with a sole corporate trustee.

Creation of Trust

Trusts may be express or verbal, however, in practice most offshore trusts are created in written form. Dispositions into trust may be *inter vivos* or testamentary. They may also be secret or semi-secret. There are special provisions to prevent trusts being set aside due to lack of capacity by a settlor under his own domestic law, eg civil law. There are, however, no statutory provisions relating to asset protection trusts.

Jersey trusts do not have to be registered and there are no filing fees or government duties to be paid at any time. There is no requirement to disclose the name of the settlor or principal beneficiary of a trust created or administered in Jersey unless the settlor or beneficiaries are Jersey resident. However, if a trustee creates a Jersey company, disclosure would be required under the company formation procedure described above. It is not possible to create a trust company in Jersey without regulatory consent. However, existing trust companies are able to create and administer managed trust companies on behalf of overseas institutions or private trust companies, which act as trustee to trusts that have a very restricted class of beneficiaries (eg family members).

Beneficiary

A beneficiary of a Jersey trust may be a natural person, a company or another trust. The beneficiary must be identifiable. A settlor of a Jersey trust may be a beneficiary of that trust.

Powers of the Trustees

Under the *Trusts (Jersey) Law* 1984, trustees, including directors of corporate trustees, are personally liable for breaches of trust, although the court may find them not so liable in certain circumstances. Trustees have an obligation to administer the trust with fidelity and diligence and to conduct its affairs as an ordinary prudent man of business would. In the case of a professional trustee, a higher standard of diligence and knowledge is expected. It is the duty of a trustee to preserve the trust fund. A Jersey trust may exist for a period of up to 100 years.

Costs

The cost of setting up and administering a Jersey trust varies widely depending on the trust company chosen but typically the cost of creating a standard form trust would be in the region of US$1,000-3,500. Ideally, a prospective trust company will be recommended by the settlor's financial/legal advisers but quotes should be obtained from several companies. However care should be taken not to select a provider by cost alone, as it is essential to ensure that the provider is sufficiently experienced so as to be able to carry out all the duties envisaged.

Financial Regulation

Jersey's finance industry is regulated by the Finance and Economics Committee. The Committee's principal duty is to defend and enhance the Island's reputation as an international finance centre. Licences to operate from Jersey are only granted to institutions of the highest reputation. The Committee ensures that legislation in Jersey keeps pace with that developed in other major financial centres. The Committee works closely with law enforcement departments worldwide and has recently adopted anti drug money laundering provisions in line with those adopted by the United Kingdom.

Edmund Bendelow is the Deputy Chairman and Chief Executive Officer of Basel Trust Corporation (Channel Islands) Limited. He is President of the Offshore Institute and a member of the Institute of Management, the International Tax Planning Association, and the States of Jersey Public Services Department Audit Committee.

JORDAN

Michael T Dabit

Introduction

Location and Time Zone

The Hashemite Kingdom of Jordan is an almost landlocked state in western Asia. It is bordered by Israel to the West, by Syria to the North, by Iraq to the East and by Saudi Arabia to the South. The capital is Amman. There are civil and religious judicial systems in Jordan. The religious courts have jurisdiction over personal matters such as marriage, divorce, inheritance and alimony.

System of Government

Jordan is a constitutional monarchy, with the king appointing the prime minister. The king has veto power over all laws, but his veto may be overridden by a two-third vote in both houses of the national assembly. The King is also empowered to appoint and dismiss judges.

Political and Legal System

There are civil and religious judicial systems in Jordan. The religious courts have jurisdiction over personal matters such as marriage, divorce, inheritance and alimony. The civil judicial system is composed of three tiers:

- The Courts of First Instance have general jurisdiction in all criminal and civil matters not expressly granted to the Magistrates court's jurisdiction. The Courts of First Instance also sit as a Court of Appeal for judgments of Magistrates Courts.
- The Courts of Appeal each have a three-judge panel. Jurisdiction of the Courts of Appeal is geographical. The Courts of Appeal hear appeals in Chambers of Magistrates Courts decisions and hear appeals of the Courts of First Instance and the Religious Courts.
- The Court of Causation which is the highest level of the judiciary consists of seven judges. Important cases are heard by a full panel. Ordinary appeals are heard by a five-judge panel.

Language and Population

Jordan's official language is Arabic although English is widely spoken. More than 90 per cent of the population are Sunni Muslims, while there are small communities of Christians and Shi'i Muslims.

Currency

The currency is the Jordanian Dinar and Fils – one JD is divided into 100 piasters or 1000 fils.

Corporate Law

Corporations and all business organisations in Jordan are governed by the *Companies Law* No 10 of 1989. As a general rule all business organisations including partnerships must be registered in the appropriate Commercial Register with the Controller of Companies of the Ministry of Industry and Trade. Business organisations must also register with the appropriate professional body of the association governing their field of activity (eg the Chamber of Commerce, the Chamber of Industry, the Construction Contracts Association, etc).

Types of Companies

The *Companies Law* provides for the following business organisations:

General partnership

The general partnership is formed by at least two and a minimum of 20 natural persons who are jointly and severally liable for partnership debts. A partner is entitled to take part in the management of the partnership although the partnership agreement normally provides for its authorised representatives and signatory. A partner may not be expelled from the partnership except by a court order. Any amendment to the partnership agreement requires the approval of all the partners and must be registered with the Controller of Companies.

The Controller shall keep a special register in which all partnerships shall be registered and have serial numbers in chronological order according to their registration dates. Any individual may, after paying the required fees (3JD), have access to the register if he obtains the prior approval of the Controller, should the latter be convinced that the said individual has a special interest in the register.

A general partnership dissolves upon the death, insanity, bankruptcy or withdrawal of one of its partners unless the partnership agreement states otherwise.

Limited partnership

A limited partnership is formed by at least one general partner and one limited partner. The total number of partners may not exceed twenty. The general partners assume unlimited personal liability for the debts of the partnership jointly and severally amongst themselves. The liability of the limited partners for the debts of the partnership is limited to their contributions to the capital of the partnership.

A limited partner may not take part in the management of the partnership nor act in its name. Failure to observe the said restrictions may render the limited partner personally liable for the debts of the partnership. A limited partnership is managed by the general partners in the same manner as a general partnership. Whereas a limited partner may freely sell or dispose of his interest in the limited partnership, the general partners are bound by the same rules governing general partnerships. The introduction of a new general partner to the limited partnership requires the approval of all the other general partners.

The bankruptcy of a limited partnership results in the bankruptcy of its general partners only. The death, insanity, bankruptcy, withdrawal or dismissal of a limited partner does not result in the dissolution of the partnership unless otherwise provided for in the partnership agreement.

Private shareholding companies with limited liability (PSC)

A PSC is formed by at least two and a maximum of fifty shareholders (whether natural or juristic). The liability of the shareholders is limited to their shares in the company's capital. The minimum authorised capital is set at JD30,000 of which at least 50 per cent should be paid up upon the incorporation of the PSC with the remaining 50 per cent to be paid within two years.

The shares of a PSC cannot be offered to the public for subscription and existing shareholders have priority over non-shareholders to purchase shares in the PSC. The shares are issued at nominal value or at a premium and are all of one class and have equal rights. The management of PSC can be entrusted to a single managing director or to a Board of Directors of 2 to 5 members who are elected for a two-year term.

A juristic shareholder can be elected to the Board of Directors and should name a natural person to represent it on the Board. Provisions can be incorporated into the Articles and Memorandum of Association entitling a shareholder (even a minority shareholder) to appoint a number of directors to represent it on the Board of Directors. The Board of Directors should have a chairman who may or may not have a casting vote depending on the agreement of the shareholders. The members of the Board of Directors or the managing director may not carry out any activities in competition with the PSC except with the approval of shareholders representing 75 per cent of the shares of the PSC.

The *Companies Law* sets out the required quorums necessary to convene valid meetings of the general authorities (both ordinary and extraordinary meetings), the authorities of such meetings as well as the required affirmative vote to pass resolutions at such meetings. In general, the shareholders are at liberty to incorporate into the Articles and Memorandum of Association appropriate provisions increasing such required quorums and voting requirements in order to safeguard the rights and interests of minority shareholders.

A PSC is obligated to annually retain 10 per cent of its net profits as mandatory reserves (with a maximum cap of 100 per cent of its authorised capital) and may retain up to 20 per cent of its net profits as voluntary reserves. A PSC is obligated to produce annual audited financial accounts and statements and to maintain completed shareholder's records. Any shareholder has the right to inspect such accounts and records and the same should be filed and registered with the Controller of Companies.

Public shareholding companies (PLC)

A PLC is formed by two or more promoters (whether natural or juristic). The liability of the shareholders of a PLC is limited to their shares in the company's capital. The minimum authorised capital (in the absence of any other legal provisions, for example, the section dealing with banks and insurance companies) is set at JD500,000 of which at least 25 per cent should be paid up upon the incorporation of the PLC with the remaining 75 per cent thereof except in the case of banks and insurance companies where the maximum is set at 50 per cent. In certain circumstances, however, the issuing committee may permit the promoters to subscribe to 100 per cent of the share capital of the PLC. The remaining shares must be offered to the public for subscription.

Contributions in kind are permitted and are subject to an evaluation by an independent committee appointed by the Minister of Industry and Trade. Shares in kind cannot be transferred for a period of two years from the date of their issue except as between the promoters themselves. The same restriction applies to promoters' shares.

The shares of a PLC are initially issued or offered at nominal value of JD1 per share. Subsequent to the registration of the PLC, shares may be issued or offered at a premium to be determined by the Issuing Committee. All shares are of one class and have equal rights. The shares become eligible for listing and trading on the Amman Financial Market (AMF) upon payment of 50 per cent of the share capital of the PLC.

The Companies Law provides that banks, financial companies, insurance companies and concession companies (companies engaged in investment and in any investment related sectors) must be incorporated as PLCs. Other laws and regulations require that certain activities may only be undertaken by PLCs as, for example, transport for tourists.

A PLC is managed by a Board of Directors consisting of 7 to 13 members who are elected for a four-year term. The members of the Board of Directors must be shareholders in the PLC and the *Companies Law* does not provide for 'Professional' directors to be elected from non-shareholders. A juristic shareholder can be elected to the Board of Directors and should name a natural person to represent it on the Board. Governmental institutions are entitled to representation on the Board of Directors in proportion to their shareholding in the PLC.

A PLC should produce audited financial accounts and statements and publish the same annually in local newspapers. A PLC should also maintain complete shareholder records.

Holding Companies (HC)

An HC is formed as a public shareholding company with the sole object of acquiring shares in other companies (other than general and limited partnerships), managing such companies and extending loans, guarantees and credit facilities thereto. HCs are subject to the same provisions governing public shareholding companies, subject, however, to a few minor exceptions.

Joint Investment Companies – Mutual Funds (JIC)

A JIC is formed either as a public shareholding company or a limited partnership in shares and hence, is governed by provisions applicable to either of the said two forms of business organisations. The objects of a JIC are confined to investing funds in securities on behalf of third parties.

The minimum authorised share capital of a JIC is set at JD1 million. The capital of a JIC is either variable or fixed. A JIC with a variable capital may issue redeemable shares, the value of which is to be determined based on the JIC's current assets. In this case, the JIC is obligated to redeem the shares upon the request of a shareholder based on the price that is announced by the JIC on a weekly basis with the knowledge of the AFM.

The shares of JIC with a fixed capital are traded on the AFM in the usual manner and their prices are determined by market forces. A JIC may not own more than 3 per cent of the shares of another JIC and its total investment in other JICs is limited to 10 per cent of its assets. A JIC may not invest more than 5 per cent of its assets in any one company and its cash and cash equivalents may not be less than 10 per cent of its assets. The *Companies Law* provides that special regulations shall be issued to govern various aspects of JICs. As at the date of writing this section, no such regulations have been issue.

Exempt companies – offshore companies (EC)

Exempt companies (offshore companies) (EC) were introduced to attract foreign investors to have a Jordanian registered entity for their operations in the region. An EC can take the form of a private shareholding company with limited liability, a limited partnership in shares or a public shareholding company. The company is registered in Jordan as a Jordanian entity, but cannot conduct any business in Jordan. ECs must be 100 per cent owned by non-Jordanians. Jordanians are prohibited from investing in such companies.

The minimum share capital of an EC depends on its form. If it is formed as a private shareholding company with limited liability, the minimum share capital is JD30,000 and JD,500,000 if it is formed as a public shareholding company. However, if the objects of the company are either banking, insurance or reinsurance, its minimum share capital is set at JD5,000,000.

An EC cannot offer its shares for public subscription in Jordan. It is not clear, however, whether an EC can be listed on the Amman Financial Market for trading between non-Jordanians. One would expect that such a move would be welcomed by the AFM. Indeed, ECs are obliged to invest a minimum of 50 per cent of their share capital in securities traded on the AFM and there are no legal restrictions against the same being traded thereon.

Foreign non-operating companies (branch or project offices)

A foreign company that has been awarded a contract in Jordan requiring execution of work therein must register a branch office with the Controller of Companies at the Ministry of Industry and Trade. Such a company is registered as a foreign operating company for purposes of the contract and for the duration thereof. If the company obtains other contracts in Jordan, then the same registration will be extended so as to cover such new contracts. If no new contracts are obtained by the company, then the Branch Office should be closed and liquidate upon the completion of the contract in respect of which the registration was effected.

Foreign non-operating companies (regional offices)

In addition to exempt companies described above (which are Jordanian registered) foreign companies are encouraged to set up regional offices in Jordan through tax and custom duty exemptions and provisions for the free movement of foreign currency. A regional office can operate from Jordan in any part of the world but not in Jordan itself; in other words, it may not generate money in Jordan. It may however, collect information generally concerning business possibilities in Jordan or in respect of a particular project.

The *Companies Law* does not elaborate on the size or type of the foreign company which may register a regional office in conformity therewith. However, it is now the policy of the Ministry of Industry and Trade to restrict this facility only to substantial and large companies of international standing in their fields.

The duration of a regional office is not limited to any period of project. A regional office enjoys the following exemptions and facilities:

- The foreign company and the regional office is exempted from local taxes, including income tax and social services tax;
- The non-Jordanian employees of the regional office are exempted from payment of income tax and social services tax on their salaries;
- A regional office may import its office equipment and furniture and business samples free of customs duties, import fees and all other related charges (except for sales tax);
- The non-Jordanian employees of the regional office may import a car every five years free of customs duties upon depositing a bank guarantee for the amount of the duty with the Ministry of Finance/ Customs. This guarantee will be discharged upon exporting the car out of Jordan or selling the car locally after paying the duty thereon;
- A regional office can have an account in Jordan in foreign currency or in Jordanian Dinars provided that the deposit are monies from foreign sources. It can pay into the account and repatriate monies out of it without exchange control restrictions;
- No fees are payable upon the registration of or in connection with the operation of a regional office;
- A regional office is exempted from the necessity of registering with the Chamber of Commerce and all other professional associations and from the payment of any fees in this regard; and
- The non-Jordanian employees of the regional office are granted residence and work permits. The number of non-Jordanian employees of the regional office may not, however, exceed that of its Jordanian employees.

Joint ventures

A joint venture (as, for example, between co-contractors) need not be registered in Jordan and, hence, is not governed by the *Companies Law*. A joint venture is typically regulated by the agreement between the joint venture parties. This obviously does not apply to a joint venture arrangement which envisages the establishment of a corporate entity as between the parties.

Supervision of Companies

All companies must strictly abide by the provisions of companies law and observe their memorandum and articles of association, and must implement the resolutions adopted by their general assemblies. The Minister of Industry and Trade and the Controller of Companies may take such measures which they deem suitable to supervise the companies in order to ensure that they comply with those provisions, contracts, regulations and resolutions. The supervision includes the following:

- Examining the accounts of the company; and
- Ensuring that the company abides by the objectives for which it was established.

Each shareholder and each partner in the companies which are registered, shall have the right to examine the information and documents related to and concerned with these companies, and which the Controller keeps. He shall also have the right to obtain an authenticated copy of any one of these documents against paying the fee stipulated in the regulations issued pursuant to companies law.

Shareholders holding not less than 20 per cent of the capital of a public shareholding company, or of a limited partnership in shares, or of a company with limited liability, may request the Controller to inspect the company's operations and the books thereof. Such a request may also be submitted by at least one quarter of the members of the Board of Directors to the Controller. Should the Controller be convinced of the justifications of this request, he shall delegate one or more experts to perform this task, at the expense of the company. Should the inspection uncover any violation that necessitates investigation and verification, then the Minister shall refer the matter to a special investigation committee which he shall form for this purpose, under the chairmanship of the Controller, and one of its members shall be a licensed auditor. The committee shall investigate and verify the violation prior to referring the matter to the court.

The Minister shall, upon a request from the Controller, assign the employees of the Companies' Controlling Division at the Ministry, to undertake an audit of a public shareholding company's accounts and activities. Those employees are entitled, in this regard, to inspect the company's registers, books and documents and shall verify them at the company's headquarters. They are also eligible to direct any inquiries to the company's employees and the company's auditors. Failure of the company to respond would be considered as a violation of the provisions of *Companies Law*.

Banks and financial institutions are exempted from the provisions mentioned above.

If any public shareholding company, or a limited partnership in shares, or a limited liability company, fails to commence its operations within one year of the date of its registration, then the Minister may, upon the request of the controller cancel the registration and he shall announce this cancellation in the official gazette. The responsibility of the promoters towards other shareholders remains in existence as if the cancellations of the company's registration did not occur. This action shall not affect the power of the court to liquidate the company whose name has been cancelled from the register.

Any person may apply to the court within three months from the date of publication of the notice in the official gazette, and if the court is satisfied that the company was carrying on its business at the time when its name was cancelled from the register, or if justice demands that its name be restored to the register, the court shall order the company's name to be restored, and the said company shall be considered as if it was not cancelled, and its existence remains in continuity.

Taxation

The Jordanian *Tax Law* No 14 of 1995 indicates that corporate income tax is a tax levied on the profits of local and foreign companies operating in Jordan. The tax rates applicable to these entities vary depending on their legal structure and nature of activities (see Table 1).

Table 1. Tax rates of various sectors

Activity	Rate
Metallurgy	15%
Manufacturing	15%
Hotels	15%
Hospitals	15%
Transportation (provided that paid up capital shall not be less than JD1,000,000)	15%
Construction contracts (provided that paid up capital shall not be less than JD1,000,000)	15%
Financial, insurance, exchange and brokerage companies and banks	35%
Others	25%

A withholding tax is levied to payments made to nonresident companies. The *Tax Law* stipulates that a resident company in Jordan making payments to nonresident parties should withhold 10 per cent of the payment on the spot to be presented to the Tax Authority within 30 days from the date it was withheld. This is a final withholding and the foreign nonresident party is expected to file a tax return and be taxed on its actual profit.

Profits distributed to shareholders shall be subject to a dividend tax at 10 per cent for the purpose of this tax and profits transferred by a branch of a foreign company to outside Jordan shall be considered as a distribution of profits. Also amounts withdrawn by partners in the form of advances or loans shall be treated as dividends, and profits distributed in the form of shares or contributions to increase capital shall both be subject to the dividend tax.

Trust Law

Creation

Trusts are created by law, by a contract with a trustee, or by an instrument of endowment. A trust may be established by the settlor in his lifetime or he may create it by his will. The will shall be subject to the provisions of the Moslem Shari'a Law and the legislative provisions drawn therefrom, and shall not be binding unless it is registered in the land registry. In respect of the heirs, the registration shall take effect from the date of the testator's death and of others from the date of registration.

A trust is usually created either orally or by a written document, a deed or a will. A case to prove the will or its revocation shall not be heard after the testator's death unless there are official documents handwritten by the deceased and signed by him.

The deposited property is the property deposited with a trustee. The validity shall be subject to the deposited property being property capable of being possessed, and by the actual or constructive receipt of the deposited property.

Role of Trustees

The trustee shall not be entitled to remuneration for preservation of the trust property unless otherwise agreed. All trusts must clearly have a trustee. A person capable of holding property may act as trustee, but certain persons may be regarded as undesirable and the court may remove them. The trustee may be appointed by the settlor, by the court, or granted this right by law.

A trustee shall hold the trust property. Something for which any trust property has been exchanged shall also be property of the trust. The trustee shall keep accounts as to all the affairs of the trust. There is no general maximum or minimum number of trustees to be appointed. A single trustee is sufficient to administer a trust.

Upon an application, the court may appoint, at its discretion, any fit or proper person as a Judicial trustee. Although he has all the normal powers of any other trustee, he may be given specific directions as to the administration of the trust.

Trustee duties are imposed by the trust instrument and the general law. The trustee must carry out his duties with diligence. He is responsible for the trust property and is liable for any loss which may occur. He shall exercise in preserving the property the care of a person preserving his own property.

Trustees have the duty to keep true and accurate accounts of all transactions. No particular form is required by law for trust accounts, but they must include all receipts and payments. The beneficiaries are entitled to examine the accounts.

A trustee shall not acquire for himself any property of the trust or a right in any such property or derive for himself any other benefit from the property or activities of the trust, and shall do nothing involving a conflict of interest between the trust and himself.

A trustee may have remuneration for his services, where the trust deed authorizes or by order of the court when a trustee is appointed by the court or by consent of all the beneficiaries.

A trustee cannot delegate his duties unless he is given authority. When a trustee fails to carry out any of the duties imposed on him by the trust deed or by law, or he exercises his discretionary powers improperly, a breach of trust occurs. A trustee is guilty of wilful default only if he knows that he is committing or intends to commit a breach of trust, or commits a breach by acting recklessly. A trustee is usually protected against personal liability for a breach of trust by lapse of time, being three years from the date at which the right of action against the trustee occurred.

Michael T Dabit is an Attorney-at-law and a member of the Jordanian Bar Association as well as the International Bar Association. His firm, Michael T Dabit & Associates, is located at Shemeisani, Al-Hindi Commercial Center, PO Box 20502, Amman 11118, Tel: 962/6-682622-682633; Fax: 962-6-682644.

LABUAN

John Koh & Co

Introduction

Location and Time Zone

Labuan is located off the northwest coast of Borneo, 18 km from the shores of the east Malaysian state of Sabah. The 92 square kilometre island is equidistant from Hong Kong, Kuala Lumpur, Singapore, Bangkok, Jakarta and Manila in the South China Sea. Local time is eight hours ahead of Greenwich Mean Time. Labuan is in the same time zone as Beijing, Hong Kong, Taipei, Shanghai and Singapore.

Political System

Labuan, together with the capital of Kuala Lumpur, is one of the two federal territories of Malaysia. Malaysia obtained its independence from British colonial rule on 31 August 1957 and has democratic parliamentary systems at both federal and state levels. Malaysia also has a unique constitutional monarchy in that the King is elected every five years on a rotational basis from the nine hereditary royal families by his fellow rulers. Malaysia is politically stable, with the ruling Barisan Nasional coalition having being in power since independence.

The Federal Government of Malaysia took over the administration of Labuan from the state of Sabah in 1984, and established Labuan as an International Offshore Financial Centre (IOFC) in 1990 with the aim of increasing Malaysia's attraction as an investment centre. Recent developments such as the establishment of a Financial Park and proposals to add to and strengthen the legal framework of Labuan IOFC legislation are evidence of the Malaysian Government's determination to promote Labuan as an IOFC.

Legal System

Malaysia has three concurrent legal systems: common law, Islamic Syariah law and the native law systems of Sabah and Sarawak. The common law system is predominant, with the others having much narrower jurisdictions both in content and persons subject to them. Malaysia shares many of the legal doctrines found in English law and the laws of former British colonies including Singapore and Hong Kong. Its criminal laws are derived from the Indian Penal Code. Generally, Labuan documentation is interpreted in accordance with Malaysian common law principles. All disputes are determined by the Malaysian court system, which is constitutionally independent. Leave of court may be obtained to conduct court proceedings on Labuan matters in English instead of the otherwise mandatory Bahasa Malaysia.

Currency
Malaysia's currency is denominated in Ringgit Malaysia (RM) and sen, and is freely convertible. One hundred sen is equal to RM1.

Population and Language
The multiracial population of Malaysia consists predominantly of ethnic Malays, Chinese and Indians, except for the East Malaysian states of Sabah and Sarawak where indigenous people form the majority. The national language is Bahasa Malaysia, but English is widely spoken and serves as the principal business language.

Economy
Labuan is a free port. The main economic activities are offshore oil and gas operations, shipbuilding and repairs, manufacturing and entrepot trading.

Infrastructure and Communications
The infrastructure of Labuan has undergone rapid upgrading in the last two years in response to the Malaysia Government's aggressive promotion of Labuan as an IOFC. A RM400 million Financial Park complex officially opened on 29 August 1996 will spread over 4.6 ha and offer approximately 198,000m^2 of commercial, office and residential space when completed.

Labuan is accessible from all major cities by air through Kuala Lumpur, Kota Kinabalu, Brunei and Singapore, with daily flights available from Kuala Lumpur and Kota Kinabalu.

Labuan IOFC Legislative Framework

Legislation
The following legislation govern offshore entities carrying on and proposing to carry on business in, through or from Labuan:

- *Offshore Companies Act* 1990 (OCA)
- *Offshore Banking Act* 1990 (OBA)
- *Offshore Insurance Act* 1990 (OIA)
- *Labuan Trust Companies Act* 1990 (LTCA)
- *Labuan Offshore Business Activity Tax Act* 1990 (LOBATA)
- *Labuan Offshore Trust Act* 1996 (LOTA)

The acts are drafted in English and are effective from 1 October 1990. They exclude offshore entities and prescribed offshore activities in varying degrees from the ambit of the Malaysian *Companies Act* 1965 (MCA) and the Malaysian *Income Tax Act* 1967 (MITA).

The concept of residency is pivotal to the IOFC legal regime. Only nonresidents are currently entitled to enjoy its benefits, although legislative changes have been proposed to also allow Malaysian residents to do so. The latter are statutorily defined as natural persons who are citizens or permanent residents of, or any other persons with established operational places of business in, Malaysia. This includes persons declared to be resident under the *Exchange Control Act* 1953 by the Controller of Foreign Exchange (Controller).

Supervisory Authority

The Labuan Offshore Financial Services Authority (LOFSA) established in February 1996 has taken over the administration and enforcement of OCA, OBA, OIA and LTCA from the LDA. LOFSA is the one-step development agency which will coordinate the functions of the Registrar of Companies (ROC) and Bank Negara Malaysia, the central bank of Malaysia, and spearhead the development of Labuan as an IOFC. The Inland Revenue Department (IRD) continues to administer and enforce LOBATA.

Proposed Changes

Proposed changes to promote a more conducive environment, in particular for offshore financial activities, currently include amendments to simplify OCA and permit offshore companies to invest in domestic companies, and proposals to establish an international stock exchange in Labuan and pass new legislation on offshore limited partnerships, the offshore securities industry and offshore Islamic financial services.

Corporate Law

Formation

Nonresidents can freely incorporate companies as Labuan Offshore Companies (offshore companies) under OCA. To enjoy the benefits of Labuan's IOFC regime, existing foreign companies incorporated by nonresidents must either redomicile in Labuan and register as offshore companies or register as foreign offshore companies. Newly incorporated and redomiciled offshore companies and foreign offshore companies can only be formed or registered by a Labuan Trust Company, which is a domestic or foreign company registered under MCA and further registered under LTCA to provide certain services to nonresidents. There are currently 16 Labuan Trust Companies. Offshore companies which are offshore banks or offshore insurers require licensing under OBA and OIA respectively.

Names

The names of offshore companies and foreign offshore companies must be approved prior to incorporation or registration. In the case of offshore companies, foreign language names are permitted provided that the characters are romanised. Chinese company names are therefore not allowed. The name must also contain the abbreviation '(L)' to distinguish it as a Labuan offshore company as well as a word or abbreviation, such as 'Limited' or 'Ltd', denoting a joint stock company limited by shares. If the proposed name resembles that of a trademark, business, person or company, prior written consent to its use must be obtained.

Incorporation of Offshore Company

New formations of offshore companies generally take one or two days if the documents are in order and properly filed by a Labuan Trust Company with the regional ROC in Labuan. Shelf companies are generally not available given the speed and ease of incorporation. Once the name of the proposed offshore company has been approved, its memorandum and articles of association should be lodged with the registrar. A statutory declaration that no promoter is a Malaysian resident may be required from an officer of the offshore company.

Registration of Redomiciled Offshore Company and Foreign Offshore Company

The Registrar of Companies also takes one or two days to process an application by a foreign incorporated company to either transfer its domicile (ie registered office) to Labuan and register as an offshore company, or to register as a foreign offshore company. An application to redomicile should be made with the consent of all shareholders, debenture holders and creditors as well as the appropriate authority in the jurisdiction of incorporation. A redomiciled offshore company is deemed to continue in Labuan as if locally incorporated. An application to register as a foreign offshore company should be accompanied by certified copies of the company's certificate of incorporation and constitutive documents, a list of directors and officers, and a memorandum of appointment or power of attorney naming a Labuan Trust Company authorised to accept service of process and notices. Registration does not create a new legal entity, nor does it affect the rights, powers, liabilities and obligations of either a redomiciled offshore company or a foreign offshore company.

Fees

A one-off initial registration fee and thereafter an annual fee is payable by offshore companies and foreign offshore companies as follows:

	Offshore Company (Incorporation/Registration to redomicile)		**Foreign Offshore Company** (Registration)
Initial Fee	Authorised capital of:		RM6,000
	• RM50,000 or less	RM1,000	
	• more than RM50,000, up to RM1,000,000	RM2,000	
	• more than RM1,000,000	RM5,000	
Annual Fee	RM2,000		RM5,000

Share Capital

An offshore company must be a company limited by shares denominated in a foreign currency. Its shares may be issued in various classes with different rights. The issue of share warrants is permitted but the issue of bearer shares is not. Shares and debentures may be issued to the general public (excluding Malaysian residents). Generally, no minimum capital requirement is imposed. An offshore company may purchase its own shares and provide financial assistance for share repurchase. Repurchased shares may be cancelled by a directors' resolution to the extent of available distributable surpluses, and shares may be issued at a discount upon approval of the Registrar of Companies. Offshore banks are required to maintain capital funds unimpaired by losses of at least RM10 million or its equivalent in any other currency. Offshore insurance companies are required to maintain minimum working funds for their reinsurance, life and general insurance, and captive insurance businesses.

Statutory Requirements

Unless otherwise stated, the following requirements apply only to offshore companies:

Shareholders

Only one subscriber to the memorandum and articles of association is required. They may be a corporation or a trust company, and do not have to be a Malaysian resident.

Directors

Only one director is required and the director or directors do not have to be Malaysian residents. If any resident director is appointed, that resident director must be an officer of a Labuan Trust Company or, in the case of offshore banks and insurers, an officer of the banking or insurance company.

Secretaries

One Malaysian resident secretary is required who must be an officer of a Labuan Trust Company.

Registered office

Every offshore company and foreign offshore company must have a registered office in Labuan, which must be situated at the principal office of a Labuan Trust Company.

An offshore company may not establish branches in any other part of Malaysia apart from Labuan, although offshore banks and insurance companies have been allowed to maintain marketing offices in Kuala Lumpur. Foreign offshore companies which also wish to have a place of or carry on business in the rest of Malaysia must also register as a foreign company.

Registers

Registers of members and of directors and secretaries must be maintained at an offshore company's registered office.

Auditors

An offshore company may appoint as its auditor any person authorised in any jurisdiction to conduct audits and who is approved and registered. The appointment must be made within 90 days of incorporation. If it neither engages in offshore banking or insurance nor invites public subscription for its shares and debentures, an offshore company does not need to appoint an auditor provided this is authorised by a shareholders' resolution.

Scope of Activities

Offshore companies and foreign offshore companies may carry on any offshore business apart from shipping and petroleum operations in Malaysia. Permitted activities include holding investments in securities, loans, deposits and immovable property, fund management, trading and licensing. All such activities must be carried out in a foreign currency, although administrative and statutory expenses may be defrayed in Ringgit Malaysia.

Management and Administration

The following only apply to offshore companies. Meetings may be called at the option of the offshore company. Members may meet by telephone or other electronic means and pass written resolutions by facsimile or telex. The notice requirements of seven days and 21 days for ordinary and special resolutions respectively may be waived by a prescribed percentage of the members. Proper accounting records must be kept in Labuan either at the registered office or such other place as the directors see fit, and if an auditor is appointed, annual audited accounts must be tabled at a general meeting no later than nine months from financial year end and lodged with the Registrar of Companies within one month of being so presented. An annual return must be filed within 30 days of an offshore company's anniversary of incorporation each year but need not be accompanied by audited accounts.

Nondisclosure Provisions

The Labuan IOFC legislation has the following secrecy provisions. Information on shareholdings, beneficial ownership, and the management and affairs of an offshore company or foreign offshore company cannot be divulged or elicited without incurring heavy penalties under OCA. All hearings apart from criminal proceedings must be heard in camera unless otherwise ordered by the court and no details may be published without leave of the court. Inspection of company files at the ROC requires court approval. OBA and OIA protect the identity of customers and policy holders respectively as well as their accounts and affairs and prohibit directors and officers from disclosing information and documents relating thereto.

However, in line with Malaysian Government policy to discourage fraudulent activities such as money laundering in Labuan, total confidentiality is not available. Disclosure can be required by law, and as previously mentioned, criminal proceedings under OCA will be heard in open court. As a matter of law, an offshore bank may open accounts only for persons whose identities are known to it. As a matter of practice, a Labuan Trust Company for purposes of verification but not for disclosure to the authorities will require disclosure of the identities of shareholders and directors (though nominees may be used) in vetting an application for incorporation or registration, and proof of the non-Malaysian resident status of settlors and beneficiaries in making a statutory declaration for preferential tax purposes.

Corporate Mobility

An offshore company may if so agreed by its shareholders, debenture holders and directors transfer its incorporation to another jurisdiction upon approval by the Registrar of Companies. A foreign offshore company may simply cease to have a place of business or cease to carry on business in Labuan and notify the registrar of this within seven days.

Incentives

There are a number of preferential tax provisions and exemptions from tax as well as liberal exchange controls (discussed below) which are incentives for offshore companies and foreign offshore companies to set up in Labuan. Other non-fiscal incentives include liberal immigration policies to facilitate expatriate employment. Employment passes valid for up to five years and multiple-entry visas may be applied for.

Three-month temporary employment permits are routinely issued whilst applications are being processed. The preferential tax rate and other incentives provided under the Labuan IOFC regime are not intended for companies carrying on industrial or manufacturing activities, which have incentives provided for them under the *Promotion of Investments Act* 1986.

Taxation

Corporate Tax Incentives

The taxation of profits derived from offshore business activities of offshore companies is governed by LOBATA, which provided preferential rates. LOBATA also covers foreign offshore companies and offshore trusts which are included in the LOBATA definition of offshore companies (henceforth collectively referred to as 'all offshore companies'). The MITA corporate tax rate however applies to offshore insurance and offshore banking business of a branch of a Malaysian insurer and bank respectively and all non-offshore business activities of all offshore companies.

Rates of tax

Profits for the basis period for a year of assessment of all offshore companies carrying on an:

- Offshore non-trading activity (ie activity relating to the holding of investments activities in securities, stock, shares, loans, deposits and immovable properties carried out on its own behalf) are not taxable.
- Offshore trading activity (ie banking, insurance, trading, management, licensing and any other activity not an offshore non-trading activity) are taxed at a preferential rate of three percent on net audited profits. Alternatively, offshore companies may elect either to be charged a fixed amount of RM20,000 for the year of assessment or to pay a flat administrative fee of RM20,000 to the Registrar of Companies instead.

All offshore companies carrying out both types of activity are deemed to be carrying on an offshore trading activity, and those not having a basis period for a year of assessment are taxed for that year of assessment at a fixed rate of RM20,000.

Tax returns and payment

Prescribed forms are required to be filed with the Director General of Inland Revenue within three months from the commencement of a year of assessment. Payment of tax must be made simultaneously.

Offshore trusts

An offshore trust qualifies for preferential tax treatment for offshore business activities under LOBATA. The identity of the settlors and beneficiaries need not be disclosed to the tax authorities unless requested, but the trustee signing the requisite statutory declarations may require proof that they are not residents. Malaysian law regards a trust as resident in Malaysia if any of the trustees are Malaysian residents, unless the trust was created and the income thereof derives wholly from and it is administered year-long outside Malaysia and at least half the trustees are non-Malaysian residents. An offshore trust is taxed on income accruing in or derived from Malaysia at a rate of 30 per cent under MITA.

The 1997 Budget proposes that the definition of an offshore trust under LOBATA be amended to be in line with the *Labuan Offshore Trusts Act* 1996 (LOTA) which was enacted in July 1996. Under LOTA, a trust may remain as an offshore trust even if any beneficiary subsequently becomes a Malaysian resident, thus enabling the trust to continue to enjoy preferential tax treatment. This proposal will take effect from the year assessment 1997.

Individual Tax Incentives

Labuan individual residents are subject to Malaysian tax but there is a 50 per cent abatement for the years of assessment 1992 to 1997 for expatriates employed in a managerial capacity and persons providing legal, financial or secretarial services to all offshore companies, as well as for infrastructure developers.

Exemptions from Income Tax

No income tax is payable by recipients on dividends derived from offshore business activities, fees and interest paid by offshore companies or by beneficiaries on distributions made by offshore trusts. Neither is it payable by offshore companies on dividends except when received from Malaysian residents.

Withholding Tax

No withholding tax is payable on tax-exempt income received from offshore companies.

Capital Gains Tax

Only real property gains tax is charged upon disposal of Malaysian property. Offshore companies can only purchase Malaysian property for use as business premises or personnel accommodation. Foreign-sourced capital gains are not chargeable to tax.

Indirect Tax

There are no sales taxes, import and export duties, excise duties or surtaxes except on petroleum products as Labuan is a free port.

Stamp Duty

All instruments made by offshore companies in connection with offshore business activities are exempt from stamp duty.

Double Taxation Treaties

Malaysia has to date signed 40 bilateral treaty agreements (some as yet unratified). Doubts have been expressed whether the Labuan IOFC legislation is covered for lack of specific reference to it in the treaties and contracting parties could refuse recognition. No authoritative clarification has been made to date, but in practice Asean nations have indirectly afforded recognition by allowing treaty advantages to offshore companies, and no other contracting parties have asked for renegotiation of terms. The advantages of exemption from withholding tax and avoidance of double taxation may be outweighed however, by the undesirability of the exchange of information provisions which erode strict secrecy. Income remitted to non-contracting nations enjoy unilateral relief.

Banking and Exchange Controls

Treatment of Nonresidents

All nonresident may freely move funds into and out of Malaysia and open foreign currency accounts in or outside Malaysia without having to complete exchange control forms or be subject to exchange control monitoring. The Exchange Control Notice dated 1 December 1994 issued by the Controller declared offshore companies to be nonresident for exchange control purposes. Offshore trusts automatically enjoy these privileges.

Trust Law

Current Legal Framework

The *Offshore Trust Act* 1996 provides a statutory framework for offshore trusts. Amongst the changes it heralds are:

- Writing will be required to create an offshore trust;
- The unenforceability of foreign claims or judgments against valid offshore trusts;
- Voiding of fraudulent offshore trusts or dispositions;
- The registration of offshore trusts;
- A fixed duration of 100 years; and
- Confidentiality provisions.

The statute governing trust companies in Labuan is the *Labuan Trust Companies Act* 1990. The Malaysian legal framework is based on English common law, and is supported by local legislation, such as the *Trustee Act* 1949, outlining the powers and duties of trustees, as well as case law. Being neither an offshore company nor a foreign offshore company, a trust with nonresident settlors and beneficiaries created in Labuan is not subject to the provisions of the *Offshore Companies Act*. Preferential tax treatment is however, accorded to offshore trusts and the concept of residency is central.

Creation

Trusts may be created orally, although disposal of purely equitable interests must be in writing. Constructive, implied and resulting trusts may be imposed by operation of law.

Settlor

The settlor must be a nonresident to qualify for preferential tax treatment and must be person able to acquire and dispose of property. The settlor cannot be bankrupt, mentally disordered or a minor.

Beneficiaries

The beneficiaries must also be nonresidents to qualify for preferential tax treatment, and must be persons capable of holding property at law. A settlor may be a beneficiary. A trust which does not directly or indirectly benefit an individual and which is not a charitable trust or a trust of imperfect obligations is invalid.

Trustees

The trustees should be nonresident individuals or trust corporations to qualify for preferential treatment, subject to one exception. A settlor may be a trustee and a sole trustee is sufficient. Only Labuan Trust Companies may provide professional trustee services in Labuan. They generally charge on a time-basis or a percentage of the value of administered assets and provide services such as share transfers and share registration, dealing with property, and management and accounting services.

Registration and Fees

Trusts are currently not required to be registered in Labuan.

Role of Trustees

Vesting

If a trustee disclaims office, the legal estate vests in any other accepting trustees but otherwise reverts to the settlor or his personal representatives. On the death of a sole or last surviving trustee, the trust property and all trust powers devolve to his personal representatives.

Management

The trust instrument and such statutory provisions as are not expressly varied or excluded thereby are the source of a trustee's powers and govern the manner in which trust assets are managed. A settlor's letter of wishes, whilst not binding on the trustees, provides them with guidance in the administration of the trust. Accounting and auditing requirements may be contained in the trust instrument but no such statutory requirements exist although an offshore trust electing to pay tax under LOBATA at three percent audited net profits is required to submit audited accounts to the IRD.

Powers

A trustee has statutory power, insofar as it is not excluded by the trust instrument, to appoint and pay an agent to perform specific executive or administrative functions. Alternatively, a trustee may delegate vested trusts, powers and discretion to another by power of attorney for a limited period. Powers of investment are conferred on trustees by statute, and trust instruments generally provide express powers to invest.

Remuneration

The remuneration of trustees can be provided for in the trust agreement, reached by agreement with beneficiaries or authorised by the courts.

Miscellaneous

The common law rule against perpetuities applies to Labuan offshore trusts. The requirements of charitable purpose trusts also apply; a trust which does not directly or indirectly benefit an individual and which is not a charitable trust or a trust of imperfect obligations is invalid. The disclosure of the existence of any trust or estate settlement or the identity of the settlor or beneficiary as well as the management thereof and affairs relating thereto is prohibited. An offshore trust may migrate into and out of Labuan if permitted by the trust instrument by appointing a trustee in another jurisdiction and nominating the law of that other jurisdiction to be the proper law of the trust.

John Koh & Co, Singapore, is a specialist law firm established in January 1995 to concentrate on cross-border corporate transactions and complex fraud and securities litigation. The firm is particularly active in the utilities, energy, telecommunications, transportation, media, aviation and food industries.

LIECHTENSTEIN

Dr Henri Leimer

Introduction

Location and Time Zone

The Principality of Liechtenstein is situated in the centre of the European Continent between Switzerland and Austria. It occupies a land area of 160 square kilometres and is Europe's fourth smallest state. It is one hour ahead of Greenwich Mean Time. The climate is alpine, with the average temperature between 0 and 17 degrees Celsius.

Political and Legal System

Liechtenstein achieved independence in 1719 and sovereignty in 1806. State authority is jointly vested in the Prince and in the people. According to its constitution, Liechtenstein is a constitutional hereditary monarchy run on a democratic and parliamentary basis. The head of state is the reigning Prince. Bills require his assent in order to become law. Liechtenstein's parliament, the Landtag, is elected by the people. Officially, the president of the Landtag is the highest representative of the people. The five-member government is constituted from a coalition of two moderate conservative political parties. Liechtenstein has a three-tier judicial system together with an administrative court to decide complaints against the government.

Currency

The currency is Liechtenstein is the Swiss Franc (CHF). One US dollar is equal to CHF 1.33.

Infrastructure and Communications

Liechtenstein is linked to the international network of roads by a motorway on the Swiss side of the Rhine. The international airport at Zurich can be reached in one and a half hours. Postal service is provided by twelve post offices.

Population and Language

There are over 30,000 inhabitants living in eleven municipalities. The majority of them are Roman Catholics. German is the official language, but Liechtensteiners speak an Alamanic dialect, which exhibits both Swiss and Austrian influences.

Finance and Commerce

All Liechtenstein banks report on the same basis as all Swiss banks to the Swiss National Bank and the Banking Commission with regard to the maintenance of capital and liquidity ratios. In addition, the Swiss National Bank acts as the lender of last resort to all Liechtenstein banks. From the foreign investment perspective, Liechtenstein's joining of the EEA in 1995 has brought benefits to the domiciliary and holding companies including the free movement of goods, services, capital and people among the member states.

Banking Secrecy

Banking secrecy is legally enshrined in the law. The Liechtenstein banking laws are among the strictest in the world in terms of safeguarding confidentiality. They are very similar to those of Switzerland.

The Foundation and Trust Settlement

The *Persons and Companies Act*, which sets out liberal company laws, together with the strict banking secrecy laws, have earned Liechtenstein the reputation as a sophisticated offshore centre. Entities which are of particular interest to asset planners include the foundation and the trust settlement.

Foundation

A foundation can be defined as a fund endowed for a specific object, which has acquired its own legal personality. The foundation does not have members, partners or participants. However, one or several beneficiaries may be designated. Founders may be natural or juridical persons, irrespective of their nationality, residence or domicile.

Object

The founders may at their own discretion determine the foundation's object; however, the object must not be contrary to law and public policy. In general, foundations do not have commercial objects. They may, however, engage in commercial activities in so far as these serve the foundation's non-commercial object and are determined in the articles. The minimum capital of a foundation is CHF30,000 (US$22,556), which may be provided by payment in cash or contributions in kind.

The governing bodies of the foundation as well as the details specifying the conduct of its business are determined in the articles. The foundation board is usually the sole and supreme governing body. However, the articles may provide for additional bodies, such as advisory boards, counsels, protectors or collators and specify their duties and powers. The beneficiaries and reversioners of the foundation as well as the type and scope of the beneficial interest may be specified in the formation deed, articles or bylaws.

Fees and Tax

Foundations qualifying as holding companies or domiciliary enterprises pursuant to the Tax Act are exempt from property, gains or profits tax. They are liable to an annual capital tax of 0.1 per cent on the foundation assets, subject to a minimum of CHF 1,000 (US$751). Other annual fees include board of directors fee of approximately CHF 2,500 (US$1,879) and representation fee of CHF 800 (US$601). The formation fee is approximately CHF 3,500 (US$2,631).

Since a Liechtenstein foundation achieves legal personality by being entered in the Public Register or by having its documents deposited with the Public Registry depending on its activity, it is of particular interest to the asset planner who prefer not to pass the legal title of his assets to an outsider or a private trust company.

Trust Settlement

Creation

Liechtenstein is the only country on the European Continent to have codified the instrument of the trust settlement in line with Anglo-Saxon model. The difference between Liechtenstein's and the UK's is that a Liechtenstein trust may be created for unlimited duration and unlimited accumulation. A trust settlement is created by a contractual relationship between one or several settlors and one or several trustees. A trust settlement does not have its own legal personality.

Settlor

The settlor may be a natural or juridical person with residence or domicile in Liechtenstein or abroad. The settlor is under obligation to comply with the provisions of the trust deed and in particular to put the trust property at the disposal of the trustee after the trust has come into existence. The settlor may also appoint an advisory board and/or protector.

Trustee

Trustees may also be natural or juridical persons with residence or domicile in Liechtenstein or abroad. The trustee administers the trust property in his/her own name as an independent legal entity. The trustee is under obligation to comply with the provisions of the trust deed and to observe the principles of due diligence. The trustee may appoint third parties to perform administrative duties. The beneficiaries are designated in the trust deed.

Fees and Tax

The law does not provide for a minimum trust property. However, the law permits the creation of trust settlements pursuant to foreign law and the transfer of foreign trusts to Liechtenstein. Trust settlements are exempt from property, gains or profits tax. They are liable to an annual capital tax of 0.1 per cent on the trust property, subject to a minimum of CHF 1,000 (US$752). The trustee fee is calculated on the basis of the assets held at the beginning of each accounting year with a minimum of CHF 5,500 (US$4135). The formation fee is approximately CHF 4,500 (US$3383).

In view of the above, Liechtenstein can be described as having two complementary trust systems: the first one based on civil law and the second one based on common law. Since Hong Kong, Singapore and Malaysia have common law systems while Taiwan, Indonesia and Japan are of civil law background, Liechtenstein may be used by individuals with diversified interest in various Asian countries.

Dr Henri Leimer is the chief representative for LGT Bank's representative office in Hong Kong.

LUXEMBOURG

Citco (Luxembourg) SA

Introduction

Location

The Grand-Duchy of Luxembourg is an independent sovereign state situated in the centre of Western Europe bordering Belgium, France and Germany. Luxembourg is a constitutional monarchy with a population of approximately 390,000 and covering an area of 2,587 square kilometres.

Luxembourg was one of the founder members of the European Union in 1957 and is also a member of the OECD and Benelux.

Currency

The monetary unit is the Luxembourg Franc (FLUX or LUF) which is at par with the Belgian Franc (also accepted as legal tender within the country).

Language

The official languages are French and German, although English is also widely spoken in business.

Legal System

The civil law system of Luxembourg is based on the Napoleonic code with similarities to both the Belgian and French legal systems. Legislative power is vested in a democratically elected parliament. The company law of Luxembourg is contained in the Code Civil and the Code de Commerce.

Corporate Law

Types of Companies

The are two types of Luxembourg limited liability companies, both with capital divided into shares:

- the Sociètè anonyme (SA), a public limited liability company or joint stock company; and
- the Sociètè à responsabilitè limitèe (SARL), a private limited liability company.

Incorporation

A Luxembourg limited liability company is incorporated by executing a deed of incorporation (which includes the articles of association of the company) before a notary in Luxembourg. The deed must then be deposited with the Chief Registrar of the District Court of Luxembourg and published in the official gazette. A Luxembourg company can usually be incorporated within a week.

Corporate Mobility

The registered office of a company must be located in the Grand-Duchy of Luxembourg. The corporate seat can be transferred to another jurisdiction by resolution of shareholders and it is also possible for a foreign company to be transferred to Luxembourg provided that the laws of the foreign jurisdiction so permit.

Capital

The minimum authorised and issued share capital for an SA is LUF1.25 million, of which at least 25 per cent must be paid up. All bearer shares must be fully paid up.

The minimum subscribed capital for a SARL is LUF500,000 which must be fully issued and paid up.

Shares

Shares of an SA may be in both registered or bearer form, although shares of a SARL must be in registered form only. Registered shares are transferred by way of a declaration signed by both the transferor and transferee and bearer shares are transferred by delivery. Transfer of registered shares is recorded in the share register.

Any transfer of shares of a SARL requires the consent of the other shareholders with a 75 percent majority. In the event that shares of a SARL are transferred, the Articles of Association of the company must be amended.

Shares of different classes, such as preferred and redeemable shares, may be issued and the rights attaching to different classes are governed by the company's statutes. Nonvoting shares and shares with no par value are permitted.

Shareholders

There must be at least two shareholders of an SA although a SARL may have a single shareholder. A SARL must have no more than forty shareholders.

Notices convening annual or extraordinary meetings of shareholders must be published twice in the local official gazette and a Luxembourg newspaper. This requirement can be waived when all of the shareholders are present or represented at the meeting.

If all shares are in registered form, general meetings may be called by registered letter to each shareholder.

Shareholders may be represented at general meetings by proxies, who are not required to be shareholders unless the company articles state otherwise.

Management

Management of both an SA and a SARL is vested in the board of directors. An SA is required to have a minimum of three directors, although a SARL is permitted to have a single director. The directors are appointed at the general meeting of shareholders and can be private individuals or corporate entities. Any appointment must be for a term no longer than six years, although re-election is possible at the end of a term of office.

Financial Statements

Financial statements must be approved by the shareholders in general meeting and filed with the Registry of the District Court within 12 months of the end of the financial year together with details of the board of directors and the statutory auditor.

Financial statements of an SA and a SARL must be audited by an independent auditor if

- the balance sheet total exceeds LUF 93 million;
- the net turnover exceeds LUF 186 million; and
- the average number of full time employees exceeds fifty.

Where these criteria are not met by an SA, the annual financial statements must be certified by a statutory auditor appointed by the shareholders. However, if a SARL does not meet the criteria, a statutory auditor is not required. Company accounting may be performed outside of Luxembourg.

Taxation

With the exception of the 1929 holding company, the following taxation rules will apply:

Tax Rates

Luxembourg companies are liable to corporation tax on their worldwide income currently at 33 percent. This rate will be reduced to 30 percent incrementally over a period of three years from May 1996. Corporate income is also subject to municipal business tax and wealth tax.

Capital Gains

Capital gains are subject to corporate tax unless they fall within one of the exceptions or are entitled to the 'affiliation privilege'. Companies can defer tax on capital gains realised on the sale of property and non-amortisable assets which form part of a permanent establishment in Luxembourg and which have been held for at least five years, if reinvested within two years.

Branches
Branches of foreign corporations are liable to full Luxembourg tax on profits attributable to the Luxembourg branch.

Foreign Source Income
Foreign Source Income is included as worldwide income subject to Luxembourg tax. Full credit is given for foreign taxes withheld from sources in tax treaty countries and also for certain types of income from non-treaty countries.

Withholding Tax
Subject to reduction under various tax treaties, rates of withholding tax are as follows:

- No withholding tax is levied on interest;
- Dividends paid to nonresident shareholders: 25 percent; and
- Royalties paid to nonresident: 10/12 percent.

Tax Treaty Arrangements
Luxembourg has tax treaties with the following countries:

Austria, Belgium, Brazil, Bulgaria, Canada, China, Czech Republic, Denmark, Finland, France, Germany, Hungary, Indonesia, Ireland, Italy, Japan, Korea, Malta, Morocco, the Netherlands, Norway, Romania, Singapore, Slovakia, Spain, Sweden, Switzerland, the United Kingdom and the United States of America.

The 1929 Holding Company

Definition
A special tax regime was introduced by legislation in 1929 for holding companies. Holding companies are defined as those companies whose activities are restricted to the taking of participating interests in any form whatsoever in other Luxembourg or foreign undertakings and the administration and development of such participating interests in a manner such that the company does not itself engage in any industrial activity nor maintain any commercial establishment open to the public. A 1929 holding company may be either a SARL or an SA.

Activities of a 1929 Holding Company
A 1929 holding company is permitted to

- subscribe, acquire, manage, and sell transferable securities in foreign or in Luxembourg companies;
- grant loans to companies in which it has a participation and provide security for third parties who have granted advances to subsidiaries;
- maintain bank accounts in any country;
- hold patents in its portfolio and grant licences to other companies to exploit the patent; and
- acquire real estate provided that it is for its own use and hold a participation in a real estate company.

However, a 1929 holding company may not

- acquire an interest in a partnership;
- advance funds to its shareholders;
- hold other intellectual property rights such as copyrights and exclusive software rights;
- invest in commodities or commodity futures, invest in gold over the limit of 10 percent of the company's net assets;
- offer services to the general public or provide services for commissions or fees;
- act as trustee or intermediary and realise transactions on behalf of third parties; or
- conduct banking, commercial or individual activity.

Restrictions

The following debt/equity ratios must be maintained:

- Liabilities other than bonds: subscribed capital; and
- Bonds: paid-in capital.

Since the holding company is exempt from direct taxation, it does not qualify under the double taxation treaties nor the provisions of the EU Parent-subsidiary Directive.

Taxation

The 1929 holding company is exempt from

- income tax;
- municipal business tax;
- wealth tax;
- withholding tax on the payment of dividend and interest;
- tax on liquidation proceeds; and
- taxation on accumulation of dividend and interest income and capital gains.

The holding company is required to pay

- Capital tax ('droit d'apport'). The tax rate is 1 percent and is calculated on the total of the subscribed capital. It is a one-off tax payable on incorporation and at the time of any increase in subscribed capital.
- Subscription tax ('taxe d'abonnement'). This is calculated at the rate of 0.2 percent of the actual value of the company's shares. If the shares are quoted, this value is based on the average quotation of the preceding year. Where the shares are not quoted, the tax is levied on the share par value.

In the event that the dividend in one year exceeds 10 percent of the share capital, the tax in the subsequent year will be due on ten times the amount of the dividend paid. If the profits realised are material and are not distributed, the value of the shares for tax purposes will not be less than par.

The Billionaire Holding Company

The 'billionaire holding company' is a special type of 1929 holding company where the aggregate of its paid-in share capital (including premium) and reserves must be at least the equivalent of LUF1 billion.

The company may opt for a special tax status and, instead of paying the taxe d'abonnement, tax is levied on distributions subject to a minimum of LUF2 million. There are no specific debt equity ratios applicable to the billionaire holding company.

Société de Participation Financière (SOPARFI)

A Societe de Participation Financiere (SOPARFI) is a company which can engage in any form of holding company activity and may be either a SARL or an SA. Since a SOPARFI is subject to the normal rates of corporate income tax, it can benefit from the Luxembourg tax treaty network as well as the European Union Parent-Subsidiary directive. A SOPARFI must maintain a debt equity ratio of 85:15.

Tax Concessions

Tax exempt dividends

Dividend income is exempt from tax if the following conditions are met:

- the distributing company is a resident company fully taxable in Luxembourg or is a nonresident company subject to income tax in its country of residence at a rate similar to the Luxembourg tax rate (deemed to be 15 percent);
- the SOPARFI holds at least 10 percent of the capital of the subsidiary or the acquisition price of the participation is at least LUF 50 million; and
- the SOPARFI has held the participation without interruption for a period of at least twelve months before the end of the financial year during which the dividend is paid. Payments received by the SOPARFI where its subsidiary is liquidated are treated as dividend.

Tax exempt capital gains

Capital gains on the disposal of the subsidiary are exempt if:

- the subsidiary is resident and fully taxable in Luxembourg or, if nonresident, is subject to income tax in its country of residence similar to the Luxembourg tax rate;
- the SOPARFI holds at least 25 percent of the capital of the subsidiary or the acquisition price of the subsidiary is at least LUF 250 million; and
- the SOPARFI has held the participation without interruption for a period of at least twelve months immediately preceding the beginning of the financial year during which the participation is sold.

Deductibility of expenses and loans

Funding costs related to exempted income are only deductible from taxable income to the extent that they exceed the exempted dividend income or capital gains. Losses realised on the sale of a participation may be deducted without limitation against other taxable income of the SOPARFI.

The SOPARFI can create a tax deductible reserve account against the value of the participation. Capital gains realised on a later sale of the participation will not be taxable in so far as they do not exceed the previously deducted reserve. Losses can be carried forward indefinitely.

Tax credit for foreign withholding taxes

Tax withheld at source on dividends paid to a SOPARFI that qualifies under the participation exemption can be used as a credit against Luxembourg corporate income tax imposed on any other taxable income that the SOPARFI may have.

The European Union Parent-subsidiary Directive

Dividends paid by a Luxembourg company to a corporate shareholder in another EC country are exempt from withholding tax provided that the following conditions are satisfied:

- the Luxembourg company is fully taxable in Luxembourg;
- the receiving company is resident in a member state of the European Union;
- the receiving company has held directly at least 25 percent of the capital of the Luxembourg company during an uninterrupted period of at least two years at the time of distribution.

Other entities

Also frequently used are the following non-corporate entities:

- Sociétés en Nom Collectif (SENC) – general partnerships; and
- Sociétés en Commandite Simple (SECS) – limited partnerships

Confidentiality

The Luxembourg Monetary Institute (IML) is responsible for monitoring the banking and financial sectors. The IML has introduced know-your-customer procedures imposing a duty on bank staff to identify the ultimate beneficial owners. The Luxembourg Penal Code prohibits banking officers from disclosing confidential information.

Citco Luxembourg is part of the Citco Group, an independent international financial services group offering trustee, fiduciary company management services, mutual fund administration and fund advisory services, and banking and custody.

MADEIRA

Dr Paulo Réfega

Introduction

Location and Time Zone

The island of Madeira is situated in the north Atlantic Ocean about 700 kilometres off the coast of North West Africa on the same latitude as Casablanca. The Madeira archipelago, made up of the Islands of Madeira, Porto Santo and several small deserted islands, was discovered by the Portuguese navigators in the 15th century and has been a Portuguese territory ever since. The islands were completely uninhabited at the time of their discovery.

Political and Legal System

Since 1976, due to political changes in Portugal, Madeira has been an autonomous region with its own parliament and locally elected government. But Madeira is still legally and politically part of Portugal and is therefore a full member of the European Union. Despite Madeira's autonomous status, most of the laws enacted by the central government and by the Portuguese Parliament are fully applicable in Madeira.

Currency

The local currency is the Escudo (PTE) which is part of the European Monetary System.

Infrastructure and Communications

Communications are good, the Island being served by an international airport with daily flights to mainland Portugal and frequent flights to other countries. Shipping is well served by deep water ports at Funchal and Porto Santo, and the Islands' telephone network is linked to mainland Portugal by cable and satellite giving easy, direct access to international networks.

Population and Language

The population is almost wholly European mainly of Portuguese origin with a small expatriate community made up mostly of British nationals. The language is Portuguese, although a good part of the population speaks English. Almost half the population of approximately 300,000 live in Funchal, the capital.

Corporate Law

Tax Concessions

By legislation first presented before the Portuguese Parliament as long ago as 1980 and enacted in 1986, the Madeira Free Trade Zone was established giving substantial tax concessions to companies incorporated on the Island.

Madeira companies, which are located within the offshore financial centre, can be structured so as to be completely exempt from all forms of Madeira taxation until 31st December 2011. Notwithstanding this attractive tax treatment, a Madeira company is considered to be the same as a normal Portuguese tax paying company and therefore falls under the taxation treaties signed by Portugal with Austria, Belgium, Brazil, Denmark, Finland, France, Germany, Italy, Japan, Mozambique, Norway, Spain, Switzerland and the United Kingdom. The terms of these treaties provide that payments from these countries can be made with a much lower rate of tax being withheld at source.

For example, royalties being paid by a UK company to a nonresident corporation or individual would normally be subject to a withholding tax of 25 per cent. However, if those same royalties are paid to a Madeira company the rate of withholding tax may be reduced to 10 per cent by virtue of the provisions of the tax treaty between the UK and Portugal. This is despite the fact that those same royalties would not be subject to tax on arrival within the accounts of the Madeira company.

In practice, not all the tax treaty partners will extend tax benefits to Madeira offshore companies. Benefits are limited by discriminatory clauses within the tax treaties or by practices of relevant revenue departments of the countries in question.

Due to the fact that Madeira companies are Portuguese companies for all intents and purposes, they automatically have a value added tax (VAT) number and are therefore ideally suited for trading activities within the European Union, where it is essential to have a VAT registration.

In addition to the normal offshore company, Madeira also allows for the incorporation of the Sociedades Gestoras de Participações Sociais (SGPS). The SGPS has been specifically designed to take advantage of European Union Directive 90/435. The terms of that Directive require that dividends paid by a subsidiary located in one EU state to a parent located in another EU state must not be subject to any form of withholding tax as long as certain conditions are met – the most important of which is that the parent company cannot be exempt from taxation in its country of incorporation. The SGPS is therefore subject to a rate of tax of 36 per cent on dividends received from subsidiaries situated in other EU states but 95 per cent of the dividend income is exempt from taxation. Thus, the effective rate of taxation on dividends is 1.8 per cent only.

The SGPS must not undertake activities other than holding shares in other companies. This type of company is therefore of considerable use to any company located outside the EU wishing to invest within the EU.

The Madeira companies described above have the following characteristics:

Taxation

This is dealt with above but, by way of summary, a normal Madeira company is exempt from all forms of taxation until 31st December 2011.

An SGPS pays tax at a rate of 36 per cent on dividends received from EU subsidiaries but 95 per cent of that income is exempt from tax making an effective rate of tax on those dividends of 1.8 per cent. The SGPS is otherwise exempt from all tax.

Shareholders

A minimum of one shareholder whose identity is a matter of public record is required. No share certificates are issued, the shareholding being described in the notarial deed when the company is set up or the structure altered.

Directors

A minimum of one director is required, who may or may not be a shareholder and, once again, whose details are on public record. Corporate directors are not permitted. The director need not be resident.

Annual reporting

As with all Portuguese companies, Madeira companies are obliged to file monthly or quarterly VAT returns and annual accounts in the Portuguese language and currency. An audit is only required for companies which have a substantial level of assets and turnover or large number of employees. This happens when, for two successive years, two of the following three limits are exceeded:

- Total assets of PTE 180 million;
- Turnover of PTE 370 million; and
- Average number of employees is 50.

Timescale

Due to the fact that the initial steps of incorporation for a Madeira company follow the same pattern as those for a Portuguese mainland company, the inevitable Portuguese bureaucracy causes substantial delays. A minimum of two months should be allowed for incorporation. In order to avoid these delays, it is possible to purchase ready incorporated Madeira companies which are able to commence business immediately. However, it should be noted that the documents evidencing any change in the structure of a Madeira company, including a change of shareholders, do involve considerable bureaucracy and will take a number of weeks to complete.

Restrictions of name and activity

Names end with the words 'Limitada' or 'Lda' and name clearance must be obtained through the Central Registry in Lisbon. Generally, names should be recognisable in the Portuguese language. Restrictions will be imposed on names indicating involvement in banking, insurance and some other financial services.

The information above refers to the type of company most commonly used, which is the 'Sociedade por Quotas' (Lda), a private limited company. These companies have a minimum capital of Esc 400,000, can have only one director, cannot issue bearer shares and are subject to fairly simple accountancy requirements.

Sociedade Anónima (SA)

Another type of company is the 'Sociedade Anónima' (SA), a public limited company that must have a minimum capital of Esc 5,000,000, must normally have at least three directors and must present audited accounts. These companies can issue bearer shares. It should be noted that an SGPS can be either an Lda or an SA.

Trust Law

Portugal is a Civil Law jurisdiction so the concept of trusts is basically alien to Portuguese law. Therefore, the Portuguese Trust Law that was created for Madeira in 1988 is based very closely on English trusts law. Thus, the concept of trustees, trust property, beneficiaries, etc is similar or the same as under English law. There are, however, several points that should be noted:

- Neither the settlor nor the beneficiary can be Portuguese residents;
- The trust cannot derive its income from sources located in Portugal with the exception of interest from bank deposits held with financial entities situated in the Madeira offshore area;
- Real estate located in Portugal cannot be held on trust; and
- The settlor must designate the law which will govern the trust and this cannot be the law of Portugal/ Madeira. Therefore the legal characteristics governing the trust will reflect those applicable to whatever foreign law is chosen. This is an unusual provision and settlors will need to ensure that the law chosen is that of a place which will readily accept jurisdiction over a trust which has a foreign trustee. Many offshore jurisdictions state within their laws that the applicable law is whatever is chosen within the trust deed so no difficulties would generally arise here.

Trust Deed

The trust deed, which must be signed before a notary, again reflects English law and the points to be contained therein do differ from those which English practitioners are used to. Thus, the trust deed must include: the designation and identification of the trust; the full identification of the settlor, the trustees and the beneficiary; the identification and description of all the property held on trust; the declaration of intent to constitute the trust; the designation of the law applicable to the trust; the purpose and type of the trust; relationship between the trustee and the beneficiaries; the powers of the trustee; the rules for appointment, retirement and removal of the trustees; and place and date of constitution of the trust and its duration.

If the trust is for more than one year, the trust deed is subject to registration, and the following details are required to be registered: name and identity of the trust and its objectives, date of creation, duration of the trust, name and office if the trustee in Madeira and termination date or manner by which the trust can be modified and terminated.

Administration

Trust administration activities can be carried out only by trust companies in Madeira. Such a company differs from the usual Madeira company in that it must be an 'SA' company, which is similar to a 'PLC' company in the UK. Its minimum capital must be 20 million Escudos (approximately £91,000) and at least 51 per cent of the capital must be represented by registered shares. It should be noted however that these companies can have any number of subscribers and shareholders (normally these companies must have at least five shareholders). The only object of the company must be trust administration activities and the setting up of trusts. Alternatively, a branch of an existing foreign trust company can be registered in Madeira.

Fees and Tax Incentives

Trust companies or their branches are entitled to the full range of tax benefits available to other companies, thus being exempt from all taxes until 2011. The setting up fee payable to the government is US$750 and the annual fee is US$2,000. The setting up of each trust is exempt from registration and setting-up fees, but is subject to an annual fee of US$600, collected by the trustee on behalf of the Madeira Government. Madeira trusts are free from all the exchange controls existing in Portugal.

Paulo Réfega is a Portuguese Avogado and a Director of International Company Services (Portugal) Lda Parque Empresarial Algarve, Apartado 246, 8400 Lagoa, Algarve, Portugal, Tel: (35182) 342 601, Fax: (35182) 342 259, E-mail: por@icsl.com.

MALTA

Anika P Savona & Dr Mark Miggiani

Introduction

Location and Time Zone

The Maltese Archipelago is strategically situated in the heart of the Mediterranean Sea about 93 km south of Italy and 290 km north of North Africa. The largest island, Malta, covers an area of 316 sq km and is located on one of the major arteries of shipping allowing it to offer a whole range of international maritime services and facilities. Malta is one hour ahead of Greenwich Mean Time (+1 GMT) and two hours ahead (+2 GMT) during the summer months, ie the last week in March to last week of September.

Political and Legal System

Malta gained independence from the United Kingdom in 1964 and is now governed by a democratically elected parliament. Malta is an active member of the British Commonwealth, the United Nations and the Council of Europe.

The legal system is a hybrid of both the continental and common law; whilst it is essentially based on the Napoleonic code, British law has had a strong influence, particularly in fiscal and commercial law. All laws are written in English and Maltese.

Currency

The official currency is the Maltese Lira (Lm) and Lm1 is divided into 100 cents.

Infrastructure and Communications

Due to its strategic location and its new financial services legislation, Malta is quickly becoming an international hub. An excellent infrastructure and a modern communication system has been essential in bolstering this activity. Its international airport services the Islands' national carrier and other airlines providing direct links to most airports in Europe and Northern Africa and also New York in the USA.

Population and Language

The Maltese are essentially a Mediterranean people. English and Maltese are the official languages although Italian is also widely spoken.

Tax Treaties

Malta has signed tax treaties with Australia, Austria, Belgium, Bulgaria, Canada, China, Cyprus, Finland, France, Germany, Hungary, India, Italy, Libya, the Netherlands, Norway, Pakistan, Poland, Sweden Switzerland, United Kingdom and the United States. At the beginning of 1996, Malta substantially revised its corporate law so as to remove the distinction between offshore and onshore companies and thereby hopes to guarantee that all Maltese companies will obtain favourable treatment under these tax treaties.

Corporate Law

It is still possible to register Maltese offshore companies until the end of December 1996 and such companies may continue to operate until 23rd September 2004 or ten years from the date of incorporation, whichever is the earlier. Offshore companies pay a fixed rate of tax of 5 per cent on worldwide income.

The new regime does away with the distinction between offshore and onshore companies and Malta now offers two types of companies of interest to the tax planner: the International Holding Company (IHC) and the International Trading Company (ITC). These entities are taxed as described below and are designed to take advantage of the tax treaties signed by Malta.

The ITC is statutorily defined as a company which is engaged solely in carrying on trading activities from Malta with persons outside Malta and has objects expressly limited to such trading activities. The ITC may not hold foreign investments or equity. An IHC is a company whose activities are limited to foreign equity participation and other similar passive income generating activities. Such entities are taxed in a particularly advantageous manner where income is received from 'participating holdings'.

Taxation

ITCs and IHCs pay tax on their worldwide income at a rate of 35 per cent, but there is a system of credit and refunds available to the shareholders which, in simple terms, reduces the net rate of tax to 4.2 per cent in the case of ITCs and between 0 and 6.5 per cent in the case of IHCs. This is an attractive system of taxation because the 35 per cent rate is actually paid at the corporate level and it is thought that tax treaty benefits will thereby be assured.

Shareholders

A minimum of two shareholders are required who may be corporate or individual. Details of the shareholders appear on public file, but anonymity can be retained by the use of nominee shareholders. Bearer shares are not permitted in the case of private companies. However, a public company may issue a warrant to bearer with respect to fully paid shares so long as it is so authorised by its memorandum and articles.

Share Repurchase Provisions

Share repurchase is allowed if the following conditions are satisfied:

- Provisions to this effect are made in the memorandum and articles;

- Authorisation is given by an extraordinary resolution which shall determine the terms and conditions of such acquisitions. The shares already held by the company itself shall be treated as having no voting rights;
- The minimal value of the acquired shares, including the shares previously acquired by the company and held by it shall not exceed 10 per cent of the issued share capital;
- No acquisitions by a company of its own shares shall be made if on the closing date of the last accounting period the net assets set out in the company's annual accounts are, or following such distribution, would become lower than the amount of issued share capital plus those reserves which may not be distributed. Furthermore, the shares may not only be acquired out of the proceeds of a fresh issue of shares made specifically for the purpose or out of profits available for distribution;
- The shares acquired must be fully paid up shares; and
- The company may not as a result of such acquisition become the only holder of its ordinary shares.

Directors

A minimum of one director is required, either corporate or individual, and details must appear on the public record in Malta. In order to establish that the company is resident in Malta, and therefore eligible for tax treaty benefits, it is necessary to have the majority of the board of directors based in Malta.

Annual Reporting

Full audited accounts are required. In the case of private exempt companies an annual return is also necessary.

Timescale

Normally it will take approximately four days from receipt of the share capital to incorporate a Maltese company. Pre-incorporated companies are not generally available.

Restrictions on Name and Activity

Names must end with the word 'limited'. There are few restrictions on the words which may be included within a company name, but those indicating a connection with the banking or insurance industries can only be used when an appropriate licence has been obtained

Local Requirements

As a matter of Maltese company law, every Maltese company must maintain a registered office address in Malta and must also appoint a licensed Maltese 'nominee company' as company secretary or sole director. The 'nominee company' is legally liable for all actions of the Maltese company and thus, must be involved fairly closely in all business operations. Although there is no strict requirement that the director(s) be resident in Malta, it is likely that tax treaty relief would not be afforded to any company which did not have a majority of directors resident in Malta. For most practical purposes it will therefore be necessary to appoint Malta resident directors.

Secrecy

Confidentiality is governed by the *Professional Secrecy Act* which has established a high common standard of confidentiality for all professional practitioners. Those who violate professional secrecy may be prosecuted under Section 27 of the Criminal Code and on conviction may be liable to a maximum fine of LM20,000 and/or a two-year prison sentence.

Trust Law

The Legal Framework

The *Trusts Act* (Act XXXV 1988) was enacted on 30 June 1989 and is based on the Jersey model. Also by virtue of Act XX 1994, Malta ratified the Hague Convention on the law applicable to trusts and on their recognition. The provisions of the Convention became an integral part of the Maltese legal system on 31 December 1995. Articles 13, 19, 21 and 22(2) of the Convention were excluded since they are in the nature of public international law provisions.

Settlor

Any 'person' other than a Maltese resident, may be a settlor. 'Person' includes a body of persons whether vested with legal personality or not.

Beneficiary

Any person, other than a Maltese resident, may be a beneficiary provided such person is identifiable by name or ascertainable by reference to a class or to a relationship to some person. Thus minors, unborn persons, the settlor or a body corporate may all be beneficiaries.

Trustees

Any person, whether physical or juridical, may be a trustee. The settlor may also be a trustee. There must be at least one trustee and if such is the case then that must be a nominee company authorised by the Malta Financial Services Centre, hereafter the Centre, to act as such. The Centre is the main regulatory authority for financial services in Malta. No exceptions can be made to this rule.

A nominee company is a company in possession of a warrant issued by the Centre authorising it to act as trustee of trusts. In order to obtain such warrant, the company must submit to the Centre, a certified copy of its memorandum and articles, if any, together with details concerning the directors. On being satisfied that the requirements of the law are met and on payment of the appropriate fees, the Centre shall issue such warrant.

A nominee company may be formed by two persons provided the following conditions are abided by:

- The company is a private one;
- The objects of the company are specifically limited to acting as a trustee with respect to trusts. It may until these remain in effect also include the acting as a nominee for an offshore company;
- The name of the company must include the word nominee;
- The issued share capital must not be less than Lm5,000;
- The share capital of the company, and any voting or controlling power therein, is neither directly or indirectly owned, held or exercisable by, or vested in a person not resident in Malta in an amount exceeding in aggregate 40 per cent; and

- The directors of the company are not less than three, of whom at least two are Maltese citizens resident in Malta who, for an uninterrupted period of five years, have been any of the following:
  a. a person holding the warrant of an advocate under the Code of Organisation and Civil Procedure;
  b. a person holding the warrant of a certified public accountant or a certified public accountant and auditor under the *Accountancy Profession Act*;
  c. an associate or fellow of the Chartered Institute of Bankers or of the Institute of Chartered Secretaries and Administrators or of the Chartered Insurance Institute of the UK or a member of such other institute or similar body recognised by the Authority for the purposes of this section; or
  d. a person who has served as a public officer in a grade not below that of assistant head of department, or in an equivalent position with a statutory body or is recognised by the Centre as a person comparable to any of the persons aforesaid.

No person who is convicted of an offence against the provisions of the Malta Financial Services Act or is otherwise disqualified from being a director of a company may be a director of a nominee company.

Resignation/Removal of Trustees

A trustee ceasing to be a trustee shall concur in executing all documents necessary for the vesting of the trust property in or under the control of the new trustee. This obligation may be enforced by power of the court.

If the transfer is not complete, the trustee shall not be released from liability to any beneficiary, trustee or person interested under the trust for any act or omission in relation to the trust property.

If the Maltese nominee company resigns, the trust is no longer considered to be a Maltese trust.

The Protector

The law makes provision for the appointment of a protector who, subject to the terms of the trust, has the power to appoint a new or additional trustee, to remove a trustee and to require the trustee(s) to obtain his consent before exercising a discretion.

The Trust Document

The trust document is the very source of the trustees' power. The general rule is that it is necessary to create a trust in writing. Thus every trust must be created voluntarily either by a will or by another written instrument and cannot be formed orally. Furthermore, a direct or indirect benefit must result to some identifiable person unless the trust is a charitable one.

Under the provisions of Maltese trusts law, one may create only express trusts evidenced in writing. Nonetheless, automatic resulting trusts and constructive trusts are also recognised by the Act.

Thus, where an express trust that was created by an instrument in writing provided for the payment of income to the beneficiary for life and the beneficiary dies, the settled property will be held on 'resulting trust' for the settlor, or where the settlor is dead, for his heirs.

Again, where a person makes or receives any profit, gain or advantage from a breach of trust, the person concerned, provided he did not acquire the property under an onerous title in good faith becomes a constructive trustee and shall be liable to deliver up the property to the beneficiaries of the trust – the express trust that was created by an instrument in writing as required by the law.

The law provides for the creation of four types of private trusts most commonly found today. The Fixed Interest Trust, the Discretionary Trust, the Accumulation and Maintenance Trust and the Protective Trust. Once created, a private trust has a life span of 100 years, whilst charitable trusts may exist in perpetuity. Income may be accumulated during the whole duration of the trust.

Registration

A trust must be registered with the Centre. Registration is effected by filing with the Centre:

- a certified copy of the trust instrument; and
- a declaration by the nominee company acting as trustee of the trust that the trust satisfies the conditions of the Act for qualification as an offshore trust.

The trust instrument must give a name to the trust by which the trust is to be known and registered. The name may be changed at any time. The instrument must also name the settlor and the beneficiaries must be identifiable.

If the settlor does not wish to be identified, a unilateral declaration of trust may be made. Here a declaration is made in writing by a nominee company stating that the settlor is a qualified person on the date of the declaration.

The registration fee of Lm200 payable to the Centre.

Fiscal and Other Benefits

The annual tax chargeable on the income of a trust is Lm200. This is payable to the Commissioner of Inland Revenue through the Centre in lieu of any income tax. No further duties are payable. Thus no death duty is paid on any asset held under a trust or by any person in respect of his interest as a beneficiary; no stamp duty is paid in respect of any document concerning a trust and no customs duty is paid on any property held under a trust when imported into Malta.

Restrictions

Trust property shall not include immovable property situated in Malta or shares, stock or debentures of a company registered in Malta or whose assets include immovable property situated in Malta. However, with the ratifying of the Convention on the recognition of foreign trusts, Maltese individuals may hold shares in Maltese companies as trustee or nominee for other persons.

The Proper Law

The proper law of a trust is determined in accordance with the Hague Convention which provides for the free choice of the applicable law by the settlor. Where the settlor does not make a valid choice, the most closely connected law will apply.

Trusts that adopt the law of Malta as their proper law are governed by the *Trusts Act* and must be registered with the Centre in order to have effect in Malta. Where the settlor chooses that a foreign law be the proper law of the trust, these trusts are referred to as foreign trusts. There is no requirement for such trusts to be registered with the Centre. However, if they are not registered, they will not qualify for the fiscal and other exemptions granted under the Act.

Powers and Obligations of Trustees

The powers of the trustee(s) are essentially discretionary and the trustee may do anything, subject to the existence of a protector, which it deems to be in the interests of the beneficiaries. It is usually the case that the settlor will write a letter of wishes to the trustees to indicate the manner in which he/she would wish the trustees to exercise their discretion. However, it is in the very nature of a trust that this is not binding. The trustee owes duties to the beneficiaries on the one hand and to the Centre on the other.

Thus, where a trustee violates his obligations by either mingling trust assets with his own property or transferring them to third parties in breach of a trust, a beneficiary will have the right to recover the original trust property and all its fruits or any other property into which the original property may have been converted. However, a bona fide purchaser of such property will be protected.

Every person is under a legal obligation to regard and deal with all documents and information relating to a trust as secret and confidential. Thus no person shall be required to divulge any information to any authority, including any court, tribunal, board or committee of inquiry.

However, where any officer of the nominee company becomes aware that the trust assets arise from criminal activity (limited to offences which are extraditable), such person is duty bound to inform the Centre. If he does not do so such person may be liable to a fine (Lm2,000-Lm10,000) and/or to imprisonment for five years. The trust assets are forfeited in favour of the Government and become its property absolutely.

Delegation of Powers of Trustees

A trustee may delegate the powers entrusted to him as stipulated by the terms of the trust, or as permitted by the *Trusts Act*.

The *Trusts Act* provides that unless the terms of the trust specifically provide otherwise, a trustee may

- delegate management of trust property to investment managers whom the trustee reasonably considers competent and qualified to manage the investment of trust property; and

- employ accountants, advocates, attorneys, bankers, brokers, custodians, investment advisors, nominees, property agents, solicitors and other professional agents or persons to act in relation to any of the affairs of the trust or to hold any of the trust property.

In case of an Investment Trust organised as a fund, the provisions of the *Investment Services Act* 1995 apply.

Court's Power

A trust validly created in accordance with the law, whether in Malta or abroad, shall, if registered under this Act, be recognised and enforceable by the courts in Malta.

On the application of a trustee or beneficiary, the court may decide to vary the terms of a trust where certain persons are affected. The law defines these persons as follows:

- any person incapacitated at law having an interest under the trust; or
- any person, ascertained or not, who may become entitled to an interest under the trust as being at a future date or on the happening of a future event a person of any specified description or a member of any specified class of persons; or
- any person unborn; or
- any person in respect of any interest that may arise to him by reason of any discretionary power given to any one on the failure or determination of any existing interest that has not failed or determined.

Thus where the court is satisfied that such variation is for the benefit of certain persons, it may approve an arrangement varying or even revoking all or any of the terms of the trust or enlarging the powers of the trustees to manage or administer any of the trust property.

Fees

In all cases, a trustee may reimburse himself or pay out of the trust all expenses properly incurred by him in connection with the trust. However, the only statutory fee is the annual registration fee of Lm200 which is paid to the Centre.

Thus, unless authorised by the terms of the trust or by the consent in writing of all the beneficiaries or by any order of the court, a trustee shall not be entitled to remuneration for services rendered. Needless to say, it is usually the case that a professional fee is agreed upon prior to the registration of the trust and this varies according to the trust document. Generally this would be a fixed fee, however, it could also be a percentage of the trust's assets under management.

Anika P Savona is a Maltese qualified lawyer and a consultant to International Company Services (S.A.) Ltd, The Terraces, 5th Floor, 34 Bree Street, Cape Town, 8001, South Africa, Tel: (27) 21 418 4237, Fax: (27) 21 418 2196, E-mail: iscca@iafrica.com.

Dr Mark Miggiani LL.D., DEI (Geneve) is the leading tax attorney in Malta.

MAURITIUS

Sydney Bathfield

Introduction

Location and Time Zone

The Republic of Mauritius is located on the Tropic of Cancer some 2000 kilometres off the east coast of Southern Africa. The island covers an area of 1850 square kilometres. It is four hours ahead of Greenwich Mean Time. This allows communication with the Far East in the morning, Europe during the day and America in the same afternoon. It is a popular tourist destination and is the third largest exporter of woollen knitted goods. Mauritius has a sub tropical climate.

Political and Legal System

Mauritius was uninhabited when colonised by the French in the 17th century. Britain took over the island in the early 19th century mostly to protect its trade route with India which was constantly attacked by French pirates operating from Mauritius. As a result, the island has a mixed legal system. Substantive law is based on the French Civil Code, while procedural and evidential laws are modelled on the English system.

Mauritius became independent in 1968, has its own constitution and has passed a number of truly Mauritian laws, often inspired by laws of other Commonwealth countries. The final court of appeal remains the Judicial Committee of the Privy Council in London. Mauritius has a Westminster style democracy, with elections held every five years.

Currency

The currency is the Mauritius rupee, which is freely convertible. The value of the rupee over the years has been slowly declining. One US dollar currently buys 21.00 rupees.

Economy

The three major economic activities are the traditional growing and milling of sugar cane with diversification during the last twenty years into tourism and light manufacture for export and, more recently, into international financial services.

Infrastructure and Communications

Mauritius has state of the art telecommunication facilities with a very good roadway network. It has an international airport with daily flights to Europe, Africa and the Far East.

Population and Language

The official language of Mauritius is English, but the spoken language is French or local patois creole. Because its people are of Hindu, African, French and Chinese ancestry, several other languages are also spoken. The total population is 1.2 million.

Corporate law

The *Companies Act* 1984 is substantially based on the UK's *Companies Act* 1948. A number of proposals put forward in the UK Companies Bill (later to become the *Companies Act* 1985) were incorporated in the Mauritius text. The *Mauritius Offshore Business Activities Authority (MOBAA) Act* of 1992 introduced a legal framework for offshore activities. A number of provisions of the *Companies Act* were disapplied with regard to offshore entities so as to facilitate the incorporation and operation of offshore entities.

The International Company and Offshore Company

The two main types of offshore structures are the International Company (IC) and the offshore company (OC). The IC need not be managed in Mauritius and is mostly used by trading and asset holding companies that do not require the benefit of double taxation agreements. The OC is mostly used as a vehicle to take advantage of the wide double taxation treaty network of Mauritius. There are requirements safeguarding the confidentiality of all information submitted to the MOBAA , hence the identity of the ultimate beneficial owner of an OC is not open to public scrutiny. The thorough due diligence procedures adopted have ensured that Mauritius has attracted 'quality' investors. In that respect, a money laundering bill is scheduled to be presented before the National Assembly very shortly.

There are variations to the OC structure which are suited to more specific types of investments. The offshore investment company is an OC with an open-structure which allows for redemption of shares not only out of profits, gains, realised revenue and unrealised revenue, but also out of the paid up capital, the share premium account or any other reserves, without causing a reduction of capital. The limited life company, although having a corporate structure, has all the characteristics of a partnership for U.S. tax purposes.

Offshore companies are presently taxed at a rate of 0 to 35 per cent. Companies incorporated after the 1st of July 1998 will be taxed at the flat rate of 15 per cent and a deemed foreign tax credit system will operate alongside to minimise actual tax liability in Mauritius.

Mauritius has so far been most successful as a provider of financial services. The sound base of Mauritian professionals who speak two European languages and often an additional Asian language, and the availability of state of the art communications, are distinct advantages.

Trust Law

There is domestic trust legislation for trusts and trust companies, and there is a separate law, the *Offshore Trusts Act* (OTA) 1992, which applies exclusively to offshore trusts. The OTA is largely based on the trusts legislation in the United Kingdom.

Settlor

The settlor of an offshore trust is defined as a 'person who provides trust property or makes a testamentary disposition on trust or to a trust'. The only restriction in respect of a settlor for an offshore trust is that he cannot be a resident of Mauritius at any time during the life of the trust. The term 'resident' in this context means a person domiciled in Mauritius and/or a body corporate incorporated or registered under the laws of Mauritius.

Beneficiary

The beneficiary of an offshore trust is widely defined as a person, whether natural or corporate, who is entitled to benefit under an offshore trust, or in whose favour a power to distribute trust property may be exercised. A settlor may be one of the beneficiaries of an offshore trust but not its sole beneficiary. Income or gains may be accumulated only if allowed by the trust deed.

Trustee

The trustee of an offshore trust is the person who holds or has vested in him, or is deemed to hold or have vested in him, property which does not form, or which has ceased to form, part of his own estate, for the benefit of a beneficiary. Thus, the trustee derives his powers from the trust deed. The trust deed can also define his duties, provided they are not in contravention of Trustees' duties as defined in the OTA.

For the purposes of an offshore trust, there must be at all times at least one trustee resident in Mauritius. As far as corporate trustees are concerned, an offshore company or an offshore bank can be registered for the specific purpose of acting as a trustee for an unlimited number of trusts. An IC may act for not more than three separate trusts. An offshore trust shall not have less than two individual trustees or one corporate trustee. A trustee may delegate his powers under the OTA as long as the deed does not specifically prevent him from doing so.

Under the OTA, where the terms of a trust contain no provision for the appointment of an additional trustee, such a trustee may be appointed by either the remaining trustee or trustees, the personal representative or liquidator of the last remaining trustee or ultimately by the Supreme Court. A trustee may resign from office by delivering a letter of resignation to co-trustees. Such a letter of resignation takes effect upon delivery of the notice except if such resignation was given to facilitate a breach of trust or reduce the number of trustees to less than the statutory minimum. A trustee may also be removed from office by order of the Supreme Court. A trustee who ceases to be a trustee is required to do everything necessary to vest the trust property in the new or the continuing trustees.

Registration Requirements

An offshore trust may be created by a verbal declaration or by an instrument in writing, a will or a codicil. However, it will only be enforceable if there is a registered declaration of trust in relation to it. The registration procedures are such that on appointment, a resident trustee of an offshore trust is required to submit to the MOBAA a declaration to the effect that

- the settlor of the trust is not a resident of Mauritius;
- the trust property does not include any immoveable property situated in Mauritius or money in a domestic bank in Mauritian currency (unless permitted under any other enactment); and
- the trust he holds qualifies as an offshore trust under the OTA 1992.

Upon receipt of the declaration, the MOBAA files the same in a Register of Offshore Trusts and the declaration will be given a reference number. Thereupon the MOBAA will send to the trustee a letter of registration notifying him of the registration of the declaration and of the registration number of the declaration. This registration number shall be the reference by which the offshore trust will be identified officially. The existence of resulting, implied and constructive trusts is recognised under the OTA.

The Trust Property

The trust property of an offshore trust can be any property not situated in Mauritius. A trustee of an offshore trust may accept property to be held on trust or to be added to the trust property from any non resident, subject to the provisions of the trust instrument. The trustees have statutory duties imposed on them with regard to their dealings with trust property. Besides the fiduciary duties which are given statutory effect, the trustees have the duty to preserve the trust property, not to profit, to keep accounts, to keep the trust property separate and to give information. There are also a number of powers, namely those concerning accumulation and advancement. The terms of an offshore trust may validly authorise the trustees to invest trust property in securities and investments with or without restrictions. However, the approval of the MOBAA will be required before a trustee can invest in securities or other investments in Mauritius.

Fees

As a rule, a trustee is not entitled to remuneration, except where terms of the offshore trust expressly provide for remuneration, with the consent in writing of every beneficiary or by an order of the Supreme Court. However, all expenses and liabilities properly incurred in connection with the offshore trust may be paid out of the trust property and a trustee may reimburse himself from the offshore trust property for all expenses incurred by him in the performance of his duty.

Forced Heirship Rules

The OTA has provisions nullifying the application of forced heirship rules which apply in certain countries. With regard to asset protection trusts, the Supreme Court may declare an offshore trust void or voidable where it is proved beyond reasonable doubt that the offshore trust was created with the intent to defraud persons who were creditors of the settlor at the time the trust property was vested in the trustee. There is, however, a delay of two years from the date of the transfer or disposal of the assets of the offshore trust within which any such action can lie.

Taxation

Offshore trusts are taxed like OCs, at a rate of 0 to 35 per cent unless the trustees submit a certificate of nonresidence to the Commissioner of Income Tax. From the 1st of July 1998 the flat tax rate of 15 per cent will also apply to trusts. Resident offshore trusts may have access to the benefit of tax treaties. Nonresident beneficiaries may elect not to be taxed.

Letters of Wishes

In recent amendments to the OTA, provisions were introduced with regard to letters of wishes, which, although acceptable, only have directory effect on the actions of the trustees. Finally, an offshore trust may have a protector, who, although having certain supervisory powers with regard to the functioning of the trust and the actions of the trustees, is not actually regarded as a trustee.

Sydney Bathfiled is the managing director of International Management (Mauritius) Ltd, Port Louis, Mauritius. He is also the executive director of the Financial Services Division of the Rogers Group, the largest trading and investment house in Mauritius.

THE NETHERLANDS

Jan-BM Rouppe van der Voort

Introduction

The Netherlands is a constitutional monarchy, ruled by a democratically chosen multi-party coalition. It is a full member country of the European Union (EU) and one of its founders. Although the official language is Dutch, English, German and French are widely spoken in the business community. The monetary unit, the Dutch guilder (Nlg), is freely convertible.

The Netherlands can in no way be considered as an offshore finance centre. However, its domestic tax system, coupled with the link with the Netherlands Antilles and the wide network of double taxation treaties to which it is a party, provide opportunities for the use of Netherlands corporations in structuring international financial transactions.

Corporate Law

Legal Entities

Two types of limited liability companies are the Limited Company (NV) and the Private Company (BV). NV and BV differ primarily in the provisions governing the transferability of shares:

- NV can issue both registered and bearer shares whilst BV can only issue registered shares;
- NV's bearer shares are freely transferable, without formalities. The transfer of BV's registered shares are subject to the provisions of the obligatory blocking clause, laid down in articles of association of the BV.
- The shares of an NV can be quoted on the Amsterdam Stock Exchange. The BV shares cannot be quoted.

An NV can be converted into a BV and vice versa. The conversion does not affect the company's existence and identity.

Incorporation

Companies are incorporated by notarial deed executed by one or more incorporators before a civil law notary in the Netherlands after the draft of deed has been approved by the Ministry of Justice; the identity of the incorporator and ultimate beneficial owner are verified; and after the initial capitalisation has been effectuated. The following information is required for incorporation:

- Proposed name of the company;
- Place of company's statutory seat within the Netherlands;
- Objective or purpose of the company;
- The authorised, issued and paid-up capital, par value of the shares;
- The company's financial year;
- Details of the company's management; and
- Information on the incorporator and ultimate beneficial owner.

Share Capital

At least 20 per cent of a company's authorised capital is to be issued and at least 25 per cent of that issued capital should be paid-up with an absolute minimum of Nlg 40,000 for a BV and Nlg 100,000 for an NV. Capital contributions may be in kind or in cash, in Dutch currency or in a foreign currency. For payments of capital in kind, an independent accountant must verify the value of the assets contributed.

Shares

Shares of an NV can be in registered or in bearer form or both. Shares of a BV must be in registered form only. There is no minimum number of shareholders. The rights attaching to different classes of shares are governed by the company's articles of incorporation. Nonvoting shares are not permitted. The shares must have a par value, which is expressed in Dutch guilders.

Management

Management is by a board consisting of at least one managing director. This board manages and represents the company, defines business policy and prepares annual accounts. It may consist of individuals or legal entities. There are no nationality or residency requirements. The managing directors share responsibility for all decisions of the board. Managing directors are appointed, suspended or dismissed by the shareholders' meeting. Managing directors may be held personally liable for the debts of the company if the company is declared bankrupt and the bankruptcy is mainly a result of mismanagement. There is a presumption of such mismanagement if the financial statements have not been filed in time or if they do not represent the actual financial position of the company.

General Meeting of Shareholders

The general meeting of shareholders must be held at least once a year, to:

- adopt resolutions;
- amend the articles of association;
- appoint, dismiss or suspend managing and supervisory directors;
- examine and approve the financial statements;
- declare dividends;
- dissolve the company and to appoint its liquidators; and
- decide to apply for bankruptcy.

Extraordinary general meetings of shareholders may be held at any time. Shareholder meetings may be held outside the Netherlands, provided the entire share capital is represented. Shareholder meetings may be held by proxy.

General Tax Regulations

Tax system

Companies incorporated under Dutch law and companies resident in the Netherlands are subject to Dutch tax on their worldwide income. Residency is determined according to the facts and circumstances. The most important one being the place of the day to day management. Nonresident companies are subject to tax on income from real estate located in the Netherlands and on income derived through a Dutch branch or permanent establishment.

Tax rates

In 1997, the corporate income tax rate is 36 per cent to be calculated on the first Nlg 100,000 taxable profits. The excess is subject to a rate of 35 per cent. From 1998, the rate is 35 per cent to be calculated on the total taxable profits.

Withholding taxes and tax treaties

There are no withholding taxes in the Netherlands on interest or royalties. Dividends paid by a company to nonresident shareholders are subject to a 25 per cent withholding tax. When a company pays to its Netherlands Antilles based parent this withholding tax is reduced (please refer to 'Dutch Sandwich'). Most of the tax treaties entered into by the Netherlands provide for a reduction of the dividend withholding tax to nil, or to between 5 per cent and 15 per cent, when a dividend is paid to or by a Dutch company.

Capital tax

Capital tax is levied on capital contributions to a Dutch company and amounts to one per cent of the equity at the moment of contribution. This tax is non-recurrent. Under certain conditions an exemption may be applicable.

Tax rulings

Dutch companies engaged in intercompany transactions may face problems in determining an arm's length pricing for tax purposes. Companies usually negotiate with the tax authorities, on an individual basis, the conditions under which intercompany transactions will result in an acceptable cost and profit allocation. In general, the application for a ruling implies the disclosure of the identity of its beneficial owners. There are three popular rulings. The various ruling activities can be used simultaneously in one legal entity.

Ruling on holding activities

In principle, it is agreed in a ruling that the Dutch holding company will report 25 per cent of the running costs (ie management fee and related expenses) of the company as a predetermined contribution to the taxable income. Please note that most Dutch tax consultancy firms enter into an agreement with the Dutch tax authorities in which it is agreed that the above mentioned predetermined contribution to the taxable income of the Dutch company does not have to be reported. The company can collect dividends from its subsidiaries and realise capital gains on sale of this investment, without incurring a Dutch tax liability if the participation exemption applies. Under Dutch law, this is the case if the company owns at least 5 per cent in the share capital of the subsidiary, the shares are not held as inventory, the investment does not qualify as a mere portfolio investment and the subsidiary is subject to a profit tax in its country of residence. The participation exemption as implemented in Dutch tax law under the EC parent subsidiary directive applies under different conditions. Therefore, the Dutch holding company should own at least 25 per cent of the share capital on an EC resident subsidiary, the legal form of the subsidiary should be listed in the annex to the EC parent subsidiary directive and the subsidiary should be subject to an ordinary profit tax in its country of residence without being exempt from it (ie no portfolio test exists in this case).

Dutch sandwich

The Dutch Sandwich is a Dutch company with a Netherlands Antilles parent. The dividend paid by the Dutch company to its parent is subject to a withholding tax of 7.5 per cent if the parent is subject to a Netherlands Antilles Corporate income tax rate of 2.4-3.0 per cent. It is subject to a withholding tax of 5 per cent if the BV's Netherlands Antilles parent is subject to a local corporate income tax rate of 5.5 per cent. These reduced withholding tax rates only apply when the parent company owns at least 25 per cent of the Dutch company's capital.

Ruling on finance activities

In a ruling on finance activities, the definition of the taxable income will be 0.125 per cent on the outstanding loans to the subsidiary, provided that this is structured as a back to back loan (parent lending to the Dutch company, the Dutch company in turn lending to subsidiary). Excess interest income will be taxed in full. Excess interest obligations are not tax deductible under the ruling, but these expenses are deductible from the normal taxable profits.

Ruling on license activities

In a ruling on license activities the taxable income will be 7 per cent of collected royalties, provided that this is structured as a back to back license (parent licensing to BV, BV licensing to subsidiary). Excess royalty income will be taxed in full. Excess royalty obligations are not tax deductible but these expenses are deductible from the normal taxable profits. If the annual income exceeds Nlg 2,000,000, the profit to be reported is as follows:

Annual income					Profit to be reported
Nlg	2,000,000	>	Nlg	4,000,000	6%
Nlg	4,000,000	>	Nlg	6,000,000	5%
Nlg	6,000,000	>	Nlg	8,000,000	4%
Nlg	8,000,000	>	Nlg	10,000,000	3%
Nlg	10,000,000	>	excess		2%

The above also applies to Dutch companies acting as a consultancy or service company, provided that this is structured as a back-to-back activity.

Annual accounts and tax returns

The annual meeting of shareholders should be held within six months after the close of the company's financial year. The financial year of a Dutch company is the calendar year, unless the articles of incorporation state otherwise. At this meeting, the shareholders review and approve the financial statements, which must be prepared in accordance with the fourth EC Directive, which has been implemented into Dutch law. The statements should comprise a balance sheet, profit and loss account, notes and a management report. The tax return is to be prepared and filed during the year following Dutch company's financial year. Extensions for filing can be obtained easily.

Disclosure and publication requirements

In case a Dutch company only has one shareholder, or in case the Dutch company issued shares which are not paid-up in full, then the name and address of that shareholder is filed at the Trade Register of the Chamber of Commerce. This Trade Register is public. In the Trade Register will also be entered the details regarding the management board, their power to represent the company, the company's details, such as date of incorporation, statutory seat and name etc.

The Dutch company has to file the approved annual accounts with the Trade Register. Depending on the size of the Dutch company, filing requirements range from a condensed balance sheet to full audited accounts. The fact whether or not the accounts have to be audited depend on the same criteria.

A Dutch company has to report on the following transactions:

- Opening of foreign bank accounts;
- Movements in foreign bank accounts (monthly);
- Foreign payments made or received by Dutch banks on behalf of the company;
- Balance sheet (annually or once every five years depending on the size and activity level of the company);
- Equity participation in foreign companies and their financing; and
- Financing transactions, borrowings and appropriation of such funds.

This information is confidential. The Central Bank is not allowed to reveal such information to other government bodies, unless criminal charges are brought, and substantiated, against the Dutch company, its management or owners.

Exchange of Information

There are no secrecy laws as such in the Netherlands. Exchange of information is governed by the many tax and other treaties to which the Netherlands is a party and by the rules of the EU.

Corporate Mobility

There are no provisions in the corporate law of the Netherlands to allow for redomiciliation of Dutch companies.

The Foundation

Characteristics

A Foundation is formed through the execution of a notarial deed. It has to be created for a specific purpose to be mentioned in its objects clause. The purpose (or part thereof) of the Foundation cannot be the making of distributions to the founder(s), beneficiaries and/or to its representatives. Distributions to other parties are only allowed if these are of a charitable or social nature. No capital is required. A foundation has no capital divided into shares or otherwise. Dutch foundations are registered with the Chamber of Commerce in a special register known as the Stichtingenregister.

The rules of the foundation (known as Statuten) must contain at least the name of the foundation, the location of the seat of the foundation, the foundation's objective, the process of appointing or discharging managers and how the foundation will be dissolved.

Management

Management of a foundation is exercised by a board of directors with at least one managing director. The board manages and represents the foundation. The board may consist of individuals or legal entities of any nationality or residency. Managing directors are appointed, suspended or dismissed as described in the Statuten. Dutch law does not prescribe a minimum of board meetings to be held during a certain period, neither does it contain a clause regarding the place of such meetings.

Tax Regulation

Capital tax

No capital tax is levied on a (possible) capital contribution to the Foundation.

Dutch corporate income tax

Unless the Foundation carries out a business, no Dutch corporate income tax will be due and thus, annual tax returns do not need to be filed.

Disclosure and Publication Requirements of Annual Accounts

There are no filing requirements. The Foundation has the obligation to keep books and records. These books are not considered public information. The public prosecutor is the only official institution, having the right to inspect the Foundation's books and records in case of serious doubt whether the Foundation or its manager(s) is acting in concert with its Statuten and/or the law.

Use of the Foundation

For international and inheritance planning, the Dutch foundation is often used as a Stitchting Administratiekantoor (Admkantoor) by acquiring the shares of a Dutch company. Upon acquisition, it issues depository receipts. This give the holders all shareholders rights except voting rights which will remain with the Admkantoor.

Jan Rouppe van de Voort is managing director of Itcon BV, an affiliate company of Citco Nederland BV. Itcon BV provides legal and administrative services in the specialised area of the exploitation of intellectual property rights. Citco Nederland BV is part of the Citco Group, an independent international financial services group offering trustee, fiduciary company management services, mutual fund administration and fund advisory services, and banking and custody.

SINGAPORE

John Koh & Co

Introduction

Location and Time Zone

The Republic of Singapore is located at the southern tip of Peninsular Malaysia, just one degree North of the equator. The 641 square kilometre island is on a major shipping lane and is one of the world's busiest container ports. It is also a regional hub for air traffic. Singapore is eight hours ahead of Greenwich Mean Time, placing it in the same time zone as Beijing, Hong Kong, Taipei, Shanghai, Kuala Lumpur and Labuan. The climate is tropical with average temperatures between 24^0C and 32^0C and high humidity throughout the year.

Political and Legal System

Singapore obtained self-government from the British in 1959, merged with Malaya and the Borneo states of Sabah and Sarawak to form the Federation of Malaysia in 1963 and separated from this group to form a republic on 9 August 1965. Singapore has a parliamentary system and an elected president. Singapore has a common law system and shares many of the legal doctrines found in English law and the laws of former British colonies including Malaysia and Hong Kong. It also has a Westminster-style constitution. Like Malaysia, its criminal laws are derived from the Indian penal code. Muslim family matters are governed by Muslim Syariah law.

Currency

Singapore's currency is denominated in Singapore dollars and cents, and is freely convertible. One hundred cents is equal to one Singapore dollar.

Population and Language

The multiracial population of Singapore is dominated by ethnic Chinese, and has Malay and Indian minority groups. English, Mandarin, Bahasa Malaysia and Tamil are the national languages, with English serving as the principal business language.

Corporate Law

Formation

The incorporation of companies in Singapore is governed by the *Singapore Companies Act* (Cap 50).

Types of companies

Three types of companies may be formed, all of which have separate legal personalities. They are companies limited by shares, which may be private limited or public limited, companies limited by guarantee and unlimited liability companies. Partnerships can also be created by contract. The most commonly used corporate entity is a company limited by shares. The company limited by guarantee is generally used by charities. The unlimited liability company is sometimes used by US corporations who wish to have the income of foreign subsidiaries treated as US partnership income.

Names

The Singapore Registry of Companies and Businesses (RCB) must first approve the name of the company before it may be registered. This process generally takes one week. Chinese names are permitted.

Incorporation

New formations generally take one week to process following the lodging of complete incorporation documents, including the memorandum and articles of association, with the RCB. Shelf companies are available. A certificate of incorporation will be issued once all is found to be in order and upon payment of the requisite fee.

Fees

The following registration fees are payable upon incorporation:

Nominal Capital	Fees
S$100,000 or less	S$1,200
More than S$100,000: (i) every S$100,000 or part thereof after the first S$100,000 up to S$1,000,000. (ii) every S$100,000 or part thereof after the first S$1,000,000.	S$1,200 plus: (i) additional S$400 (ii) additional S$300 up to a maximum of S$35,000.
No share capital	S$600

Registered foreign company

A foreign company may alternatively set up a foreign branch and register to do business in Singapore. Once registered with the RCB, such a foreign branch may carry on business in Singapore, but despite having a presence in Singapore will not have separate legal personality from its head office. The liabilities of the Singapore branch will be treated as the liabilities of the head office.

Share Capital

Every Singapore incorporated company must have share capital, but that need not be denominated in Singapore dollars. There is no fixed par value. There are no prescribed minimum authorised, issued or paid-up capital, but as the lowest registration fee payable is S$1,200 and at least two shareholders are required it is common for the 'minimum' authorised capital to be S$100,000 and the issued share capital to be S$2. Different classes of shares may be issued. The issue of bearer shares and share warrants are prohibited. A Singapore company may not deal in or purchase its own shares nor provide financial assistance for the purchase. Shares are not permitted to be issued at a discount. Proceeds from shares issued at a premium are deposited in a share premium account.

Statutory Requirements

Shareholders

Two subscribers to the memorandum and articles of association are required unless the company is being set up as a wholly-owned subsidiary, in which case the parent company may be the sole shareholder. Details required to be disclosed by the shareholders are identity, nationality, identity card or passport number, address and number of shares allotted. This does not extend to disclosure of the beneficial owner behind a corporate shareholder.

Directors

A minimum of two directors is required, one of who must be 'ordinarily resident' in Singapore. An ordinary resident is undefined but taken to mean a citizen or permanent resident of Singapore. An expatriate holding a valid employment pass from the Comptroller of Immigration in Singapore is also accepted by the RCB as being ordinarily resident in Singapore.

Secretaries

Each company is required to have one secretary, a qualified person with a principal place of residence in Singapore. A qualified person includes an advocate, solicitor or a certified public accountant. Most legal firms and certified public accountants serve as company secretaries.

Registered office

Every Singapore company must have a registered office in Singapore. As the secretary has to maintain the statutory books of the company, it is common for the firm providing secretarial services to also provide the location of the registered office.

Registers

Registers required to be kept at the registered offices are those of members, directors, secretaries and managers; directors' shareholdings; substantial shareholdings; debenture holders; charges; and participatory interests.

Auditors

Auditors, who must be a firm of public accountants practising in Singapore, must be appointed by the company within three months of incorporation.

Scope of Activities

Singapore companies may carry out such businesses as are authorised by the objects clause in their memorandum of association. Companies which are formed for the purpose of providing recreation and amusements, or promoting commerce, industry, art, science, religion or like objects not involving the acquisition of gains cannot acquire land without the approval of the Minister. Companies with foreign beneficial shareholders cannot buy land. Foreign persons may however purchase apartments in any building with six or more storeys as well as units in any building approved as a condominium.

Management and Administration

Management of the company is vested in the Board of Directors. Day-to-day management may be delegated to a management team. Shareholders do not have a direct say in the running of the company. Every company is required to hold an annual general meeting of shareholders (AGM) each year at which the audited accounts for the previous financial year prepared by the company's accountants are tabled and adopted. Thereafter, a set of audited accounts and an annual return showing the particulars of shareholders, directors and any existing registered charges must be filed with the RCB within one month of the AGM.

Nondisclosure Provisions

There are no secrecy provisions for safeguarding the identity of shareholders.

Corporate Mobility

There are no provisions for a foreign company to redomicile in Singapore or for a Singapore company to relocate to another jurisdiction.

Incentives

There are a number of specific financial incentives to encourage incorporation in Singapore, the most important of which is the Operational Headquarters Structure (OHQ). A company satisfying qualifying criteria, such as having a substantial operational presence in Singapore supporting a regional network of business activities, may apply for OHQ status. This carries a 10 per cent tax rate on income and an exemption from tax on dividends received. Dividends paid to the parent company are similarly exempt.

Singapore is a stable, cost efficient and carefully administered jurisdiction with modern and highly efficient infrastructure. Further, a comprehensive series of double taxation treaties and investment protection agreements, as well as strong government encouragement, provide attractive external business opportunities. Provided it is correctly structured and administered, a Singapore company having external investments and operations may not be liable to tax on profits generated from offshore activities.

Taxation

Corporate Taxation

The current level of corporate tax is a flat rate of 26 per cent on profits, less allowable deductions. Generally, income is taxable when it accrues in or is derived from Singapore through a Singapore permanent establishment or is received in Singapore from sources outside Singapore. Income of Singapore unlimited liability companies may be treated as US partnership income.

Goods and Services Tax

The tax rate of three per cent covering almost all goods and services was introduced on 1 April 1994 and will not be changed until at least 1999. Exemptions are granted to businesses with an annual turnover of less than S$1 million and on the sale and rental of residential property.

Capital Gains Tax

There is no capital gains tax in Singapore. However, capital gains derived from multiple trading transactions may be characterised by the Internal Revenue Department as income and thus be liable to income tax.

Stamp Duty

There is no stamp duty on agreements and contracts. However, there is a flat 0.2 per cent stamp duty on share transfers under the Singapore *Stamp Duties Act*, except on transfers of shares of a private company wherein 75 per cent or more of its net tangible assets comprise residential property at the date of transfer (ie residential property company). Stamp duty on the latter and all other property transfers are:

Consideration	Stamp Duty (for every S$100 or part thereof)
The first S$18,000	S$1
The next S$18,000	S$2
Thereafter	S$3

Taxes on Disposal of Real Property

A package of income tax and stamp duty measures designed to curb property market speculation with effect from 15 May 1996 on all disposal of property,

- imposes stamp duty on all sales and sub-sales of property and an additional charge on vendors who dispose of residential property or shares in a residential property company within three years of acquisition; and
- deems chargeable to tax gains from the disposal of a residential property or shares in a Residential Property Company within three years of acquisition.

Excise Tax

There is no excise tax in Singapore

Property Tax

Industrial, commercial and let-out residential properties are subject to a 12 percent property tax. Properties to be redeveloped are subject to a local development tax which rate is determined by the plot ratio and whether there is to be a change of use.

Double Taxation Treaties

Singapore has 37 bilateral double taxation treaties, which exempt taxpayers from withholding tax and permit them to avoid double taxation. However, the exchange of information provisions mean that in taking advantage of such advantages, total secrecy of business and financial dealings cannot be maintained.

Investment Protection Treaties

Singapore is party to the multilateral Convention on the Settlement of Investment disputes. Singapore is also party to a number of bilateral investment protection treaties with countries including the People's Republic of China (PRC), the Asean countries and Vietnam. The Singapore-PRC treaty of 1986 protects investment by the state and companies of both contracting parties in each others' countries against expropriation and nationalization and provides for compensation in the event of war, a state of national emergency or insurrection.

Banking and Exchange Controls

Suspension of the Exchange Control Act

The *Exchange Control Act* has been suspended since 1 June 1978 by a circular issued by the Monetary Authority of Singapore (MAS). Requirements for approvals and the imposition of limits and restrictions for all forms of payments or capital transfers were abolished. In view of the Singapore government's efforts to promote Singapore as an international financial centre, the suspension is unlikely to be reversed.

Repatriation of Capital and Profits

A foreign investor is free to repatriate capital, including the proceeds realised from liquidation of an enterprise. Dividends, branch profits, interest, royalties, advisory fees, license fees, management fees and amounts payable under guarantees may also be freely repatriated, and no additional remittance is imposed on these earnings after tax has been paid on the income accruing in or derived from Singapore.

Incentives and Loans

In addition to the suspension of exchange controls, MAS has also provided tax incentives for fund management. The approval of MAS is required when Singapore dollar loans in excess of S$5 million are made to nonresident Singaporeans.

Bank Secrecy

Singapore's *Banking Act* provides for stringent secrecy provisions that prohibit disclosure of any information relating to Singapore bank deposits. Unauthorised disclosures are prescribed as offences under the *Banking Act*.

Trust Law

Current legal framework

The legal framework for trusts in Singapore is based on English common law and is supported by local legislation. No preferential tax treatment is available.

Creation

Trusts may be created orally although dispositions of purely equitable interests must be in writing. Constructive, implied and resulting trusts may be imposed by operation of law.

Settlor

The settlor must be a person able to acquire and dispose of property and cannot be bankrupt, mentally disordered or a minor.

Beneficiaries

The beneficiaries must be persons capable of holding property at law. A trust which does not directly or indirectly benefit an individual and which is not a charitable trust or a trust of imperfect obligations is invalid.

Trustees

A body corporate may be a trustee, as may the settlor. Professional trustee services are available from trust companies.

Registration and Fees

There are no registration requirements nor any fees to be paid in establishing a trust apart from professional fees.

Role of Trustees

Vesting

If a trustee disclaims office, the legal estate vests in any other accepting trustees but otherwise reverts to the settlor or his personal representatives. On the death of a sole or last surviving trustee, the trust property and all trust powers devolve to his personal representatives.

Management

The trust instrument and such statutory provisions as are not expressly varied or excluded thereby are the source of a trustee's powers and govern the manner in which trust assets are managed. A settlor's letter of wishes, whilst not binding on the trustees, provides them with guidance in the administration of the trust. Accounting and auditing requirements may be contained in the trust instrument but no such statutory requirements exist.

Powers

A trustee has statutory power insofar as it is not excluded by the trust instrument to appoint and pay an agent to perform specific executive or administrative functions. Alternatively, a trustee may delegate by power of attorney for a limited period the trusts powers and discretion vested in the trustee. Powers of investment are conferred on trustees by statute, and trust instruments generally provide express powers to invest.

Remuneration

The remuneration of trustees can be provided for in the trust agreement, reached by agreement with beneficiaries or authorised by the courts.

Miscellaneous

The common law rule against perpetuities applies to trusts in Singapore as do the requirements of charitable purpose in relation to purpose trusts. As mentioned above, a trust which does not directly or indirectly benefit an individual and which is not a charitable trust or a trust of imperfect obligation is invalid. There are no disclosure requirements, thus assuring privacy. A trust may migrate into and out of Singapore, if permitted by the trust instrument, by appointing a trustee in another jurisdiction and nominating the law of that other jurisdiction to be the proper law of the trust.

Fraudulent dispositions may be set aside under general legal principles if intent to defraud is proved. This limitation period of six years runs from the date of discovery of fraud to the date when fraud could reasonably have been discovered. A trust may be used in estate duty planning.

John Koh & Co, Singapore, is a specialist law firm established in January 1995 to concentrate on cross-border corporate transactions and complex fraud and securities litigation. The firm is particularly active in the utilities, energy, telecommunications, transportation, media, aviation and food industries.

SWITZERLAND

Dominique Liardet

Introduction

Location and Time Zone

Switzerland is situated in the centre of Western Europe and borders on five countries. Switzerland is one hour ahead of Greenwich Mean Time.

Language

The national languages and the percentages of population speaking them are German (65 per cent), French (18 per cent), Italian (10 per cent), Romanch (1 per cent) and others (6 per cent). The use of English is widespread, particularly in business circles.

Political and Legal System

Switzerland is a federal state composed of 20 cantons and 6 semi-cantons. Political and administrative responsibilities are divided among federal, cantonal and municipal levels of government.

The country benefits from its political neutrality and from its well-trained, educated population with a strong work ethic. It is highly industrialised and its economy is based upon the free enterprise system.

Economy

As a country with a high quality of life and a commitment to open markets and freely convertible currencies, Switzerland has traditionally been the preferred location for the headquarters of many important international business organisations, such as Nestlé, Novartis, Michelin, Hewlett-Packard and Cartier.

Switzerland has one of the most highly developed and efficient banking systems in the world, with over 500 banking institutions. The bank secrecy in Switzerland is world famous. The country is also widely recognised for good telecommunications.

Currency

Switzerland's currency is denominated in Swiss Francs (CHF) and is freely convertible. It is fully-backed and is one of the world's strongest currencies.

Infrastructure

It has a very dense road and railway network with multiple connections to all bordering countries. As a result, major cities within the country and in adjacent lands are easily accessible.

Corporate Law

Establishing a Business in Switzerland

In Switzerland, a business can be established as one of the following:

- a stock corporation;
- a limited liability company;
- a co-operative; or
- an association of partners with unlimited liability.

The latter two types of business enterprises are rarely used.

Swiss Company Law

Swiss company Law is embodied in the Swiss Code of Obligations (the Code). The Code details all the various forms of business enterprises in Switzerland.

Corporation

The corporation is the most common form of business enterprise in Switzerland. The corporation is characterised by the existence of minimum capital divided shares, which are usually freely transferable, and by the fact that it confers a limited liability on its shareholders. Shares may be bearer or registered and paid either in cash or in kind.

At least three incorporators, either individuals or legal entities, are necessary to form a corporation. However, a corporation with a single shareholder is permitted.

Incorporators and shareholders are not subject to any nationality or residence requirements. Directors must be shareholders (one fiduciary share is enough) and the majority of the directors must be Swiss citizens residing in Switzerland. A lawyer or a nominee can be appointed as a director.

Authorised capital must be at least CHF 100,000, of which one fifth of the par value of shares or at least CHF 50,000 of the capital must be paid up prior to the incorporation meeting. All shares must be subscribed at the time of formation.

The articles of incorporation must include details of the corporation's name, residence, purpose, capital stock (number and face value of bearer shares and/or registered shares), shareholders meetings, board of directors and the auditors, as well as the forms of notification for meetings.

Limited liability company

A limited liability company is not a common business form. It has the characteristics of both a corporation and a partnership. It is an association of two or more persons or legal entities with a minimum authorised capital of CHF 20,000, up to a maximum of CHF 2,000,000. Each member's interest must be in multiples of CHF 1,000. By the date of formation, at least 50 per cent of the capital contributions, in cash or kind, must be paid up and disclosed in the articles of association. All partners are expressly registered in the Commercial Register. At least one of the managers must reside in Switzerland.

Merger provisions

Merger is accepted in Switzerland. The merger of companies is usually structured as either an 'absorption' or a 'consolidation'. In practice the main impediment to acquisitions is the inclusion of provisions in the articles of incorporation of the target company that restrict the transfer of shares.

Administrative regulations

The board of directors is responsible each year for preparing the company's annual report to shareholders. It contains the annual financial statements, a report of the course of the business and the financial statements of the company. Under the law, active disclosure, that is publication, is required only for companies with publicly quoted shares or bonds.

All companies must be audited annually, though limited liability companies have the choice. The auditors examine the books and the annual financial statements and submit their report at the shareholders' meeting. All companies must also file an annual or biannual tax return, depending on which canton the company is registered in.

Disclosure requirements

Companies must disclose in the Commercial Register:

- the company's legal address;
- a statement of acceptance of office and duties by the board members and auditors; and
- the nature of the initial capital contribution of the incorporators (whether in cash or in kind).

Investment Incentives

The federal government and most cantons offer a broad range of investment incentives to attract new companies, to encourage existing companies to expand production facilities or to develop innovative technologies. The incentives include tax breaks, various financial incentives (which are negotiable) and favourable provisions for depreciation and reserve allocations.

Taxation of Swiss Companies

Switzerland's tax structure is complex. There are distinct tax levels:

- federal;
- cantonal; and
- municipal taxes.

The tax is levied on companies and other legal entities having their domicile in Switzerland and nonresident companies having specific economic relationship with Switzerland such as trading activities and real estate holding.

General Taxation

Federal tax law is standard throughout Switzerland. Since tax laws and rates vary widely from canton to canton and from commune to commune, the choice of domicile is an important element in tax planning.

In principle, Swiss business enterprises are assessed on their net profit and net equity as shown by the statutory financial statements prepared in accordance with generally accepted accounting principles in Switzerland.

The taxable base is the annual worldwide income, after the deduction of business expenses. In most cantons, taxes are deductible but in others, profit before taxation is the taxable base.

Capital gains are generally included in the taxable base for their full amount. A gain or a loss from the sale or exchange of assets is treated as ordinary income or expense. The basis for determining the gain or loss is the book value.

Swiss income tax rates are progressive. The progression is determined on the basis of the earnings capacity (ratio of income to shareholders' equity). The federal income tax is levied at progressive rate ranging from 3.63 per cent to 9.8 per cent. Swiss federal tax periods cover one year.

Likewise, cantonal tax rates are progressive. Progressivity also depends on profitability, with fixed minimum and maximum rates. Depending on the canton, the maximum combined rates range from approximately 6 per cent to 27 per cent of pre-tax profits. Equity tax rates range from approximately 0.3 per cent to 1.3 per cent.

Privilege holding

Holding companies are entities which hold substantial participation in the capital of other companies. Their income essentially consists of dividend income. As long as dividend income (such as trading income, interest and commission income) does not exceed a certain percentage of total income (generally between 51 per cent and 80 per cent), it will retain its status as a holding company and therefore be exempt from any tax on dividend income.

Privilege industrial and commercial holding companies

Privilege industrial and commercial holding companies are normal commercial and industrial companies which also hold equity investments in other companies and which may qualify for relief from income taxes on their investment income. To qualify for such relief, the investment must represent at least 20 per cent of the investor's capital or have a carrying value of not less than CHF 2,000,000.

Special Tax Status of 'Offshore' Companies

Certain types of foreign controlled companies which are commonly named offshore companies benefit from special tax concessions in various cantons. Federal tax law does not grant special tax status to offshore companies They are however, exempt from income tax in various cantons.

Domiciliary companies

The company must be foreign controlled. It may not carry on business activities within Switzerland. Some cantons allow offshore companies to rent offices and hire personnel within Switzerland. Under the law of most cantons, a domiciliary company may not own real estate in Switzerland, except for its own use.

Mixed companies

Certain foreign-owned companies are principally engaged in activities outside Switzerland, but do not qualify as holding or domiciliary companies.

Cantons may also grant exemption or reduction of tax on such companies if they qualify for mixed company status. As a rule, the following conditions must be met:

- The company must be foreign controlled;
- At least 80 per cent of the company's total income must be derived from foreign sources; and
- The company must have close relationships to foreign entities.

Service companies

Companies that maintain Swiss offices and staff for the sole purpose of performing services for affiliated foreign groups may obtain a special tax ruling classifying them as service companies. This ruling is applicable for both federal and cantonal tax purposes. These services may relate to management, marketing, publicity, technical assistance or finance. In general, such companies may not derive income from third parties (that is, outside their corporate group).

Withholding Tax

A federal withholding tax at a rate of 35 per cent is imposed mainly on profit distribution by Swiss resident companies. This tax is refundable to recipient companies. Switzerland has concluded many income tax treaties to avoid and reduce double taxation on dividends paid outside Switzerland. Withholding tax could be avoided by using in Switzerland a branch of a foreign company. No withholding tax is levied on royalties paid to foreign beneficiaries.

Value Added Tax (VAT)

Individuals and corporations exercising a gainful business or professional activity only in Switzerland are subject to VAT. In addition, all persons are subject to VAT in respect of their imports of services from abroad.

The taxable base is any remuneration paid in cash or in kind in return for the supply of goods and services and in the case of imported goods, the value for the purposes of customs duty increased by the customs duty. Input tax, ie the tax paid on purchases of goods and services, can be deducted. The standard rate is 6.5 per cent.

Social Security Contributions

A social security contribution is due and paid by the company and amounts to 13.1 per cent of paid-out salaries. It is the so-called 'AVS-AC' basic contribution. These contributions are shared between employer and employee.

Fraudulent Transfers

Banks may not accept funds from individuals or companies if they have reason to believe that the money was acquired in a manner that could constitute a criminal act under Swiss law (laundering, drug or other suspicious money is criminal). All financial intermediaries (lawyers, directors, bankers, etc) are responsible for checking the origin of the funds. Failure to do so may result in civil and criminal proceedings being taken against the intermediary.

Incorporation Fee

Presently, incorporation costs for a company with a capital of CHF 100,000 range between CHF 5,500 to CHF 7,000 including notary, Commercial Register, publications costs and others.

Dominique Liardet is a Swiss Attorney-at-law with professional experience in Geneva and San Francisco. She has specialised in trust fiduciary work since 1987 when she joined the Citco Group. She has been heading the Geneva office of Citco (Suisse) SA since 1989.

TURKS & CAICOS ISLANDS

Paul Winder

Introduction

Location and Time Zone

The Turks and Caicos Islands (TCI) are a British dependent territory lying 927 kilometre south east of Miami, with the Bahamas some 48 kilometres to the north west. There are eight principle inhabited islands. The islands are five hours behind Greenwich Mean Time and are in the same time zone as the Bahamas, Florida, Georgia, South Carolina, North Carolina, Virginia, Pennsylvania, New York and all other east American states. The climate is Caribbean, with average temperatures between 85°F and 95°F. For nine months of the year the islands are cooled by the Eastern trade winds.

Political and Legal System

The Turks and Caicos Islands were administered by Jamaica until 1962. Upon withdrawing from the Federation of the West Indies, the Turks and Caicos Islands were left a dependent territory of the United Kingdom.

The Turks and Caicos government is democratically elected and the ruling party provides the chief minister. The Islands are governed by an executive council of ministers appointed from an elected legislature. Britain appoints a governor and maintains responsibility for defence and foreign affairs. The legal system is based upon English common law with local modifications.

Currency

The Turks and Caicos Islands' official currency is the US dollar and there are no exchange controls.

Infrastructure and Communications

The Turks and Caicos Islands have two international airports. Cable and Wireless recently spent in excess of $15 million updating the telecommunication system, thus making it one of the most advanced international systems in existence. There are two hospitals on the Islands and a good standard of medical care is upheld. Due to the increase in the number of high net worth individuals moving to the Islands, property prices are increasing although not in drastic proportions.

Population and Language

The Islands have an estimated population of 13,000. The inhabitants include Turks Islanders, Bahamians, Haitians, Dominicans, British, Canadians, Australians and New Zealanders. The main language is English.

An increasing number of professional organisations are immigrating to the islands, thus making the standard of business second to none in the offshore finance sector.

Corporate Law

The Turks and Caicos Islands Exempt Company

One of the foundations upon which the TCI's success as an offshore centre has been built is the *Companies Ordinance* 1981. This legislation was closely modelled on the equivalent Cayman Islands law, is extremely flexible and provides for a minimum of disclosure. Meetings need not take place in the islands, the objects may be unrestricted and details of shareholders and directors need not appear on any public record.

An exempt TCI company receives a certificate issued in the name of the governor which guarantees that the company will be exempt from all forms of taxation, both in respect of its own operations and on the shares in the company, for a period of 20 years from its date of incorporation.

Companies may be incorporated with a translation of the English name appearing on the Certificate of Incorporation. The name may be represented in any foreign language or characters. Additionally, a foreign language translation of the memorandum and articles of association may be officially registered alongside the English version. Thus, for example, the Certificate of Incorporation could bear both an English name and a translation of that name in Chinese characters. A Chinese character version of the memorandum and articles of association could also be registered.

Taxation

There are no direct taxes such as income tax, corporation tax, capital gains tax, profit tax, gift tax or death duties.

Shareholders

An exempted company need only have one shareholder and shares can be issued in bearer or registered form. There is no requirement to file shareholder details on any public records.

Directors

A minimum of one director is required who may be a resident or a nonresident and corporate directors are permitted. There is no requirement to file details of directors on any public records.

Annual Reporting

There is also no requirement to file accounts or a detailed annual return. Each company must file a short statement indicating that it has traded mainly outside the Islands and that the company has complied with various statutory requirements. Exempt companies are permitted to hold bank accounts and trading accounts on the Islands. However, if a company physically trades on the Islands, a business licence is required. Only ordinary resident companies can hold land or property on the Islands.

Timescale

Incorporation can be achieved within 24 hours. However it does take approximately one week for documents to arrive from TCI. Pre-incorporated companies are available for immediate purchase.

Restrictions on Name and Activity

The following words cannot be used either in English or any other language: Assurance, Bank, Building Society, Commonwealth, Cooperative Society, Fidelity, Friendly Society, Guarantee, Indemnity, Insurance, Reinsurance, Trust, Trustee, Underwriter, Royal, Imperial, Empire, Municipal and Chartered or any derivatives of any of those words without the written consent of the financial secretary. The name of an exempt company need not indicate that the company is limited.

Local Requirements

As a matter of local company law the company must maintain a registered office address within the TCI and must also appoint a TCI resident as registered agent.

Secrecy

Both the *Companies Ordinance* and the *Confidential Relationships Ordinance* 1979 make it an offence punishable by a maximum fine of US$50,000 and/or a prison sentence of up to three years for anybody to reveal confidential information, including details of the owners and directors, about a TCI exempt company or to threaten to reveal such information.

There is an excellent professional infrastructure with a large number of legal firms that are active in the Islands' offshore financial services. These are supported by accountancy firms and banks such as KPMG, Coopers and Lybrand, Barclays and Bank of Nova Scotia. In addition to these there are a growing number of company formation, trust management and captive insurance companies within the jurisdiction.

There are a range of incentives available to new businesses in certain specialised areas through the government's investment advisers, TCI Invest, to attract more businesses to the jurisdiction. These range from import duty holidays on capital equipment to waivers of land taxes for new land purchases.

Two drug-related legislation are the *Control of Drugs Ordinance* 1976 and the *Control of Drugs (Trafficking) Ordinance* 1988. An *All Crimes Money Laundering Ordinance* is due to be introduced soon.

Trust Laws

The *Trusts Ordinance* 1990 was enacted in TCI to cater to modern demands and includes features from other jurisdictions and some original provisions suggested and drafted by local offshore practitioners.

The *Trusts Ordinance* does not specify any restrictions as to who the settlor may be. It also specifically allows the settlor to be either the trustee or the beneficiary but not all three together, as this would constitute a sham trust. A TCI trust may come into existence in any manner, ie orally, written (including a will or codicil) or arise by conduct. Implied, resulting and constructive trusts whilst not being specifically provided for within the legislation may come into existence depending on the circumstances in each individual case.

All trusts must comply with the *Trusts Ordinance* and all trustees must comply with the *Trustees (Licensing) Ordinance* 1992. However, it is optional as to whether the trust details are filed at the companies registry.

The powers of the trustees are specified within the Ordinance and there must be a minimum of two trustees unless the sole trustee is a corporation. Letters of wishes are frequently used, but have no legal standing within the jurisdiction. A trustee can delegate powers to investment managers and to professional persons in relation to any affairs of the trust. A trustee does have the right to apply to the court for direction in the manner in which he should act in connection with the trust. The court can make an order to vary the terms of the trust as it thinks fit.

Appointment and Resignation of a Trustee

The terms of a trust can specify the procedure for appointing a trustee or the last remaining trustee. A trustee may resign in writing providing it does not result in there being no trustee or fewer than the number of trustees required by law. Trustees can be removed by an order of the court or by a provision within the terms of a trust.

Powers of the Trustee

The powers of the trustee are only as per the terms of the trust although consent may have to be obtained from the protector before exercising a power or discretion.

Revocability

Trusts within the jurisdiction may be revocable wholly or in part and this is stipulated within the legislation and adds clarity to this particular area of law which has been questioned in many other jurisdictions.

Change of Power

It is possible to change the proper law of a TCI trust provided that none of the trust terms are invalidated and that it is consistent with the intention of the settlor.

Duration

The legislation abolishes all rules regarding perpetuity and accumulation periods. This gives the Islands a major advantage as competitive jurisdictions impose limits on the life of the trust normally to 100 years or less, and also limit the period during which the trust can accumulate income without distribution.

Protectors

Protectors have fiduciary responsibility to the trust and are given statutory recognition as being persons whose consent the trustees must obtain before exercising power of discretion. The legislation specifically provides that the protector shall not be deemed to be a trustee. This is an extremely welcome move as previously there had been little authority to refer to regarding the role of protectors. Practitioners frequently advised against their use even though the preference of the client may have been to have such an officer written into the trust deed.

Disclosure

A trustee is not required to disclose information to any person except for accounting information which need only be revealed to the beneficiaries. Disclosure of other information would cause a breach of the *Confidential Relationships Ordinance* 1979 which can result in a prison sentence of up to three years and a maximum fine of up to US$50,000.

Protective Trusts

The legislation provides that the interest of a beneficiary may be reduced or terminated in the event of that beneficiary becoming insolvent or any of his property becoming liable to sequestration by a creditor.

Accumulation and Advancement

Direction and authority may be taken from the terms of a trust for all or part of the income of the trust. If the beneficiary is a minor then the trustee may accumulate the income attributed to the minor, apply the income to the education, maintenance or benefit of the minor or discharge payment to a parent or legal guardian of the minor. Advancements can be made prior to an event occurring upon which a beneficiary would become absolutely entitled to the advancement. No advancement shall be made that exceeds the presumptive share of the beneficiary in the trust property.

Asset Protection

Where an individual makes a disposition to a trust and that individual is (a) not insolvent at the time of making the disposition and (b) does not become insolvent by reason of the disposition, then that disposition is not voidable at the insistence of any other party. In addition, the burden of proof that the disposition was made in contradiction of conditions (a) or (b) rests upon the person asserting that fact.

As can be seen from the foregoing, the state of mind of the settlor when settling the trust is irrelevant. Many other offshore jurisdictions will allow a trust to be broken if it can be shown that the settlor had fraudulent intent when setting up the trust, ie it was the settlor's intention to put assets beyond the reach of a current or future creditor. What is in the mind of a settlor when setting up a trust is always going to be difficult to prove so it is advantageous that the TCI legislation focuses purely on solvency rather than intent.

Other items of interest to the settlor are that there are no restrictions on the setup of noncharitable purpose trusts and there are anti-forced heirship provisions within the ordinance.

Paul Winder is a Director of International Company Services (TCI) Limited, PO Box 107, Oceanic House, Duke Street, Grand Turk, Turks & Caicos Islands, British West Indies, Tel: (1 809) 94 62828, Fax: (1 809) 94 62825, E-mail: tci@icsl.com.

URUGUAY

Geoffrey Hooper & Mark Sexton

Introduction

The Uruguayan democracy has matured gradually since the conception of the nation state in 1825. The official language of Uruguay is Spanish reflecting the population, which is largely of Spanish origin. Nonetheless, it is a nation of immigrants who have brought with them their different cultures and customs. French, German, Italian and English are spoken in many quarters, and there are small but notable Japanese and Korean communities. This cultural blend has assisted in the development of an unusually tolerant but conservative democracy by Latin American standards.

Apart from a period of instability in 1973-84, the nation has established itself as a regional bastion of stable democracy, thus explaining references to it as the 'Switzerland of South America'. It has a pleasant, temperate climate and boasts extremely low rates of crime by Latin American standards. The international airport is easily reached via Buenos Aires or Sao Paulo, and some direct flights. For these reasons, Uruguay is increasingly being seen by foreign investors as an attractive base from which to penetrate the larger markets of Argentina and Brazil.

The Government of Uruguay is keen to encourage foreign investors since it is often the case that domestic businesses are unable to provide the necessary capital to develop projects to their full potential. The authorities have been particularly receptive to Asian investors, who are increasingly being seen as a driving force for incoming investment in the Uruguayan economy. Korean, Japanese and Malaysian companies have made notable investments in Uruguay in the last five years, with particular focus in the areas of shipbuilding, car assembly plants, mining, hotels and tourism and finance.

The country has quality beaches which draw Argentine and Brazilian tourists, and some Europeans searching alternative locations from which to escape the winter of the northern hemisphere. The principle export of Uruguay is beef, the quality of this product being a source of national pride. Record beef prices have been assisted by demand in Europe, particularly the United Kingdom, Germany and Spain, and by the development of economic links between Mercosur and the Asean countries, and the Far East generally. Uruguay is three hours behind Greenwich Mean Time.

Offshore Structures

Investors seeking to derive tax advantages under Uruguayan legislation should consider the various options listed below.

SAFI (Sociedad Financiera de Inversión)

SAFI is a foreign investment company and is the Uruguay equivalent of the offshore company. The principal activity of this company is to invest outside Uruguay in securities for its own account or for the account of third parties. It is also allowed to engage in offshore trading and in practise is applied to a wide range of activities in industry, commerce and services with little supervision from the authorities.

Taxation and other costs

A SAFI is subject to a 'unique tax' or license fee calculated in the following fashion:

Shareholders equity + [liabilities - (shareholders equity x 2)] = taxable base

Taxable base x 0.3 per cent is the tax payable

Other than the above tax, there is a one-off charge of around US$700 for incorporating companies. There is a similar charge for the liquidation of a company. In general terms, this charge will increase for companies with higher authorised capital and does not include subscribers' fees, fees due for basic consultancy services, general expenses nor costs incurred for any special provisions the client may request.

Company incorporation

The most common method of company incorporation is to purchase a shelf company. These are readily available and may be put into operation within 24 hours. It is then possible to change the name, authorised capital and other details of the company by amendment of the statutes and in accordance with the requirements of the principal.

A SAFI requires only one shareholder and one director. The shareholder or shareholders may appoint up to seven directors and there is no obligation for any of these to be Uruguayan.

Share certificates are usually issued in bearer form, although nominative shares can also be issued. The par value of shares must be at least US$1.00. The minimum authorised capital is US$50,000, of which five per cent must be paid in.

It is also possible to incorporate a company from scratch, although this is a relatively lengthy process, typically two months. During the period prior to completion of all incorporation formalities the shareholders bear full responsibility for the liabilities of the company. Limited liability will only take effect after the new company's statutes have been published in an approved newspaper, this being the last formality in the incorporation process.

It is a legal requirement for a company to maintain the following statutory books:

- Register of annual general meetings (AGM). AGMs must be held in Uruguay with at least 50 per cent of the issued share and paid-up share capital represented at the meetings. Usually the local domiciliary agent acts as custodian and holds this meeting by proxy;
- Minute books of shareholder and director meetings;
- Inventory;
- Correspondence file; and
- Accounting ledger. Financial statements must be presented to the tax authority four months prior to the close of the financial year. Directors are at liberty to elect the financial year end.

Names

There are not many restrictions regarding the choice of name for a SAFI. The word 'bank' is unacceptable but the words 'trust' (there is no trust law), 'finance', 'insurance' are permissible. Chinese investors will also be encouraged to know that Chinese names are acceptable, although Chinese characters are not. The names of well-known multinational companies are also likely to meet disapproval. It is possible to reserve names of companies for a period of ten days for a small fee (currently around US$18). The important point to note is that names are usually checked for approval just prior to proceeding with incorporation.

Sociedad Anónima de Zona Franca (SAZF)

The other principal vehicle of interest to investors seeking tax incentives is the Sociedad Anónima de Zona Franca (SAZF), a company incorporated in one of the five free trade zones in Uruguay. Unlike the SAFI, companies operating from these free trade zones have zero rate of taxation, provided that none of their merchandise or services are destined for the domestic market.

Each free trade zone operates independently. Two of the zones are state owned, two privately owned, and one privately managed but state owned. There are restrictions on the number of foreign employees each company may employ and employees are subject to compulsory social security contributions. Other than rent of the premises and the hire of machinery there are no other compulsory contributions to restrict capital growth.

Although slow to react to the opportunities presented by the free zones on their inception in 1988, major multinational companies are relocating there in increasing numbers including PepsiCo, Merill Lynch and Banco Frances, amongst others.

Trust Law

There is no trust law in Uruguay and the concept of trust is not one recognised by Uruguayan authorities. However, it is possible to incorporate a company with the word 'trust' in the name. Investors requesting this service must be clear that such a company would not be bound by any trust law and would incorporate as a normal offshore company.

Geoffrey Hooper is group managing director of Winterbotham Trust Company, PO Box 12.129, Blance Viale 5910 11.500 Montevideo, Uruguay. He has worked for 14 years in offshore banking and financial services in South America. Mark Sexton joined the company in 1996 as Mr Hooper's personal assistant.

IN-BOUND INVESTMENT

Canada

New Zealand

United Kingdom

United States of America

CANADA

Richard Hay

Immigration Laws

General

In Canada, immigration is a matter of shared jurisdiction between the federal and provincial governments. However, the federal government has primary jurisdiction over immigration as the provincial governments can only make laws in relation to immigration into that province to the extent that such laws are not repugnant to Acts of the federal Parliament. So far, only the province of Quebec has exercised this right by virtue of the *Act Respecting the Ministere des Communautés culturelles et de l'Immigration*, the structure of which emphasises a foreign national's ability to integrate into Quebec culture.

The *Immigration Act* sets out the basic requirements, policies and principles of Canadian immigration law. The Regulations to the *Immigration Act* provide for a variety of classes and subclasses of immigrants. These may be broken down into four major categories or classes namely:

- Members of the family class;
- Convention refugees;
- Assisted relatives; and
- Independent immigrants.

The last category can be further subdivided into four sub-categories:

- Entrepreneurs;
- Investors;
- Self-employed persons; and
- Independent workers.

The Regulations set out specific selection criteria for each class and subclass of applicant which serve as a framework for evaluating the applicant's ability to establish himself successfully in Canada. In most cases, the criteria are applied by way of a point system. The nine factors utilised in the point system and the way in which points are awarded are set out as Schedule I to the Regulations:

- Education;
- Specific vocational preparation;

- Experience;
- Occupational demand;
- Arranged employment or designated occupation;
- Demographic factor;
- Age;
- Knowledge of English and French languages; and
- Personal suitability.

In addition to the above categories, points may be available as a result of immigration levels that are established from time to time by the Minister. The province of Quebec also has a points system although the selection criteria differ from the federal grid.

Entrepreneur Category

The Regulations define an entrepreneur as an immigrant who intends and has the ability to establish, purchase or make a substantial investment in a business or commercial venture in Canada that will make a significant contribution to the economy and whereby employment opportunities will be created or continued in Canada for one or more Canadian citizens or permanent residents, other than the entrepreneur and his dependants, and who intends and has the ability to provide active and ongoing participation in the management of the business or commercial venture. The success or failure of the entrepreneur's application will hinge primarily upon the viability of a business proposal which the applicant must submit in conjunction with the application.

To qualify as an entrepreneur, the applicant must have the ability, financial and otherwise, to become involved in a Canadian business enterprise that will create employment and must be prepared to actively participate in the management of that business. The latter requirement usually means that the business activity proposed must bear some relationship to the business or employment background of the applicant. It is generally acknowledged that the entrepreneurial applicant must have sufficient economic resources to make an initial capital investment of at least $150,000 (Canadian), unless the business being proposed requires unusually low initial capitalisation. The visa granted is generally subject to conditions and a two-year time frame to comply with the conditions.

Investor Category

The Immigrant Investor Programme was established to provide a means for admitting people with business skills and experience who are prepared to make a minimum investment in business in Canada. To qualify, an immigrant investor must be at least 18 years of age and must have accumulated a prescribed net worth by his or her own efforts.

The key feature is that the investor must make an irrevocable investment for a minimum lock-in period of five years. The amount of the minimum investment depends on three factors: the date on which the investment is made or the date in which the investment was approved by a province, the province of investment, and whether or not the investor seeks to obtain a guarantee or collateral on property of a fixed value.

It is essential that the investment contribute to the creation or continuation of employment opportunities for Canadian citizens or permanent residents other than the investor and the investor's dependants. The following methods of investment are provided in the Regulations:

- Eligible business; and
- Approved fund.

Canadian Residence

Residency

For Canadian tax purposes, residence is the relevant factor. Canadian citizenship and domicile are not relevant for purposes of establishing a Canadian tax nexus. As the *Income Tax Act (Canada)* (the Act) does not provide for a general definition of 'residence', Revenue Canada takes the following criteria into account in making a determination of residence:

- The maintenance of a dwelling in Canada for personal use by the individual;
- The residence of the individual's spouse and dependants;
- The length of time during which the individual is physically present in Canada in a taxation year; and
- The individual's personal, social and economic ties with Canada.

In addition, an individual may be deemed resident in Canada without regard to the above if, for example, he or she was a 'sojourner' and physically present in Canada for 183 days or more. Alternatively, an individual physically present for a shorter period may be considered 'ordinarily resident' on the basis of the criteria noted above. As Canada taxes on a part-year basis in some circumstances, an individual who becomes resident during a taxation year would become liable for tax for that period, not the entire tax year. However, if he or she is considered a 'sojourner' then he or she will be exposed to Canadian tax liability for the entire taxation year.

Summary of Canadian Tax Exposures

Income Tax

A Canadian resident is liable to combined federal and provincial income taxes at progressive rates up to a maximum of approximately 53 per cent on worldwide income, depending on the province of residence. Seventy-five per cent of capital gains are included in taxable income, resulting in a top rate for capital gains of approximately 40 per cent. Income and capital gains of a Canadian resident are taxable irrespective of remittance to Canada.

Gift and Estate Taxes

Canada has no gift or estate tax as such, though accrued capital gains are recognised in the event of a gift or on death, subject to spousal rollovers.

A resident of Canada is treated as having disposed of, immediately before death, all his capital property at the fair market value of such property at that time. A nonresident is subject to these rules only in respect of taxable Canadian property. Such deemed disposition would give rise to capital gains which would be subject to Canadian tax.

Capital Gains Tax

Canada operates a 'closed' system for capital gains. Thus, as a general rule, individuals are subject to Canadian capital gains tax on the appreciation on capital property which accrues while the individual is resident in Canada.

The general rule is that an immigrant receives, for capital gains tax purposes, a 'fair market value' tax basis for his capital property on the date he takes up residence in Canada, with the result that on a subsequent disposal (or deemed disposal) only the gains which accrued while the individual was resident in Canada are subject to tax. In addition, an individual who departs from Canada is generally deemed to dispose of property on departure from Canada, subject to several important exceptions as follows:

- Where the individual has resided in Canada for less than five years out of the previous ten the deemed disposition rule will not apply to property owned by the taxpayer at the time he last became resident in Canada;
- Property acquired by a taxpayer by inheritance or bequest after he last became resident in Canada is not subject to the rule providing for deemed disposition on departure; and
- Ordinary property that the taxpayer has elected, under prescribed rules, to treat as 'taxable Canadian property' is subject to special treatment. Such an election has the result of deferring the date of deemed disposition until the actual date for disposition of the property. Accordingly, the taxpayer gets the advantage of deferring the tax payable, but if the property continues to appreciate he would be subject to the capital gains tax liability on increased amounts.

'Taxable Canadian property', as defined, is subject to special rules and nonresidents of Canada are generally subject to tax on capital gains realised following the disposition (or deemed disposition) of property in this category. 'Taxable Canadian property' includes shares in private Canadian companies and interests in Canadian real estate.

Tax Treatment of Offshore Vehicles

Companies

Non-Canadian source income of a Canadian resident is usually taxable in Canada in the year in which it is received or becomes receivable by the Canadian resident. For example, where interest is earned on foreign deposits, rent is earned from foreign properties or foreign source royalties are accrued, tax is payable in Canada regardless of whether the income is paid or remitted to Canada. In the case of dividends, tax is payable when an amount is received as, on account or in lieu of payment of the dividend.

In order to limit tax avoidance and deferral opportunities through the use of offshore companies, a resident is subject to Canadian tax on passive income (referred to as 'foreign accrual property income' or 'FAPI') arising in closely-held non-Canadian companies ('foreign affiliates') if such income has not been distributed to the Canadian resident. In effect, the Act 'looks through' the corporate entity to tax passive income of a nonresident company in the hands of Canadian residents who control the company either alone, or in combination with non-arm's length parties or with four or fewer other Canadian residents.

Offshore Trusts

A trust which is a nonresident of Canada (ie normally one which is controlled and managed by trustees resident outside Canada) is generally subject to tax only in respect of certain Canadian source income. However, in order to limit opportunities for tax avoidance through the use of non-Canadian resident trusts by Canadians the Act contains rules which, in the case of a discretionary trust, deem the trust to be resident in Canada and taxable on its FAPI in particular circumstances. This regime applies where at least one of the beneficiaries of the trust is a resident of Canada (or a controlled foreign affiliate of a Canadian resident, or a non-arm's length corporation or trust) and the nonresident trust has acquired property directly or indirectly in any manner whatever from such beneficiary or a related person and such transferor has been resident in Canada at some time in the previous 18 months and resident in Canada in the past for more than five years in total. The FAPI rules do not extend to nonresident trusts settled by residents in Canada exclusively for nonresident beneficiaries or to nonresident trusts with Canadian beneficiaries which were settled by nonresident individuals who have not resided in Canada for a total of at least five years.

If the trust is not discretionary, it is considered to be a controlled foreign affiliate of each of its beneficiaries resident in Canada with a 10 per cent or greater interest in the trust where it meets the tests set out above. Each such beneficiary is required to include in income his proportionate share of the FAPI of the trust.

Where a Canadian resident beneficiary becomes entitled to a payment of income (including capital gains) from the trust, the amount is included in computing his income regardless of whether or when the income is actually received. In a fully discretionary trust, the trustee may be permitted under the terms of the trust not to distribute current income and instead to accumulate it and add it to trust capital for distribution, as capital, in a later year. This procedure opens the possibility of instigating taxation of non-Canadian income accruing in the trust.

The Act contains a number of complex attribution rules which may attribute trust income to the settlor. In the absence of further planning to mitigate attribution exposures these rules may apply:

- Where the settlor who becomes a Canadian resident is a beneficiary of the trust;
- Where the settlor attempts to maintain legal control over trust assets;
- Where the underlying corporations are used in certain structures; and
- Where income (as opposed to capital) is distributed to Canadian resident beneficiaries.

Reporting Requirements for Foreign Property

Draft legislation was released jointly by the Canadian Ministers of Finance and Revenue on 5 March, 1996 to impose enlarged reporting obligations on Canadian resident taxpayers with interests in foreign properties, companies and trusts. The amendments, tabled for public comment at this stage, implement proposals originally announced in the February, 1995 Federal budget. The new rules are expected to be introduced in a bill and will apply for taxation years commencing in 1996. The first returns are due in April 1997.

The proposed amendments, tabled with explanatory notes and drafts of the information returns, will generally require reporting by Canadian residents in respect of

- Transfers or loans to foreign trusts;
- Distributions from or indebtedness to foreign trusts;
- Interests in specified foreign property with a cost exceeding CDN$100,000; and
- Shares held in foreign affiliates

Penalties for failure to file returns range up to CDN$12,000 (or CDN$24,000 where a demand for an information return has been served and not complied with). An additional penalty, generally equal to 10 per cent of the cost of the foreign property less the penalty otherwise imposed, may also apply.

Anti-avoidance Rules

In addition to numerous technical anti-avoidance rules applicable in particular circumstances the Act also contains a general anti-avoidance rule (the GAAR).

Under the GAAR, if any transaction is found to be an 'avoidance transaction' the Minister of National Revenue has the power to disregard the other provisions of the Act and assess tax as is reasonable in the circumstances in order to deny any 'tax benefit' which would otherwise result from the 'avoidance transaction'. A 'tax benefit' for purposes of this rule is a reduction, avoidance or deferral of any tax or other amount payable under the Act (eg interest on tax payable) or an increase in the refund of tax or of any other amount to which a taxpayer is entitled. An 'avoidance transaction' is any transaction which (either alone or in context of a series of transactions of which it forms a part) but for the GAAR would result in a tax benefit, unless it can be shown that the transaction or series of transactions was undertaken or arranged primarily for bona fide purposes other than to achieve the tax benefit in question.

As the GAAR is a rule expressly intended to counter abuse of the Canadian tax system, it will not apply in cases where a tax benefit arises if it may reasonably be considered in all the circumstances that the transaction does not result in a misuse of the provisions of the Act as a result of which the tax benefit arises or is an abuse of the provisions of the Act read as a whole.

Planning for Immigrants

A discretionary trust controlled and managed by non-Canadian resident trustees funded exclusively by an individual taking up residence in Canada for the first time will, subject to anti-avoidance and attribution rules, generally be permitted to accumulate 'offshore' capital gains and income free of Canadian tax until the beginning of the taxation year in which any individual contributing property to the trust has been resident in Canada for a cumulative total of 60 months during his lifetime. Accordingly, if an individual took up residence in Canada for the first time in 1997 and remained resident in Canada for tax purposes, a nonresident trust settled by him would not generally be subject to Canadian tax on offshore income and gains until the 2001 taxation year (ie the year commencing on 1 January 2001). It is possible that distributions of capital in a properly structured trust may be distributed to Canadian resident beneficiaries without a Canadian tax exposure, though they will still be subject to reporting obligations.

As a result of these rules, a properly structured trust can assist a new immigrant to avoid Canadian tax on income and capital gains from offshore sources for up to 60 months on property transferred to the trust which was beneficially owned by the immigrant to Canada. (By contrast, as noted above, income from property which the immigrant owns personally is subject to tax at a top rate of approximately 53 per cent). After 60 months, a trust funded in whole or part by the immigrant will be deemed resident in Canada and be taxable on its passive income where the trust includes specified family members as beneficiaries and at least one of those beneficiaries is resident in Canada.

Departure Taxes

As noted above under the heading 'Capital Gains Tax', on giving up Canadian residence, an emigrant will be deemed to dispose of each property owned, with certain exceptions, for proceeds equal to its fair market value. Tax will generally be payable on capital gains accrued from the time that the immigrant takes up residence in Canada.

Richard Hay is the private capital tax partner in the London office of Stikeman, Elliott. He is an author and speaks frequently in Europe and Asia on the subject of international tax planning.

NEW ZEALAND

Michael J Reynolds

The New Zealand foreign trust regime was first introduced by amendment in 1988 and was then consolidated in the *Income Tax Act* 1994. A New Zealand foreign trust provides the opportunity for establishing a trust which enjoys the credibility of tax residence in New Zealand, a high tax OECD jurisdiction, whilst remaining tax free.

Foreign Trust Assessability Based on Settlor Residence

The 1988 Amendment changed the test for assessability of trust income from the residency of the trustee to the residency of the settlor. A settlor is widely defined to include any person or entity who or which provides goods or services to a trust for less than market value or acquires goods or services from a trust for greater than market value. The settlor provisions also extend to a principal behind a nominee settlement. The *Income Tax Act* 1994 identifies three types of trusts for taxation purposes:

- qualifying trusts;
- non-qualifying trusts; and
- foreign trusts.

Qualifying Trust

A qualifying trust is a domestic trust with a New Zealand resident settlor and New Zealand resident trustees. It is assessable for New Zealand tax on its worldwide income.

Non-qualifying Trust

These trusts attract a penal rate of tax. They include qualifying trusts that have not satisfied their obligations under the *Income Tax Act* and also any offshore trust on which a settlement has been made by a tax resident of New Zealand.

Foreign Trust

A trust is treated as a foreign trust for New Zealand tax purposes if no settlor of the trust has been a New Zealand tax resident from the later of 17 December 1987 or the date on which a settlement was first made on the trustees, until the date on which a distribution is made. This is the case even if there are New Zealand resident trustees and/or beneficiaries.

New Zealand resident trustees of a foreign trust will not be assessable for tax in New Zealand other than on income sourced in New Zealand.

There are provisions dealing with the assessability of distributions made from a foreign trust to a New Zealand resident beneficiary, but a nonresident beneficiary will not be subject to New Zealand tax on any distributions unless the income is sourced in New Zealand.

Although tax residency for assessability purposes is based on the residence of the settlor, a trust which has no New Zealand resident settlor (a foreign trust) is not considered to be nonresident. This leaves the New Zealand resident trustee's tax residence unaffected and enables access to New Zealand's Double Taxation Treaty network. Before examining the Double Tax Treaty issues in more detail, an examination of New Zealand trust law is appropriate.

General New Zealand Trust Law

The Trustee Act 1956

The principal statute governing New Zealand trusts is the *Trustee Act* 1956. That Act is based upon various countries' *Trustee Acts* in force at that time (including the English *Trustee Act*) and is supplemented by United Kingdom common law through the New Zealand High Court which has inherent equitable jurisdiction. The 1956 Act has been amended several times. The most important amendment is the 1988 *Trustee Amendment Act* which substantially modified the duties and responsibilities of New Zealand trustees and, in particular, adopted the 'prudent man' rule of United States jurisprudence thereby greatly extending a trustee's discretion to invest.

Two further interesting provisions in the *Trustee Act* are Sections 49 and 50:

Advisory Trustee (Section 49)

An Advisory Trustee may be appointed either by the 'responsible trustee' or by the person having power to appoint new trustees. The 'responsible trustee' is the trustee or trustees of the trust at the time the advisory trustee is appointed. The trust fund remains vested in the 'responsible trustee' who may consult the Advisory Trustee on any matter relating to the trust. The Advisory Trustee may also advise the responsible trustee on any matter relating to the trust but is not treated or responsible as a trustee in respect of the trust.

Where any advice is given by the Advisory Trustee, the responsible trustee may follow the same and act thereon and shall not be liable for anything done or omitted by reason of following that advice.

This provision means that a New Zealand resident trustee can be guided in its actions by an overseas Advisory Trustee without the Advisory Trustee being deemed a trustee of the trust. In addition, s 49 provides that an Advisory Trustee may be remunerated in accordance with the provision in the trust instrument for remuneration of the responsible trustee.

Custodian Trustee (Section 50)

Any corporation may be appointed as a Custodian Trustee of any trust in any case where that company could be appointed to be a trustee. In such a case the trust property may, subject to the trust instrument, be vested in the Custodian Trustee as if it were the sole trustee. The sole function of the Custodian Trustee is to get in and hold the trust property and invest the funds and deal with assets as the responsible trustee directs in writing. This section is subject to any provisions in the trust instrument and also provides for remuneration of the custodian trustee in the same manner as for the advisory trustee.

The custodian trustee and advisory trustee provisions permit flexibility in New Zealand foreign trust structuring, while protecting professional and client relationships.

The Perpetuities Act 1964

The *Perpetuities Act* 1964 permits the standard common law period of a life in being and 21 years but also provides for a trust instrument to specify an alternative fixed perpetuity period not exceeding 80 years from the date of the instrument. The *Perpetuities Act* also provides that, notwithstanding the Common Law rule against accumulations, trustees may accumulate income pursuant to a specific power to so accumulate set out in the trust instrument. Accordingly, if so empowered, trustees may accumulate income for the life of the trust.

Double Tax Treaties

The use of trusts and tax treaties is a growing area of international corporate, estate and tax planning. However, as noted by Baker and Maurice in their article 'Trusts and Treaties', the application of tax treaties to trusts raises a large number of questions with very few answers. Only about 10 per cent of tax treaties make any reference to trusts and of that 10 per cent, most make only a passing reference.

When considering the application of New Zealand treaties to trusts, it remains pertinent to go back to first principles to test the application of a treaty. Once those principles are satisfied, then the particular characteristics of the trust and the treaty should be reviewed to assess the overall application of that treaty to the particular trust.

Steps to Test Applicability of Tax Treaties to Trusts

Is the trust or the trustee a person within the definition of 'person' in the particular treaty?

Some treaties expressly include a trust within the definition of a 'person'. While that may give initial comfort by ensuring that a trust has access to a particular treaty, it could also have the effect of causing a trust to have dual residency by virtue of the tax residency of a trustee and also by the tax residency of the trust.

New Zealand tax treaties generally define a 'person' to include an individual, a company and any other body of persons. The *Income Tax Act* 1994 (section OB1) defines a 'person' as including a company, a local or public authority and also an unincorporated body of persons.

A 'body of persons' is not separately defined in the general definitions, but a 'body' is defined within the Withholding Tax Part of the Act (Part N) section NF 10(6), which provides that for the purposes of that section, a 'body' means an unincorporated body of persons, and includes a partnership, a joint venture, and the trustees of a trust.

Although there are gaps in the definitions, many of New Zealand's tax treaties make reference to the trustee of a trust being regarded as the beneficial owner of dividends, interest and royalties. Such a reference indicates that the New Zealand Government anticipates that a trustee of a trust could be a 'person' under a New Zealand tax treaty.

New Zealand academics generally agree that a New Zealand resident trustee (being either a corporate or personal trustee and liable to taxation in New Zealand) of a New Zealand Foreign Trust qualifies as a 'person' for the purposes of the New Zealand Treaty network.

Is the trust or the trustee a resident of one or more of the treaty states (contracting state)?

Most New Zealand tax treaties define the term 'resident of a contracting state' as any person who, under the laws of the contracting state, is liable to tax therein by reason of his domicile, residence, place of head office or any other criterion of a similar nature.

A New Zealand incorporated company acting as a trustee in New Zealand is tax resident in New Zealand and therefore liable to tax by virtue of having its place of incorporation and head office in New Zealand, a permanent establishment in New Zealand and further by having day-to-day management and control exercised in New Zealand.

While some commentators take the view that such liability of the trustee is sufficient to meet the test for residence of a New Zealand trust for treaty purposes, it also follows that a New Zealand resident trustee of a New Zealand foreign trust is liable to tax in New Zealand as a trustee and therefore qualifies as resident for tax treaty purposes notwithstanding that the trustee is exempt from assessment of trust income because it is not New Zealand sourced.

It is important to remember that the exemption from tax on non-New Zealand sourced income earned by a foreign trust relates to the assessability of that income and not to the liability of the trustee and thus does not of itself affect the tax residency of the trustee either in its own right or as a trustee of a foreign trust.

If in the worst case a tax treaty is not available, the trustee of a New Zealand foreign trust will still not be assessable for tax on non-New Zealand sourced income.

Advantages of New Zealand Foreign Trusts

The key advantages of New Zealand foreign trusts include:

- The credible appeal of a successful high tax OECD jurisdiction as a base;
- New Zealand has an increasingly cosmopolitan population with various ethnic communities;
- The high standard of professional services and commercial infrastructure;
- A time zone that overlaps Asia and the Americas;
- Common law and equity similar to the United Kingdom;
- A legal profession and judiciary experienced in equity with final appeal to the Privy Council;
- Statutory provisions (the *Trustee Act* 1956 (as amended) and the *Perpetuities Act* 1984) which ameliorate or extend certain common law rules, for example, the limitation of the rule against accumulations, the extension of a trustee's powers of investment and the provision for advisory and custodian trustees;
- No tax reporting or registration requirements with the New Zealand authorities provided the trust fund has no New Zealand sourced income or distributions to a New Zealand resident beneficiary. Trustees could elect to report if that is preferred;
- Potential access to New Zealand's extensive tax treaty network; and
- The ability to use offshore holding companies (situated and administered in suitable jurisdictions) owned by a New Zealand resident trustee, to hold assets for the trust without those offshore companies being treated as Controlled Foreign Companies for New Zealand tax purposes.

Michael Reynolds is managing director and a founding shareholder of Anchor Trustees Ltd. He is a graduate of the University of Auckland and a barrister and solicitor.

UNITED KINGDOM

Mark Lea

Taxation in the UK

Taxation in the UK is triggered by residence, ordinary residence and domicile. Residence and ordinary residence are a question of physical presence in the UK. Domicile is a different concept. It is the intention to create one's permanent home in a particular country or state, coupled with evidence to support this.

Residence and Ordinary Residence

Residence and ordinary residence relate to a tax year. The tax year runs from 6th April to the following 5th April. If an individual is present in the UK for 183 days or more in any tax year he is resident in the UK for that tax year. This is also true if he is present in the UK for an average of 90 days or more per annum over four consecutive years. If he has a property in the UK which is available for his use and he is present in the UK for any length of time during a tax year, then he will be resident in the UK for that tax year. This draconian test is now substantially limited. It does not apply to an individual who is employed full time outside the UK and the duties of that employment are wholly carried on outside the UK. It also does not apply to an individual who comes to the UK as a temporary resident, which means he does not intend to stay in the UK for three years or more. Ordinary residence means habitual residence. If an individual comes to the UK intending to stay there for three years or more or to work there for two years or more, then he will be treated as resident and ordinarily resident in the UK from the day of his arrival.

Domicile

Residence and ordinary residence are the tests which control income tax and capital gains tax. It is domicile which controls inheritance tax, a tax on chargeable gifts made during an individual's lifetime or on his death. Domicile may also limit an individual's exposure to income tax and capital gains tax. The present UK law of domicile provides initially for a domicile of origin. Every individual receives this at birth; it is usually the domicile of his father at that time. At the age of 16, an individual can abandon his domicile of origin for a domicile of choice. The burden of proving this is heavy and is beyond reasonable doubt. If a domicile of choice is later abandoned and another domicile of choice is not obtained, then the individual's domicile of origin revives. Women who married before 1 January 1974 automatically took their husbands' domiciles by dependency on the date of their marriage. There was an intention to change the UK Law of Domicile. On 16 January 1996 the Lord Chancellor announced in the House of Lords that the proposed changes would not be affected. He said that the present Law of Domicile was too well entrenched and the changes would cause too many difficulties. If the law had been changed, there would no longer have been a domicile of origin. Therefore it could not revive. Domicile would in future be based upon the country with which one is most closely connected. This is a frequent test of residence in other jurisdictions. An individual would still take his father's domicile at birth and would be able to adopt a domicile of choice from the age of 16 onwards. The test for a change would be merely a balance of probabilities. Domicile of dependency would be abolished. Whether or not the Finance Bill 1998 seeks to change domicile or the benefits which non UK domicile provides remains to be seen.

To obtain the benefits of not being domiciled in any part of the UK, it is necessary not merely to show that an individual is domiciled outside the UK, but to show beyond reasonable doubt that another domicile of origin or of choice is relevant. There are substantial taxation benefits if an individual is not domiciled in any part of the UK. Only assets situated in the UK are liable to inheritance tax. Income which arises outside the UK is only liable to income tax if it is remitted to the UK. The net proceeds of capital gains realised outside the UK are only chargeable to capital gains tax if remitted to the UK.

If an individual creates a trust outside the UK at a time when he is not domiciled in any part of the UK and the assets within that trust are not situated in the UK and remain so, then those assets will be 'excluded property' and outside the scope of inheritance tax throughout the life of the trust. For this purpose it will not matter if the individual who created the trust subsequently becomes domiciled in some part of the UK. The capital gains realised by the trustees of such trust cannot be assessed either upon the settlor (the creator of the trust) or upon the beneficiaries of the trust while the settlor remains domiciled outside the UK.

The only way of testing the domicile of an individual who is neither resident nor ordinarily resident in the UK, is for him to create a trust outside the UK with assets not situated in the UK. The value of those assets must be such that there would be an immediate charge to inheritance tax if he is domiciled in some part of the UK. If the individual is already resident or ordinarily resident in the UK, then his domicile can be tested by reference to non UK source income, which would only be liable to UK income tax if remitted to the UK.

Income Tax

Income tax is a tax on the income of individuals; companies pay corporation tax on their profits. Income tax was introduced by the Prime Minister, William Pitt, to help finance the Napoleonic War. It necessitated taxpayers revealing their income. This was most unpopular. A subsequent prime minister, Henry Addington, reintroduced the tax in 1803. He chose to classify an individual's income by reference to its source. Each source was dealt with under a separate schedule. Each schedule had separate rules for determining liability and calculation. This system still applies. Income tax was last introduced by Sir Robert Peel in 1842. This was done as a three-year temporary measure.

Under the self-assessment system, individuals are required to make tax returns. The deadline for submitting a return is the later of 31 January following the tax year and three months after the issue of a notice requesting submission of the return. If the taxpayer chooses not to make a self assessment of his income and gains, the Inland Revenue will make an assessment on his behalf if he submits his return before 30 September following the end of the tax year or, if later, two months following the issue of the notice requiring him to make the return. Trustees also have to make tax returns in respect of trust income and gains. Under the self-assessment system, their position is similar to that for individuals. Failure to make returns or to comply with notices requiring information gives rise to penalties. What is so far said concerns individuals and trustees who are resident in the UK. Nonresidents only need to make tax returns, or to have them made on their behalf, in respect of UK source income. However, the Inland Revenue has wide powers to seek information to determine whether or not there has been tax avoidance.

Tax Avoidance

Tax avoidance is a very broad subject which the UK Inland Revenue are well versed in. Apart from two particular sections of the *Income and Corporation Taxes Act* 1988 (ICTA), which are now mentioned, there are other statutory provisions; for example, provision designed to assess the proceeds of the sale of UK land, which is purchased with the intention that it be sold or developed at a profit. The two sections of ICTA which are probably considered most in the context of individuals, who are not ordinarily resident in the UK, are Sections 739 and 740. These are perhaps the main weapons in the Inland Revenue's armoury in this context. Both sections postulate a transfer of assets with the result that income arises to a person who is neither resident nor domiciled in the UK. The object is to prevent an individual or his spouse who is ordinarily resident in the UK, from avoiding UK taxation in this way.

In *Inland Revenue Commissioners v Willoughby and another*, s 739 was tested. Professor Willoughby made a transfer of assets into an international portfolio bond. Income arose to the insurance company concerned in the Isle of Man. The Inland Revenue sought to assess Professor Willoughby as the transferor. He argued successfully that the section could not apply because he was not ordinarily resident in the UK at the time he made the transfer and because his action fell within exceptions. The exceptions were twofold: where the transfer is not made with the intention of avoiding UK taxation and where there is a genuine commercial transaction not designed to avoid tax. He argued successfully that he was, in effect, providing for his pension and nothing should prevent him from doing this in the most tax efficient way. He successfully distinguished that from tax avoidance. The taxpayer's achievement was arguably short-lived. In s 81 *Finance Act* 1997 the provisions of s 739 were strengthened. For income arising by reason of such a transfer on or after 26 November 1996, it is immaterial where the transferor was ordinarily resident when he made the transfer. It does not matter when the transfer was made. If a purpose of such a transfer was to avoid any form of direct taxation the exceptions would not apply. In order to be assessable under s 739, the transferor must have power to enjoy the income or be entitled to receive a 'capital sum', which is in any way connected with the transfer. 'Power to enjoy the income' has a very wide meaning. It does not merely include benefit from income but the increase in the value of assets by reason of the income, any benefit received because of that income, the possibility that he may become entitled to enjoy the income because of an exercise of a power to that effect or because he can directly or indirectly control the way income is applied. 'Capital sum' includes the payment or repayment of a loan and any other payment, which is not in the nature of income and which is not paid for full consideration. There is a specific provision, which ensures that non UK domiciliaries, who are entitled to the benefit of the remittance rules in respect of non UK source income do not suffer by reference to s 739.

Section 739 is solely concerned with the assessment of the transferor. If that section applies, then s 740 cannot; the two sections are mutually exclusive. Section 740 again postulates a similar transfer. It is concerned with benefits received by individuals, who are not ordinarily resident in the UK, out of or by reason of the assets transferred. Such benefits may be, for example, loans at less than a commercial rate or the occupation of a house at less than the full market rent. Benefits can only be measured by reference to income which arises because of the transfer to persons neither resident nor domiciled in the UK. Therefore, if there is no income, it is not possible to make an assessment either under s 739 or under s 740. The Inland Revenue has a further armoury of statutory provisions to attack trusts and companies but the test referred to here holds true. For non UK domiciliaries inheritance tax is, at present, really voluntary and while they remain not domiciled in any part of the UK, there is limited exposure to capital gains tax and to income tax.

On 25 November 1997 the UK Government issued a Green Paper. This is a document intended to provide discussion. It is clear from this that a general and sweeping anti-avoidance provision is to be introduced.

Other Criteria

Assuming that non-UK domicile is not available, other criteria apply to UK tax planning. The use of a properly drafted and tax efficient will is essential. In this, it needs to be remembered that unless the donor spouse is domiciled in some part of the UK and the donee spouse is not, everything which one spouse leaves to the other is exempt from inheritance tax. Since the first £215,000 of chargeable gifts bears a nil rate of tax, care must be taken to see that the benefit of this is not lost within the spouse exemption. Investment may be made in assets which are exempt from or which bear a reduced rate of inheritance tax. There are some exemptions from the tax. Everyone is allowed £3,000 worth of tax free gifts per annum. Otherwise it is a question of 'give it away or pay'. Gifts can be 'potentially exempt'. These are gifts to individuals or to certain trusts. If the donor lives for seven years after making the gift, then it will be outside inheritance tax. Reduced rates of tax apply after the fourth year. A discretionary trust may be used to receive the nil rate band, the benefit of which will be restored after seven years.

Pre-immigration planning will be concerned not only with long-term inheritance tax planning but also with the avoidance and mitigation of capital gains tax and income tax. It is important to act soon enough; this means in the tax year preceding that of immigration to the UK. Gains from disposals of assets will be tax free if made in a tax year throughout which the individual is neither resident nor ordinarily resident in the UK. Hence 'bed and breakfasting' of assets, like stocks and shares which can easily be reacquired will assist. Gains can be 'washed out' with regard to other assets, which cannot easily be reacquired; trusts can be used for this purpose. Losses should be realised after residence is established. Care should be taken as to the timing of terminal payments for employment. If realty is retained in the UK, it will be important to see if it qualifies for principal private residence relief for capital gains tax purposes. The continuing tax efficiency of existing trusts needs to be looked at. The reason and need for all insurance policies should be reviewed; probably some of them should be written in trust and are not. This may also be true of any death in service benefit. Tax efficient investment should be considered. Spouses should see that their income producing assets are split between them, perhaps with the use of suitable Declarations of Trust, so that the benefits of two personal allowances, the lower rate of income tax and the standard rate of income tax are not lost. There are two ways to beneficially own realty jointly and a check should be made to see that the right method has been adopted.

Having tasted the delights of the UK and found them wanting, there are two particular factors to be borne in mind when departing. If trusts are exported, then there is a deemed disposal of the assets in trust for capital gains tax purposes. If you have been resident in the UK for income tax purposes for 17 or more out of the last 20 UK tax years, then until this ceases to be the case, you will remain UK domiciled for inheritance tax only. For inheritance tax, you will not abandon UK domicile until three years after this would otherwise have happened under the general law.

Tax is not the only consideration. The practical implications are frequently more important. Long-term protection of the family and asset protection may override secondary tax considerations. The tax considerations of being resident in the UK will be of little significance if the individual has no right of abode in the UK. Assuming that the individual is neither a British nor a Commonwealth citizen with right of abode nor an EEA national who is entitled to enter and remain in the UK, then, leaving aside special and limited categories, the usual reasons for admission will be the establishment of a business, permitted employment or as an investor. Each category requires a number of conditions to be met. Care and preplanning are needed. An investor covers someone of sufficient independent means who wishes to reside in the UK. Among the conditions of entry for an investor are that he shall have under his control and disposable in the UK not less than £1 million. Of this, £750,000 has to be invested in UK Government securities or in permitted UK registered companies. The person concerned has to intend to make the UK his main home, which is tantamount to a declaration that he seeks to be domiciled in some part of the UK.

Since 1971 Mark Lea has been involved in offshore and international comparative taxation as well as UK taxation. For eight years ending in 1995 he was a Partner with Wilsons, Solicitors in Salisbury specialising in taxation. He is now based in Hong Kong as a Consultant with Crump & Co, Hong Kong Solicitors. He is also a Consultant to City of London Solicitors, Walker Martineau, who have longstanding connections with and experience in the Asia Pacific region.

United States of America

Mary Ellen Hutton

In the past few years, significant changes to US Federal tax laws have affected the application of US Federal income tax, estate tax and generation-skipping tax. Since these changes have wide-reaching effects, care must be exercised when planning for persons who have both US and foreign connections in the offshore trust planing context.

Inbound and Outbound Grantor Trusts

On August 20, 1996, US President Bill Clinton signed into law legislation which changed the rules pertaining to inbound and outbound grantor trusts as well as the reporting requirements for both grantors and beneficiaries associated with such trusts.

These measures target perceived abuses related to various types of foreign trusts. The changes affect so-called inbound grantor trusts, created by nonresident aliens (NRAs) of the United States for the benefit of US persons, and outbound grantor trusts (and more specifically asset protection trusts), in which US persons create, or transfer property to, trusts located outside the United States. The current laws are summarised below.

Foreign Trust Defined

Prior to August 20, 1996, a trust was determined to be either domestic or foreign based on a facts and circumstances test. The August 20, 1996 measures modify the definition of a foreign trust by expressly defining a foreign trust as any trust other than a domestic trust. To qualify as a domestic trust, a trust must meet two tests:

1. a court within the United States is able to exercise primary supervision over the administration of the trust; and
2. one or more US fiduciaries have authority to control all substantial decisions of the trust.

Inbound Grantor Trusts

Under prior law, if an NRA grantor created a foreign grantor trust, the income from such a trust (other than US source income) was not subject to US income tax and distributions by such a trust to US persons were also not taxed to such persons as income. This planning technique had been used for a number of years and was sanctioned by the US Treasury in Revenue Ruling 69-70 in 1970.

Under current legislation, generally only US persons will be treated as owning assets in a foreign trust for US income tax purposes. However, the rules do provide exceptions for trusts which are revocable by an NRA grantor (or revocable with the consent of certain people who are related to the grantor) or, if the trust is not revocable, for trusts which may only make distributions to the grantor or the grantor's spouse during the grantor's lifetime. The new law further excepts compensatory trusts if a trust distribution would be taxable as compensation for services rendered. In addition to these exceptions, the new law also grandfathers foreign trusts in existence on September 19, 1995, provided that such trusts are treated as owned by the grantor under s 676 or 677 of the Internal Revenue Code (ie the trusts are either revocable or the grantor or the grantor's spouse are in the class of beneficiaries.)

Any income from a foreign trust which fails to meet one of these exceptions if paid to a US person will be taxed to the recipient as income. Foreign trusts that do not fall into one of these exceptions will be treated as non-grantor trusts (ie those trusts in which the grantor or settlor is either deceased, or in which he no longer has any rights or possible interest). As a result, the United States will tax all income distributed to US persons at ordinary rates until all income in the trust is distributed, and will impose interest at market rates on amounts of income earned in prior years and accumulated in the trust when such accumulated income is deemed distributed. Note, however, that even if a foreign trust's income will become subject to US income tax as a result of the new law, there may still be US estate tax and other advantages to keeping the trust in place.

If a US beneficiary (or his or her relatives) receives a loan from a foreign trust, the value of such loan will be taxed as a constructive distribution to that beneficiary. Limited grandfathering is granted for loans of cash and marketable securities entered into prior to September 19, 1995.

The legislation authorises the Treasury to recharacterise direct or indirect gifts from corporations (presumably including gifts from 'corporate grantor trusts') and partnerships if such recharacterisation would prevent the avoidance of tax.

Outbound Grantor Trusts

As discussed earlier, the creation of a foreign trust by a US person or the transfer of property to such a trust, or the receipt of a distribution by a US person from any foreign trust whether created by a US person or otherwise, gives rise to a series of reporting requirements on the part of transferors and of US beneficiaries which are discussed in more detail below.

The rules also provide that an NRA who becomes a US resident within five years after directly or indirectly transferring property to a foreign trust will be treated as having transferred such property (and any undistributed income) to the foreign trust on the date he or she became a US resident. Thereafter, unless no US person could ever benefit from the trust and no other grantor trust powers are retained, the US resident will continue to be subject to US Federal income tax on all the income of the trust. This provision is designed to prevent the use of foreign trusts as 'pre-immigration' planning structures to avoid US income tax. However, there continue to be substantial US gift and estate tax advantages to the creation of irrevocable trusts as a pre-immigration planning technique.

Information Reporting Requirements as to Foreign Trusts

The August 20, 1996 measures impose information reporting requirements, and attendant compliance penalties, on US persons with respect to their transfers to, their ownership of, and their interests in, foreign trusts. Moreover, to the extent provided in regulations, these new requirements will also affect the obligations of US persons to report their transfers to, their ownership of, and their interests in, domestic trusts that have substantial activities, or hold substantial property, outside of the United States.

Reporting requirements as to certain reportable events

Expanded information reporting requirements will apply to certain reportable events involving foreign trusts that occur after August 20, 1996. First, a US person who creates a foreign trust must report the creation of the trust to the IRS. Second, upon the death of a US citizen or resident, the deceased's executor must report the deceased's death to the IRS if:

- the deceased was treated as an owner of part of a foreign trust under the grantor trust rules; or
- part of a foreign trust was included in the deceased's gross estate.

Third, a US person who transfers money or property, whether directly or indirectly, to a foreign trust must report the transfer to the IRS. The preceding rule also applies to a transfer to a foreign trust by reason of death, in which case the reporting obligation falls upon the deceased's executor. Moreover, the fact that another US person may be treated as an owner of part of a foreign trust under the grantor trust rules is disregarded in determining whether a reportable transfer to the trust has occurred.

The required written notice must generally be given on or before the ninetieth day after the occurrence of the reportable event. The notice must contain all information required by regulations, including the amount of any money or other property transferred in connection with the reportable event, the identity of the relevant trust, and each trustee and beneficiary, or class of beneficiaries, of the relevant trust.

Reporting requirements of US Grantors of foreign trusts

If, at any time during any taxable year of a US person that begins after December 31, 1995, the person is treated as the owner (ie grantor) of any portion of a foreign trust under the grantor trust rules, the person shall be responsible for ensuring that the foreign trust files a return setting forth a full and complete accounting of the trust's activities and operations for the relevant taxable year, the name of the trust's US agent, and any other information as prescribed by regulations. Moreover, the US person must also ensure that the foreign trust furnishes the proper information, as prescribed by regulations, to each US person who is treated as an owner of part of the trust or who receives, directly or indirectly, any distribution from the trust.

A foreign trust's US agent is a US person authorized to act as the trust's limited agent solely for purposes of the application of certain provisions of US tax law pertaining to:

- requests by the IRS to examine records or produce testimony related to the proper treatment of amounts required to be taken into income by a US person under the grantor trust rules; or

- summonses issued by the IRS for such records or testimony. If a foreign trust does not appoint a US agent, the IRS may determine, in its discretion, the proper amount to be taken into income by a US person under the grantor trust rules with respect to the trust.

Reporting requirements of US Beneficiaries of foreign trusts

If a US person receives, after August 20, 1996, directly or indirectly, during any taxable year of the person, any distribution from a foreign trust, the person must file an information return regarding the trust for the relevant taxable year. The fact that another US person may be treated as an owner of part of the trust under the grantor trust rules is disregarded in determining whether a reportable distribution from the trust has occurred. The return must include:

- the name of the trust;
- the aggregate amount of distributions the person received from the trust during the taxable year; and
- any other information prescribed by regulations.

If adequate records are not provided to the IRS to determine the proper tax treatment of a distribution to a US person from a foreign trust, the distribution will be treated a taxable accumulation distribution.

Applicable penalties

In addition to any criminal penalty under US law, if any return or notice required to be filed with respect to a foreign trust is not filed on or before the appointed time, or does not include the required information or includes incorrect information, the person required to file, or to ensure the filing of, as the case may be, the return or notice shall pay a penalty equal to thirty-five percent, or five percent in the case of a US person required as the owner of part of a foreign trust under the grantor trust rules, to ensure the filing of a return, or notice by the trust, of the gross reportable amount. The term 'gross reportable amount' means:

- with respect to a so-called reportable event (eg the creation of a foreign trust by a US person), the gross value of the property involved in the reportable event determined as of the date of such event;
- with respect to a US person required as the owner of a portion of a foreign trust under the grantor trust rules to ensure the filing of a return or notice by the trust, the gross value of the portion of the trust's assets, as of the close of the relevant taxable year, treated as being owned by such person; and
- with respect to a US person receiving distributions from a foreign trust, the gross amount of the reportable distributions.

If any failure continues for more than ninety days after the day on which a notice of the failure is mailed to the person required to pay a penalty as described above, the person must pay an additional US$10,000 penalty for each thirty day period, or fraction thereof, during which the failure continues after the expiration of the ninety day period. This additional penalty amount may not, with respect to any failure, exceed the gross reportable amount at issue.

No penalty shall be imposed if the failure was due to reasonable cause and not wilful neglect. However, the fact that a foreign jurisdiction would impose a civil or criminal penalty on the relevant taxpayer, or any other person, for disclosing the required information is not reasonable cause for the failure. Accordingly, bank secrecy laws will not excuse a failure to satisfy the relevant requirements.

Notice of large gifts received from foreign persons

Information reporting requirements are imposed on US persons, other than certain qualified tax-exempt charitable organisations, with respect to foreign gifts received after the enactment date in taxable years ending after such date. For purposes of the new requirements, the term 'foreign gifts' means amounts received from persons, other than US persons, which the recipient treats as gifts or bequests.

If the total aggregate value of foreign gifts received by a US person during any taxable year exceeds US$100,000 with respect to gifts from foreign individuals or estates or US$10,000 with respect to gifts from foreign corporations or partnerships, the person must furnish, at the time and in the manner as prescribed by regulations, all required information regarding each foreign gift received during the relevant taxable year. The reporting threshold will be subject to a cost-of-living adjustment.

If a US person fails to furnish the required information with respect to a foreign gift within the prescribed time period, including extensions, the tax consequences of the receipt of the gift shall be determined by the IRS, and the US person must pay, upon notice and demand and in the same manner as a tax, an amount equal to five percent of the amount of the foreign gift for each month during which the failure continues, not to exceed twenty-five percent of the amount of the gift in the aggregate. However, the penalty will not apply if the failure to report the foreign gift was due to reasonable cause and not wilful neglect.

Expatriation Provisions

Applicability

Individuals who relinquish their US citizenship on or after February 6, 1995 and so-called 'long-term' permanent resident aliens (green card holders) whose residence terminates on or after that date, face tightened treatment under s 877 for the Internal Revenue Code. A 'long-term resident' is any individual who is a lawful permanent resident of the United States in at least eight taxable years out of the period of fifteen taxable years ending with the taxable year in which the termination of residence occurred.

Presumptions

As was the case prior to the enactment of the current law, an expatriate who within ten years of the taxable year expatriates and has as at least one of his principal purposes the avoidance of US taxes, will continue to be taxed on his or her US source income for a period of ten years, following his or her year of expatriation unless his or her departure did not have for one of its principal purposes the avoidance of tax (s 877 of the Internal Revenue Code). The recent changes provide a presumption that a tax-avoidance motive exists if either

- an individual's average annual US federal income tax liability for the previous five years exceeds US$100,000; or
- such individual's net worth on the date of expatriation or termination of residence is at least US$500,000. Both these amounts are to be indexed for inflation in the years following 1996.

Exceptions

Certain categories of expatriating persons are not, however, subject to these presumptions if, within the one-year period beginning with the date of loss of citizenship, such persons submit a ruling request to the IRS as to whether such loss has as a principal purpose the avoidance of taxes. These categories of persons are as follows:

- individuals who are born with dual citizenship and who retain their non-US citizenship;
- individuals who (no later than the close of a reasonable period after loss of citizenship, which period is not defined in the legislation) become citizens of the country where they, their spouses or either of their parents were born;
- individuals not present in the United States for more than thirty days in any of the ten years prior to loss of citizenship;
- individuals who surrender their citizenship before they reach age 18 1/2; and
- such other individuals which the Secretary of the Treasury may describe by regulation.

Similar exceptions apply to departing long-term aliens.

Increased scope of taxation

The current law broadens the scope of US source income subject to taxation under s 877 to include income or gains realized from a foreign corporation owned, at any time within two years prior to expatriation or termination of residence, more than fifty percent by a former citizen or long-term resident. The current law also taxes immediately gains on exchanges of property giving rise to US source income for property giving rise to foreign-source income, unless the taxpayer enters into a ten year gain recognition agreement with the IRS, by which any income or gain derived from the property acquired in the exchange during such ten year period would be taxed as US source income or gain. The IRS is also authorised to issue regulations which would cause immediate taxation upon the removal of appreciated tangible personal property from the United States or upon any other occurrence which results in a change of the source of the income or gain from the United States to any other jurisdiction.

Informational filings

Expatriating citizens and long-term residents terminating their residence are required to provide detailed information concerning their assets and liabilities, foreign citizenship and residence and foreign address to the Department of State and the IRS. Any person failing to make such a statement will be subject to a penalty for each year during any portion of which such failure continues in an amount equal to the greater of five percent of the tax required to be paid under s 877 for the taxable year ending during such year or US$1,000. The names of expatriating persons shall be published in the Federal Register.

US Federal Generation-skipping Tax

The US Federal generation-skipping transfer tax (the 'GST tax') is generally designed to tax transfers of property or interests in property from grandparents to grandchildren as if the property or interest in property had first passed to the intervening child. If the transfer had in fact been made first from the grandparent to the child, and then from the child to the grandchild, the US Federal estate or gift tax may have been imposed separately on each transfer. In the absence of the GST tax, transfers from grandparents to grandchildren would only be subject to the estate or gift tax once (or perhaps not at all in the case of transfers of non-US property by nonresident aliens of the united States). The GST tax, which may apply to transfers also subject to the US estate or gift tax, is imposed at a flat rate based upon the maximum US estate tax rate (presently 55 per cent).

The IRS issued regulations (the 'Regulations') concerning the application of the GST tax in the context of NRA transferors on December 26, 1995. The Regulations provide that the GST tax will only apply if a transfer by an NRA is subject to either US Federal gift or estate tax. As a result of the Regulations, provided that a trust is created by an NRA and is not directly funded with any US assets or otherwise subject to US Federal gift tax, and provided that the trust is not subject to US Federal estate tax by reason of the death of the grantor, then the trust should not be subject to US Federal GST tax. This favourable GST tax status is a valuable benefit, in that a trust created by an NRA grantor can be designed to benefit multiple generations of the grantor's family without US Federal estate tax or GST tax upon the deaths of the trust beneficiaries. That is, none of the property in the trust would be subject to GST tax upon the death of any trust beneficiaries until such time as the trust terminates and the trust property is distributed to the 'final' beneficiaries outright. The longer a GST trust is kept in place, the greater the tax benefit.

Conclusion

Although the US Federal tax laws which affect offshore trusts and estates planning have changed significantly in the past few years, the impact of these changes may be minimized with proper planning or restructuring. These continue to be substantial US gift, estate and generation-skipping tax advantages to using trusts as a structuring technique.

Mary Ellen Hutton is a partner of Bryan Cave LLP and has advised international and American clients in the areas of tax and trust planning for 18 years. Bryan Cave LLP is one of the 20 largest law firms in the United States. The firm's core practice areas include corporate and business law, litigation, employment and labour relations law, securities, banking and real estate, immigration and tax law.

CORPORATE REGULATIONS & TRUST LAW – A SUMMARY

ALDERNEY	Corporate Regulations
What are the types of companies allowed?	• Companies limited by shares • Companies limited by guarantee • International companies (IC) • General partnerships • Exempt status companies • Hybrid companies
Are there redomiciliation/corporate migration provisions?	Provision does not exist for migration of companies at present but is expected
Is share repurchase allowed?	Yes
How many directors are required?	One (1)
Are resident directors required?	No
How many shareholders are required?	One
Are corporate directors allowed?	Yes
Are bearer shares permitted?	No
Are no par value shares permitted?	Yes
Are nonresident companies permitted?	Yes
Is tax free status guaranteed? How long for?	Yes, no time limit
Are Chinese company names allowed?	There is no provision for this but it is not prohibited
Contact details for the regulatory body governing companies in this jurisdiction	The Registry of Companies Queen Elizabeth II Street St Anne, Alderney, CI
Is beneficial ownership disclosure required?	Required as a condition for incorporation
What is the incorporation fee? What is the annual fee?	Incorporation must be made through an advocate. The total incorporation cost is usually about £500 + annual cost £500.
Is foreign currency accounting allowed?	Yes
Is an annual return required?	Yes – but for a private company after the first return this is very simple
Is an audit required?	Not for private company

ALDERNEY — Trust Law

Is there a trust law? What is the perpetuity period?	No. Alderney trusts are governed by the law of Equity. There is no perpetuity period.
Are there anti-Saunders v Vautier provisions?	Covered by Equity not statute
Are purpose trusts permitted?	No
Are there fraudulent transfer provisions?	Yes under customary law
Are there anti-forced heirship provisions?	No
Are there community property provisions in domestic law?	No
Are there private trust company provisions?	These are not excluded and can be formed as ordinary companies.
What are the registration requirements, if any?	None

ALDERNEY — Treaty Networks

Alderney has limited income tax treaty between Guernsey and UK.

ANGUILLA	Corporate Regulations
What are the types of companies allowed?	• Limited liability companies • Companies limited by guarantee • International business companies (IBC) • General partnerships • Limited partnerships • Exempt status companies • Hybrid companies
Are there redomiciliation/corporate migration provisions?	Yes, by filing and paying the appropriate fees
Is share repurchase allowed?	Yes
How many directors are required?	One (1)
Are resident directors required?	No
How many shareholders are required?	One (1)
Are corporate directors allowed?	Yes
Are bearer shares permitted?	Only in IBC
Are no par value shares permitted?	Yes
Are nonresident companies permitted?	Yes
Is tax free status guaranteed? How long for?	Yes, for an unlimited period
Are Chinese company names allowed?	No
Contact details for the regulatory body governing companies in this jurisdiction	Director of Offshore finance Ministry of Finance Anguilla, West Indies Fax: 809-497-5728
Is beneficial ownership disclosure required?	Not without a court order
What is the incorporation fee?	US$250 – Government fee for IBC
What is the annual fee?	US$200 – Government fee for IBC
Is foreign currency accounting allowed?	Yes
Is an annual return required?	Not for IBC
Is an audit required?	Not for IBC

ANGUILLA — Trust Law

Is there a trust law?	*Trust Ordinance* 1994
What is the date of enactment?	1 January 1995
What is the perpetuity period?	Abolished
Are there anti-Saunders v Vautier provisions?	No
Are purpose trusts permitted?	Yes
Are there fraudulent transfer provisions?	No
Are there anti-forced heirship provisions?	Yes
Are there community property provisions in domestic law?	No
Are there private trust company provisions?	*Offshore Banks and Trust Companies Ordinance* 1991
What are the registration requirements, if any?	A trust company doing offshore trust business must receive a trust company licence. Trusts need not be registered.
What are the exceptions to the registration requirements, if any?	If the settlor is a resident of Anguilla (eg an Anguillian company), no licence for trustee is required.

ANTIGUA & BARBUDA — *Corporate Regulations*

What are the types of companies allowed?	• Limited liability companies • International companies (IC) • Exempt status companies • Chartered companies Being drafted: • Companies limited by guarantee • General partnerships • Limited partnerships • Hybrid companies
Are there redomiciliation/corporate migration provisions?	Inward and outward migration allowed
Is share repurchase allowed?	Yes
Is dual listing permitted?	No
How many directors are required?	Minimum one
Are resident directors required?	No, except for banks, insurance and trust companies
How many shareholders are required?	Minimum one
Are corporate directors allowed?	Yes
Are bearer shares permitted?	Yes, except for banks, insurance and trust companies
Are no par value shares permitted?	Yes
Are nonresident companies permitted?	Yes
Is tax free status guaranteed? How long for?	Yes – 50 years
Are Chinese company names allowed?	Yes, with English translation
Contact details for the regulatory body governing companies in this jurisdiction	Director of International Business Corporations Ministry of Finance High Street, St Johns, Antigua, West Indies
Is beneficial ownership disclosure required?	No, except for banks, insurance and trust companies
What is the incorporation fee? What is the annual fee?	Government fee: US$250.00 US$250.00
Is foreign currency accounting allowed?	Yes
Is an annual return required?	No, except for banks, insurance and trust companies
Is an audit required?	No, except for banks, insurance and trust companies

BAHAMAS	**Corporate Regulations**
What are the types of companies allowed?	• Limited liability companies • Unlimited liability companies • Companies limited by guarantee • International companies (IC) • General partnerships • Limited partnerships • Exempt status companies • Hybrid companies • Chartered companies
Are there redomiciliation/corporate migration provisions?	Yes, a foreign company may be registered in the Bahamas; an IBC may conduct business anywhere.
Is share repurchase allowed?	Yes
Is dual listing permitted?	No, by virtue of ss 65-66 of IBC Act as amended
How many directors are required?	Two for private companies and three for public companies. For an IBC, only one is required.
Are resident directors required?	No
How many shareholders are required?	A minimum of two
Are corporate directors allowed?	Yes
Are bearer shares permitted?	They are under the IBC Act but not the regular Companies Act
Are no par value shares permitted?	Yes
Are nonresident companies permitted?	Yes
Is tax free status guaranteed? How long for?	Twenty years
Are Chinese company names allowed?	Yes
Contact details for the regulatory body governing companies in this jurisdiction	The Registrar General P.O. Box N-532, Nassau, Bahamas
Is beneficial ownership disclosure required?	Only when ordered by the court
What is the incorporation fee?	Incorporation fee is $750.00
What is the annual fee?	Annual licence fee is $350.00 for Bahamian company and $1,000.00 for non-Bahamian, and $100.00 for IBCs.
Is foreign currency accounting allowed?	Yes, with Central Bank approval for domestic companies. IBCs are allowed to hold foreign currency accounts.
Is an annual return required?	Yes, for a regular company
Is an audit required?	Yes, but not for an IBC

BAHAMAS — *Trust Law*

Is there a trust law?	There are several statutes; the most recent is the *Trust (Choice of Governing Law) Act.*
What is the date of enactment?	1989
What is the perpetuity period?	Trust deeds usually refer to 80 years. The Common Law applies.
Are there anti-Saunders v Vautier provisions?	No
Are purpose trusts permitted?	Only in limited circumstances
Are there fraudulent transfer provisions?	Yes
Are there anti-forced heirship provisions?	Yes. *The Trust (Choice of Governing Law) Act*
Are there community property provisions in domestic law?	Yes
Are there private trust company provisions?	Yes
What are the registration requirements, if any?	A payment of $3.50 per page

BAHAMAS — *Treaty Networks*

Bermuda has an exchange of information treaty with the U.S.A. under the *USA-Bermuda Tax Convention Act* 1986.

BARBADOS	Corporate Regulations
What are the types of companies allowed?	• Limited liability companies • International companies (IC) • General partnerships • Limited partnerships • Exempt status companies
Are there redomiciliation/corporate migration provisions?	Yes, redomicile by filing articles of continuance
Is share repurchase allowed?	Yes
Is dual listing permitted?	No
How many directors are required?	One (three if public company)
Are resident directors required?	Only for exempt insurance company and offshore bank
How many shareholders are required?	One
Are corporate directors allowed?	Yes
Are bearer shares permitted?	No
Are no par value shares permitted?	Yes
Are nonresident companies permitted?	Yes
Are Chinese company names allowed?	No
What is the regulatory body governing companies in this jurisdiction?	The Registrar of Companies
Is beneficial ownership disclosure required?	Not for IBC
What is the incorporation fee?	For IBC: US$1000
What is the annual fee?	Approximately US$750
Is foreign currency accounting allowed?	Yes
Is an annual return required?	No
Is an audit required?	No if gross assets less than US$500,000.

BARBADOS — *Trust Law*

Is there a trust law?	*International Trusts Act* 1995
What is the perpetuity period?	Maximum period of 100 years for international trust
Are there anti-Saunders v Vautier provisions?	No
Are purpose trusts permitted?	Yes
Are there fraudulent transfer provisions?	Yes
Are there anti-forced heirship provisions?	Yes
Are there community property provisions in domestic law?	Yes
Are there private trust company provisions?	Yes
What are the registration requirements, if any?	None

BARBADOS — *Treaty Networks*

Barbados has income tax treaties with:

Canada, Finland, Norway, Sweden, Switzerland, UK and USA.

BELIZE	Corporate Regulations
What are the types of companies allowed?	• Limited liability companies • International companies (IC)
Are there redomiciliation/corporate migration provisions?	Yes, redomiciliation allowed under the provisions of the International Belize Companies Act 1990 through continuance.
Is share repurchase allowed?	Yes
Is dual listing permitted?	No
How many directors are required?	One (1)
Are resident directors required?	No
How many shareholders are required?	One (1)
Are corporate directors allowed?	Yes
Are bearer shares permitted?	Yes
Are no par value shares permitted?	Yes
Are nonresident companies permitted?	Yes
Is tax free status guaranteed? How long for?	Not guaranteed
Are Chinese company names allowed?	No
Contact details for the regulatory body governing companies in this jurisdiction	Central Bank of Belize Bishop Street
Is beneficial ownership disclosure required?	No requirement to file shareholders and directors' details but no specific legislation restricting disclosure.
What is the incorporation fee?	US$1300
What is the annual fee?	US$850
Is foreign currency accounting allowed?	Yes
Is an annual return required?	No
Is an audit required?	No

BELIZE	Trust Law
Is there a trust law?	Yes
What is the date of enactment?	23 April 1992
What is the perpetuity period?	120 years
Are there anti-Saunders v Vautier provisions?	No
Are purpose trusts permitted?	Yes
Are there fraudulent transfer provisions?	Yes
Are there anti-forced heirship provisions?	No
Are there community property provisions in domestic law?	No
Are there private trust company provisions?	No
What are the registration requirements, if any?	None

BERMUDA — Corporate Regulations

What are the types of companies allowed?	• Limited liability companies • Unlimited liability companies • Companies limited by guarantee • International companies (IC) • General partnerships • Limited partnerships • Exempt status companies • Hybrid companies • Company incorporated by Act of Parliament
Are there redomiciliation/corporate migration provisions?	• Incorporation of Bermuda holding company and reorganisation of underlying interests • Section 99 scheme of arrangement • Section 104/104A amalgamation
Is share repurchase allowed?	Yes
Is dual listing permitted?	Bermuda law does not prohibit but also depends on listing rules of stock exchanges involved
How many directors are required?	Minimum two (2)
Are resident directors required?	No longer required but remains an option
How many shareholders are required?	One shareholder is permitted
Are corporate directors allowed?	No
Are bearer shares permitted?	No
Are no par value shares permitted?	No
Are nonresident companies permitted?	Yes, referred to as exempted companies
Is tax free status guaranteed? How long for?	Until March 2016
Are Chinese company names allowed?	Use of Chinese names is not prohibited so long as it is used in conjunction with its English name; but there is no facility for registration of Chinese names.
Contact details for the regulatory body governing companies in this jurisdiction	Bermuda Monetary Authority Sofia Building, 48 Church Street Hamilton HM 12, Bermuda Tel: 441-295-5278; Fax: 441-292-7471 The Registrar of Companies Government Administration Building 30 Parliament Street, Hamilton HM 12, Bermuda Tel: 441-295-5151; Fax: 441-292-6640
Is beneficial ownership disclosure required?	Any beneficial ownership disclosed to the Bermuda Monetary Authority is strictly confidential.

BERMUDA	Corporate Regulations (continued)
What is the incorporation fee?	Professional fees US$2,750 exclusive of disbursements
What is the annual fee?	Ranges on a sliding scale from US$1,680 to US$25,000 depending on share capital and share premium account (see Table 1).
Is foreign currency accounting allowed?	Yes, so long as in accordance with generally accepted accounting principles.
Is an annual return required?	Yes, by 31 January of every year
Is an audit required?	Yes, but may be waived with the consent of the directors and shareholders

BERMUDA	Trust Law
Is there a trust law?	Yes. Trustee Act and later enacted Acts
What is the date of enactment?	1975
What is the perpetuity period?	Normally 100 years
Are there anti-Saunders v Vautier provisions?	No
Are purpose trusts permitted?	Yes, Trusts (Special Provisions) Act 1989
Are there fraudulent transfer provisions?	Yes, Conveyancing Amendment Act 1989
Are there anti-forced heirship provisions?	Yes, s 11, Trusts (Special Provisions) Act 1989
Are there community property provisions in domestic law?	No, community property is not recognised.
Are there private trust company provisions?	Yes
What are the registration requirements, if any?	Those usual for a company

BERMUDA — Treaty Networks

Bermuda has an exchange of information treaty with the USA under the USA-Bermuda Tax Convention Act 1986.

BRITISH VIRGIN ISLANDS — *Corporate Regulations*

What are the types of companies allowed?	• Limited liability companies • Unlimited liability companies • Companies limited by guarantee • International companies (IC) • General partnerships • Limited partnerships • Exempt status companies • Hybrid companies • Chartered companies
Are there redomiciliation/corporate migration provisions?	Redomiciliation into and out of BVI allowed
Is share repurchase allowed?	Yes
Is dual listing permitted?	Yes, if permitted by the relevant stock exchanges
How many directors are required?	Minimum of 1
Are resident directors required?	No
How many shareholders are required?	Minimum of 1 – the registered agent subscribes.
Are corporate directors allowed?	Yes
Are bearer shares permitted?	Yes
Are no par value shares permitted?	Yes
Are nonresident companies permitted?	Yes under Cap 285
Is tax free status guaranteed? How long for?	Cap 291 Companies are exempt from all BVI tax
Are Chinese company names allowed?	Yes
Contact details for the regulatory body governing companies in this jurisdiction	Director of Financial Services Financial Services Dept Government of the British Virgin Islands Road Town, Tortola, British Virgin Islands Tel: (1809) 494 6430; Fax: (1809) 494 5016
Is beneficial ownership disclosure required?	No, not without the consent of the director or Court order
What is the incorporation fee? What is the annual fee?	*Cap 291 Companies:* US$300 government registration fee and annual fee of US$300 if the authorised capital does not exceed US$50,000. *Cap 285 Companies:* US$200 registration fee for the first US$10,000 of authorised capital and US$15 for each additional US$10,000.
Is foreign currency accounting allowed?	Yes
Is an annual return required?	No
Is an audit required?	No

BRITISH VIRGIN ISLANDS — Trust Law

Is there a trust law?	Yes
What is the date of enactment?	The *Trustee Ordinance* 1961 – amended by the *Trustee Amendment Act* 1993 together with an English common law underlay.
What is the perpetuity period?	Any period not exceeding 100 years, with a wait and see period
Are there anti-Saunders v Vautier provisions?	No
Are purpose trusts permitted?	Yes
Are there fraudulent transfer provisions?	No, the Statute of Elizabeth has not been overridden
Are there anti-forced heirship provisions?	Yes
Are there community property provisions in domestic law?	No
Are there private trust company provisions?	Yes, the most utilised of these being a BVI company owned by family members can be trustee of a British Virgin Islands trust where the beneficiaries are family members.
What are the registration requirements, if any?	Trusts are not required to be registered
What are the exceptions to the registration requirements, if any?	A US$50.00 trust duty is payable

BRITISH VIRGIN ISLANDS — Treaty Networks

There is a relief of double taxation treaty in place with both Japan and Switzerland.

CAYMAN ISLANDS	Corporate Regulations
What are the types of companies allowed?	• Limited liability companies • Unlimited liability companies • Companies limited by guarantee • General partnerships • Limited partnerships • Exempt status companies • Hybrid companies • Chartered companies
Are there redomiciliation/corporate migration provisions?	Yes, inward and outward corporate mobility allowed
Is share repurchase allowed?	Yes
Is dual listing permitted?	No company may have two domiciles
How many directors are required?	One (1)
Are resident directors required?	No
How many shareholders are required?	One
Are corporate directors allowed?	Yes
Are bearer shares permitted?	Yes, exempted companies only
Are no par value shares permitted?	Yes, exempted companies only
Are nonresident companies permitted?	Yes
Is tax free status guaranteed? How long for?	Yes, 30 years
Are Chinese company names allowed?	Yes, provided they do not include restricted names
What is the regulatory body governing companies in this jurisdiction?	The Registrar of Companies
Is beneficial ownership disclosure required?	Not without an order of the court
What is the incorporation fee?	US$500 for exempted companies US$427 for nonresident companies
What is the annual fee?	US$500 for exempted companies US$427 for nonresident companies
Is foreign currency accounting allowed?	Yes
Is an annual return required?	Yes
Is an audit required?	No

CAYMAN ISLANDS	Trust Law
Is there a trust law?	Yes
What is the date of enactment?	1967
What is the perpetuity period?	150 years for ordinary trust, none for pension trusts
Are there anti-Saunders v Vautier provisions?	Yes
Are purpose trusts permitted?	No, law is in the process of being passed
Are there fraudulent transfer provisions?	Yes
Are there anti-forced heirship provisions?	Yes
Are there community property provisions in domestic law?	No
Are there private trust company provisions?	Yes
What are the registration requirements, if any?	None, exempted trusts may be registered

COOK ISLANDS	*Corporate Regulations*
What are the types of companies allowed?	• Limited liability companies • Unlimited liability companies • Companies limited by guarantee • International companies (IC) • General partnerships • Limited partnerships • Hybrid companies
Are there redomiciliation/corporate migration provisions?	Provisions allow redomiciliation into and out of the Cook Islands
Is share repurchase allowed?	Yes
Is dual listing permitted?	Yes
How many directors are required?	One
Are resident directors required?	No
How many shareholders are required?	One
Are corporate directors allowed?	Yes
Are bearer shares permitted?	Yes
Are no par value shares permitted?	Yes
Are nonresident companies permitted?	Yes, they must be registered as foreign companies
Is tax free status guaranteed? How long for?	Yes, for the life of the company
Are Chinese company names allowed?	Yes
Contact details for the regulatory body governing companies in this jurisdiction	The Secretary Cook Islands Monetary Board PO Box 594, Cook Islands. Tel: (682) 20798; Fax: (682) 21798
Is beneficial ownership disclosure required?	Only with consent of authorised person
What is the incorporation fee?	USD1,000
What is the annual fee?	USD 500
Is foreign currency accounting allowed?	Yes
Is an annual return required?	Yes, unless members resolve otherwise
Is an audit required?	No

COOK ISLANDS	Trust Law
Is there a trust law?	Yes, International Trusts Act
What is the date of enactment?	1984
What is the perpetuity period?	Any period not exceeding 100 years, with a 21 year wait and see period
Are there anti-Saunders v Vautier provisions?	Yes
Are purpose trusts permitted?	Yes
Are there fraudulent transfer provisions?	Yes
Are there anti-forced heirship provisions?	Yes
Are there community property provisions in domestic law?	Yes
Are there private trust company provisions?	Yes
What are the registration requirements, if any?	• Certificate from trust company that upon registration the trust will be an international trust • A notice of the name and registered office of the trust • USD200.00 government registration fee

COSTA RICA	Corporate Regulations
What are the types of companies allowed?	• Limited liability companies • Unlimited liability companies • General partnerships • Limited partnerships • Chartered companies
Are there redomiciliation/corporate migration provisions?	No
Is share repurchase allowed?	Yes
How many directors are required?	3
Are resident directors required?	No
How many shareholders are required?	Two at the moment of incorporation, however, one individual may own all outstanding stock thereon
Are corporate directors allowed?	Yes
Are bearer shares permitted?	No, however, they may be endorsed openly
Are no par value shares permitted?	No
Are nonresident companies permitted?	Yes
Is tax free status guaranteed? How long for?	There is no tax free status
Are Chinese company names allowed?	No, unless it is the name of one or both of the partners
What is the incorporation fee?	Generally, corporations with Share Capital of ¢1.000 (approximately US$5) to ¢100.000 (US$500) are quoted at US$500-US$700. Costs increase according to the amount of Share Capital. Incorporation duties, stamp taxes, corporate books and legal and notarial fees are included in said costs.
What is the annual fee?	None
Is foreign currency accounting allowed?	Yes
Is an annual return required?	Yes
Is an audit required?	Not necessary

COSTA RICA — Trust Law

Is there a trust law?	Yes
What is the date of enactment?	1964
What is the perpetuity period?	Thirty (30) years
Are there anti-Saunders v Vautier provisions?	No
Are purpose trusts permitted?	Yes
Are there fraudulent transfer provisions?	Yes
Are there anti-forced heirship provisions?	No
Are there community property provisions in domestic law?	No
Are there private trust company provisions?	No
What are the registration requirements, if any?	None, except in the case of real estate property

COSTA RICA — Treaty Networks

Costa Rica has a 'Tax Information Exchange Agreement' with the US.

CYPRUS	***Corporate Regulations***
What are the types of companies allowed?	• Limited liability companies • Companies limited by guarantee • General partnerships • Limited partnerships
Are there redomiciliation/corporate migration provisions?	No
Is dual listing permitted?	Yes
How many directors are required?	One (1)
Are resident directors required?	No
How many shareholders are required?	Two (2)
Are corporate directors allowed?	No
Are bearer shares permitted?	No
Are no par value shares permitted?	No
Is tax free status guaranteed? How long for?	There is no tax free status
Are Chinese company names allowed?	No
What is the regulatory body governing companies in this jurisdiction?	Central Bank of Cyprus
Is beneficial ownership disclosure required?	Mandatory on incorporation but not a matter of public record
What is the incorporation fee?	CPY£650
What is the annual fee?	CPY£750
Is an annual return required?	Yes
Is an audit required?	Yes

CYPRUS — Trust Law

Is there a trust law?	Yes, Trustee Law 1955
What is the perpetuity period?	100 years
Are there anti-Saunders v Vautier provisions?	No
Are purpose trusts permitted?	Yes
Are there fraudulent transfer provisions?	Yes
Are there anti-forced heirship provisions?	Yes
Are there community property provisions in domestic law?	No
Are there private trust company provisions?	Yes
What are the registration requirements, if any?	No requirement to register

CYPRUS — Treaty Networks

Cyprus has tax treaties with the following:

Canada, France, Germany, Sweden, United Kingdom, United States.

Note: Tax treaty benefits are limited by discriminatory clauses within the tax treaty or by practices of the relevant revenue departments of the country in question.

GIBRALTAR — *Corporate Regulations*

What are the types of companies allowed?	• Limited liability companies • Unlimited liability companies • Companies limited by guarantee • International companies (IC) • Limited partnerships • Exempt status companies • Hybrid companies • Chartered companies (limited by guarantee with share capital)
Are there redomiciliation/corporate migration provisions?	Only by Ordinance: • In from the European Union, the European Economic Area, any Commonwealth country, any British dependent territory, Hong Kong, Panama and Liberia • Out only to the European Union and the European Economic Area
Is share repurchase allowed?	No
Is dual listing permitted?	Yes
How many directors are required?	• 1 or more for private companies (subject to the secretary being a distinct person) • 2 or more for public companies
Are resident directors required?	No
How many shareholders are required?	• 1 to a max of 50 for private companies (if permitted by the Articles of Assoc) • 7 or more for public companies
Are corporate directors allowed?	Yes
Are bearer shares permitted?	• No for private companies (subject to opinion that Exempt Companies may) • Yes for public companies
Are no par value shares permitted?	No
Are nonresident companies permitted?	Yes
Is tax free status guaranteed? How long for?	25 years – exempt companies
Are Chinese company names allowed?	Yes, if written phonetically in Latin
Contact details for the regulatory body governing companies in this jurisdiction	The Registrar of Companies Companies House (Gibraltar) Limited 317 Main Street, Gibraltar Tel: (350) 78193; Fax: (350) 44436
Is beneficial ownership disclosure required?	Only by order of Court

GIBRALTAR	Corporate Regulations (continued)
What is the incorporation fee?	• £500 to £750 depending whether ordinary, exempt or qualifying • £300 to £650 depending on services provided
What is the annual fee?	• £26 annual return filing fee • £200 to £225 annual exempt tax
Is foreign currency accounting allowed?	Yes, except for Swiss Francs
Is an annual return required?	Yes
Is an audit required?	Yes

GIBRALTAR	Trust Law
Is there a trust law?	English principles of equity, some statutes.
What is the perpetuity period?	100 years
Are there anti-Saunders v Vautier provisions?	No
Are purpose trusts permitted?	Only charitable
Are there fraudulent transfer provisions?	Yes
Are there anti-forced heirship provisions?	No
Are there community property provisions in domestic law?	No
Are there private trust company provisions?	Licence required if offering trustee services to the public
What are the registration requirements, if any?	None. Optional for Asset Protection Trusts to take advantage of amendments to the Bankruptcy Ordinance.

GUERNSEY	Corporate Regulations
What are the types of companies allowed?	• Limited liability companies • Unlimited liability companies • International companies (IC) • General partnerships • Limited partnerships • Exempt status companies Enabling legislation has been drafted for hybrid companies.
Are there redomiciliation/corporate migration provisions?	No. Enabling legislation has been drafted. Enactment due late 1996/early 1997.
Is share repurchase allowed?	No, Enabling legislation is planned
Is dual listing permitted?	Yes
How many directors are required?	One
Are resident directors required?	No
How many shareholders are required?	Two
Are corporate directors allowed?	Yes
Are bearer shares permitted?	No
Are no par value shares permitted?	No. Enabling legislation has been drafted. Enactment due late 1996/early 1997.
Are nonresident companies permitted?	Yes, provided beneficial owners are non resident
Is tax free status guaranteed? How long for?	Annual application for tax exempt status is required
Are Chinese company names allowed?	No
What is the regulatory body governing companies in this jurisdiction?	Guernsey Financial Services Commission
Is beneficial ownership disclosure required?	Beneficial ownership disclosure is required, but confidential to Regulatory Authority
What is the incorporation fee?	£550
What is the annual fee?	£110 Annual Return Fee £500 Exempt Company Licence Fee
Is foreign currency accounting allowed?	Yes
Is an annual return required?	Yes
Is an audit required?	Not necessarily depending on the company activities

GUERNSEY — *Trust Law*

Is there a trust law?	Yes. The Trusts (Guernsey) Law 1989 as amended
What is the date of enactment?	21 March 1989
What is the perpetuity period?	100 years
Are there anti-Saunders v Vautier provisions?	No
Are purpose trusts permitted?	Yes but there must be an identifiable or ascertainable beneficiary. Specific legislation under discussion.
Are there fraudulent transfer provisions?	Yes the Directors of a corporate trustee are deemed to be guarantors of the trustee in respect of a breach of trust.
Are there anti-forced heirship provisions?	Yes
Are there community property provisions in domestic law?	No
Are there private trust company provisions?	Not specifically. Private or managed trust companies may be formed with the approval of the Guernsey Financial Services commission.
What are the registration requirements, if any?	None

GUERNSEY — *Treaty Networks*

Guernsey has double tax agreements with the UK and Jersey.

ISLE OF MAN	Corporate Regulations
What are the types of companies allowed?	• Limited liability companies • Unlimited liability companies • Companies limited by guarantee • International companies (IC) • General partnerships • Limited partnerships • Exempt status companies • Hybrid companies • Chartered companies
Are there redomiciliation/corporate migration provisions?	None at present; legislation pending
Is share repurchase allowed?	Yes
How many directors are required?	Two
Are resident directors required?	Yes, if the company has exempt status
How many shareholders are required?	One for private companies; two for public companies
Are corporate directors allowed?	No
Are bearer shares permitted?	No
Are no par value shares permitted?	No
Are nonresident companies permitted?	Yes
Is tax free status guaranteed? How long for?	There is no tax free status
Are Chinese company names allowed?	No
Contact details for the regulatory body governing companies in this jurisdiction	Isle of Man Financial Supervision Commission 1-4 Goldie Terrace, Douglas, Isle of Man, IM1 1EB.
Is beneficial ownership disclosure required?	No
What is the incorporation fee?	£160 minimum
What is the annual fee?	Annual Return filing fee: £45 Nonresident company duty: £660 Exempt company duty: £300 International company duty: £300 minimum
Is foreign currency accounting allowed?	Yes
Is an annual return required?	Yes
Is an audit required?	Only for resident companies

ISLE OF MAN — *Trust Law*

Is there a trust law?	Case law modified by statute. The Trustee Act 1961 is the primary legislation.
What is the perpetuity period?	80 years
Are there anti-Saunders v Vautier provisions?	No
Are purpose trusts permitted?	Yes
Are there fraudulent transfer provisions?	Yes
Are there anti-forced heirship provisions?	Yes
Are there private trust company provisions?	Must be approved by the High Court.
What are the registration requirements, if any?	None

ISLE OF MAN — *Treaty Networks*

The Isle of Man has an income tax treaty with United Kingdom.

JERSEY	**Corporate Regulations**
What are the types of companies allowed?	• Limited liability companies • International companies (IC) • General partnerships • Limited partnerships • Exempt status companies Legislation pending: • Unlimited liability companies • Companies limited by guarantee • Hybrid companies
Are there redomiciliation/corporate migration provisions?	None, legislation pending
Is share repurchase allowed?	Yes
Is dual listing permitted?	Yes in practice
How many directors are required?	Public companies – minimum two Private companies – minimum one
Are resident directors required?	No
How many shareholders are required?	Public companies – Minimum two Private companies – Minimum one
Are corporate directors allowed?	No
Are bearer shares permitted?	No
Are no par value shares permitted?	No, legislation pending
Are nonresident companies permitted?	Yes, but beneficial owners must be nonresident
Is tax free status guaranteed? How long for?	Companies owned by non-residents are tax exempt without time limit in return for the payment of an annual fee.
Are Chinese company names allowed?	No, English translation is possible however
Contact details for the regulatory body governing companies in this jurisdiction	States of Jersey Company Registrar Tel: +44 1534 603000; Fax: +44 1534 603610
Is beneficial ownership disclosure required?	Yes, but this is confidential to the Regulatory Authorities and is not divulged to other parties without a Jersey Court order.
What is the incorporation fee?	Professional fee: £450-1500 Registration fee: £120 Duty on issue of shares: £50 minimum
What is the annual fee?	Annual return: £120; Exempt Tax: £600
Is foreign currency accounting allowed?	Yes
Is an annual return required?	Yes
Is an audit required?	Public company – Yes; Private company – No.

JERSEY — Trust Law

Is there a trust law?	Yes. The Trusts (Jersey) Law 1984
What is the perpetuity period?	100 years
Are there anti-Saunders v Vautier provisions?	No
Are purpose trusts permitted?	Yes
What are the most common types of trust?	Discretionary Trust Charitable Trust Interest in Possession Trust Accumulation and Maintenance Trust
Are there fraudulent transfer provisions?	No, but the Bankruptcy (Desastre) (Jersey) Law 1990 does provide assistance on public policy.
Are there anti-forced heirship provisions?	Yes
Are there community property provisions in domestic law?	No
Are there private trust company provisions?	No. In practice private trust companies are permitted in certain circumstances.
What are the registration requirements, if any?	None
Can the settlor be a beneficiary?	Yes
Can beneficiaries by added/removed?	Yes
Does a beneficiary have to be informed that a trusts exists and that he/she has an interest thereunder?	No

JERSEY — Treaty Networks

Jersey has double tax treaties with the UK and Guernsey and a limited treaty with France relating to aircraft and shipping profits.

JORDAN	Corporate Regulations
What are the types of companies allowed?	• General partnership • Limited partnership • Joint venture • Limited liability company • Limited partnership in shares • Public shareholding companies • Offshore companies (exempt companies) • Foreign companies
Is share repurchase allowed?	A shareholder selling his or some of his shares is allowed to repurchase those shares if he wishes.
Is dual listing permitted?	Dual listing is not permitted by virtue of Sections 65 and 66 of IBC Act as amended.
How many directors are required?	• General partnership: One director either from among the partners or outside the partners. • Limited Partnership: managed by the General Partners in the company. • Joint venture: the management is according to the agreement between the partners. • Limited liability company: One director or a Board of Directors not less than two and not more than five. • Public shareholding company: a Board of Directors not less than seven members and not more than thirteen.
How many shareholders are required?	No specific number of shareholders required.
Are Chinese company names allowed?	No
What is the incorporation fee? What is the annual fee?	Incorporation fees and annual fees differ from one company to another
Is foreign currency accounting allowed?	No
Is an annual return required?	Yes
Is an audit required?	Yes

JORDAN — Trust Law

Is there a trust law?	No
Are there anti-Saunders v Vautier provisions?	No
Are purpose trusts permitted?	Yes
Are there fraudulent transfer provisions?	Yes
Are there anti-forced heirship provisions?	Yes
Are there community property provisions in domestic law?	Yes
Are there private trust company provisions?	No
What are the registration requirements, if any?	None

LABUAN	***Corporate Regulations***
What are the types of companies allowed?	• Limited liability companies • Limited partnerships (legislation proposed)
Are there redomiciliation/corporate migration provisions?	Application by a Labuan Trust Company on behalf of transferring company to Registrar of Companies, accompanied by supporting materials in particular showing requisite consent of shareholders, debenture holders and creditors of the transferring company as well as the authorization of the proper authorities of the jurisdiction of incorporation.
Is share repurchase allowed?	Yes
Is dual listing permitted?	No, Labuan stock exchange cannot list on Kuala Lumpur Stock Exchange
How many directors are required?	One (1)
Are resident directors required?	No, but if any resident director is appointed, he must be an officer of a Labuan Trust Company
How many shareholders are required?	One (1)
Are corporate directors allowed?	Yes
Are bearer shares permitted?	No
Are no par value shares permitted?	No
Are nonresident companies permitted?	Yes
Is tax free status guaranteed? How long for?	No formal tax free status
Are Chinese company names allowed?	No
Contact details for the regulatory body governing companies in this jurisdiction	Labuan Offshore Financial Services Authority (LOFSA) Level 17, Main Office Tower Financial Park Labuan, Jalan Merdeka 87000 Federal Territory of Labuan Tel: (6087) 413 166 Fax: (6087) 413 328 Regional Registrar of Companies Ministry of Domestic Trade and Consumer Affairs Lot B Level 4 Wisma Oceanic Jalan OKK Awang Besar 87008 Federal Territory of Labuan Tel: (6087) 414 100 Fax: (6087) 414 152
Is beneficial ownership disclosure required?	May be required by law
What is the (i) incorporation fee? (ii) annual fee?	Offshore companies/redomiciled companies: (i) RM1,000-RM5,000 (ii) RM2,000 Foreign offshore companies: (i) RM6,000. (ii) RM5,000.

LABUAN	Corporate Regulations (continued)
Is foreign currency accounting allowed?	Yes
Is an annual return required?	Yes
Is an audit required?	Yes, unless company does not engage in offshore banking or insurance or invite public subscription for shares and debentures, and shareholders resolve not to appoint auditors.

LABUAN	Trust Law
Is there a trust law?	*Offshore Trusts Act* 1996
What is the perpetuity period?	100 years
Are there anti-Saunders v Vautier provisions?	No
Are purpose trusts permitted?	Not unless charitable.
Are there fraudulent transfer provisions?	No
Are there anti-forced heirship provisions?	No
Are there community property provisions in domestic law?	Yes
Are there private trust company provisions?	No
What are the registration requirements, if any?	None

LABUAN — Treaty Networks

Malaysia has double taxation treaties with:

Albania, Australia, Austria, Bangladesh, Belgium, Canada, China , Denmark, Finland, France, Germany, Hungary, India, Indonesia, Italy, Japan, Mauritius, Mongolia, the Netherlands, New Zealand, Norway, Pakistan, Papua New Guinea, Philippines, Poland, Romania, Singapore, South Korea, Sri Lanka, Sudan, Sweden, Switzerland, Thailand, USSR, United Kingdom, Yugoslavia, Zimbabwe.

Also limited agreement with the United States of America and unratified agreement with Iran.

LIECHTENSTEIN	Corporate Regulations
What are the types of companies allowed?	• Limited liability companies • Unlimited liability companies • General partnerships • Limited partnerships The Establishment (Hybrid companies)
Are there redomiciliation/corporate migration provisions?	Escape clause possible
Is share repurchase allowed?	Generally no
Is dual listing permitted?	Yes
How many directors are required?	One
Are resident directors required?	Yes
How many shareholders are required?	One
Are corporate directors allowed?	Yes
Are bearer shares permitted?	Yes
Are no par value shares permitted?	Yes
Are nonresident companies permitted?	No, but companies with no commercial activity in Liechtenstein are not subject to profit tax
Is tax free status guaranteed? How long for?	As long as the companies do not have commercial activity in the country
Are Chinese company names allowed?	No
Contact details for the regulatory body governing companies in this jurisdiction	Companies Registration Office Oeffentlichkeitsregisteramt FL-9490 Vaduz, Liechtenstein
Is beneficial ownership disclosure required?	No
What is the incorporation fee?	Approximately CHF4,100 plus a stamp duty of 3% on paid-up capital
What is the annual fee?	Approximately CHF4,800 including Board of Directors fee, registration fee and capital tax
Is foreign currency accounting allowed?	Yes
Is an annual return required?	Yes
Is an audit required?	Yes

LIECHTENSTEIN — Trust Law

Is there a trust law?	Yes
What is the date of enactment?	April 10, 1928
What is the perpetuity period?	Limit must be stated but no specific period is set by law
Are there anti-Saunders v Vautier provisions?	No
Are purpose trusts permitted?	Yes
Are there fraudulent transfer provisions?	Yes, Conveyancing Amendment Act, 1989
Are there anti-forced heirship provisions?	No
Are there community property provisions in domestic law?	No
Are there private trust company provisions?	No, but private trust companies are allowed
What are the registration requirements, if any?	Trust created for a period of longer than 12 months must be recorded in the public register
What are the exceptions to the registration requirements, if any?	Trust with the Trust Deed deposited with the Public Register is exempt from registration

LIECHTENSTEIN — Treaty Networks

Liechtenstein has only one income tax treaty with Austria, but it does not apply to domiciliary enterprises and holding companies.

LUXEMBOURG — *Corporate Regulations*

What are the types of companies allowed?	• Limited liability companies • General partnerships • Limited partnerships
Are there redomiciliation/corporate migration provisions?	Yes, by shareholders' resolution
Is share repurchase allowed?	No
Is dual listing permitted?	No
How many directors are required?	3 for SA, 1 for SARL
Are resident directors required?	No
How many shareholders are required?	2 for SA, 1 for SARL
Are corporate directors allowed?	Yes
Are bearer shares permitted?	Only for SA
Are no par value shares permitted?	Yes
Are nonresident companies permitted?	No
Is tax free status guaranteed? How long for?	There is no tax free status
Are Chinese company names allowed?	No
Is beneficial ownership disclosure required?	Yes
What is the incorporation fee? What is the annual fee?	Variable, depending on type of company and its capital
Is foreign currency accounting allowed?	Yes
Is an annual return required?	No
Is an audit required?	Depending on size and turnover of company

LUXEMBOURG — *Treaty Networks*

Luxembourg has signed income tax treaties with:

Austria, Belgium, Brazil, Bulgaria, Canada, China, Czech Republic, Denmark, Finland, France, Germany, Hungary, Indonesia, Ireland, Italy, Japan, Korea, Malta, Mauritius, Morocco, Netherlands, Norway, Romania, Singapore, Slovakia, Spain, Sweden, Switzerland, UK, USA.

MADEIRA	Corporate Regulations
What are the types of companies allowed?	Limited liability companies
Are there redomiciliation/corporate migration provisions?	Redomiciliation/corporate migration allowed
Is share repurchase allowed?	Yes
Is dual listing permitted?	No
How many directors are required?	One
Are resident directors required?	Yes, one
How many shareholders are required?	One
Are corporate directors allowed?	No
Are bearer shares permitted?	Yes for Sociedades Anónimas
Are no par value shares permitted?	No
Are nonresident companies permitted?	No
Is tax free status guaranteed? How long for?	Until 2011
Are Chinese company names allowed?	Foreign names are allowed but with roman alphabet
Contact details for the regulatory body governing companies in this jurisdiction	S.D.M., Rua Imperatriz D. Amélia, Apartado 4164 9052 Funchal Tel: 351 91 225466; Fax: 351 91 228950
Is beneficial ownership disclosure required?	No
What is the incorporation fee?	US$2,750
What is the annual fee?	US$1,750
Is foreign currency accounting allowed?	No
Is an annual return required?	Yes
Is an audit required?	Audits required for S.A.

MADEIRA — Trust Law

Is there a trust law?	Yes
What is the date of enactment?	3rd October 1988
What is the perpetuity period?	Depends on the jurisdiction chosen
Are there anti-Saunders v Vautier provisions?	Depends on the jurisdiction chosen
Are purpose trusts permitted?	Yes
Are there fraudulent transfer provisions?	Depends on the jurisdiction chosen
Are there anti-forced heirship provisions?	Depends on the jurisdiction chosen
Are there community property provisions in domestic law?	Depends on the jurisdiction chosen
Are there private trust company provisions?	Yes
What are the registration requirements, if any?	Trusts must be registered
What are the exceptions to the registration requirements, if any?	None

MADEIRA — Treaty Networks

Madeira has double taxation treaties with:

Austria, Belgium, Brazil, Denmark, Finland, France, Germany, Italy, Japan, Mozambique, Norway, Spain, Switzerland and the United Kingdom.

MALTA — *Corporate Regulations*

What are the types of companies allowed?	• General partnerships • Limited partnerships • Limited liability companies • International trading companies • International holding companies • Limited liability companies with variable share capital • Offshore companies may be registered until the end of 1996 and will have standing until 2004
Are there redomiciliation/corporate migration provisions?	Redomiciliation provisions only exist with respect to offshore companies. Offshore companies may be redomiciled in a jurisdiction with a similar legal system and which accepts the possibility of redomiciliation.
Is share repurchase allowed?	Yes
Is dual listing permitted?	Applications for dual listing are pending, awaiting the publications of bye-laws by the Centre.
How many directors are required?	Minimum of 1
Are resident directors required?	No
How many shareholders are required?	Minimum 2 for both public and private companies and 1 for private exempt companies.
Are corporate directors allowed?	Yes
Are bearer shares permitted?	Private companies – No; public companies – Yes
Are no par value shares permitted?	No
Are nonresident companies permitted?	No
Is tax free status guaranteed? How long for?	In the case of offshore companies there is a 10 year guarantee for tax free status for holding companies and 5% taxation for trading companies.
Are Chinese company names allowed?	The phonetic equivalent of Chinese company names may be registered.
Contact details for the regulatory body governing companies in this jurisdiction	Malta Financial Service Centre Attard, Malta Tel: 35644-1155; Fax: 35644-1188
Is beneficial ownership disclosure required?	Licensed nominees are permitted. Beneficial ownership is not communicated to any authority.
What is the incorporation fee?	Varies between US$300 and US$500
What is the annual fee?	US$75

MALTA	Corporate Regulations (continued)
Is foreign currency accounting allowed?	Yes
Is an annual return required?	Yes
Is an audit required?	Yes

MALTA	Trust Law
Is there a trust law?	Yes. The Offshore Trusts Act [ACT XXXV 1988]
What is the date of enactment?	30 June 1989
What is the perpetuity period?	100 years, unless terminated sooner
Are there anti-Saunders v Vautier provisions?	No
Are purpose trusts permitted?	Not specifically, but arguably possible
Are there fraudulent transfer provisions?	Yes
Are there anti-forced heirship provisions?	Not for non-Maltese domiciliary
Are there community property provisions in domestic law?	Not for non-Maltese domiciliary
Are there private trust company provisions?	No
What are the registration requirements, if any?	Registration shall be effected by filing with the Malta Financial Services Centre: i) a certified copy of the trust instrument ii) a declaration by the Nominee Company acting as trustee of the trust that the trust satisfies the condition of the Act in order that it may be an offshore trust.
What are the exceptions to the registration requirements, if any?	There is an exception in the case of constructive trusts

MAURITIUS	***Corporate Regulations***
What are the types of companies allowed?	• Limited liability companies • Unlimited liability companies • Companies limited by guarantee • International companies (IC) • Offshore companies (OC) • Investment companies (for open ended structures) • Limited life companies (with characteristics of a partnership for US tax purposes)
Are there redomiciliation/corporate migration provisions?	Yes, Applicable only to OC and IC
Is share repurchase allowed?	Applicable only to OC and IC
Is dual listing permitted?	Applicable only to OC
How many directors are required?	Minimum 2 directors
Are resident directors required?	Yes, at least 2 for OC acceding to DTA benefits.
How many shareholders are required?	OC: minimum of two individual shareholders or one corporate; IC: minimum of one
Are corporate directors allowed?	Only for IC
Are bearer shares permitted?	Only for IC
Are no par value shares permitted?	Only for IC
Are nonresident companies permitted?	Only for IC
Is tax free status guaranteed? How long for?	Indefinitely for IC; OC incorporated before July 1988 can elect to pay tax at rates of 0-35%; OC incorporated after July 1988 will be imposed 15% tax with relief from deemed foreign tax credits.
Are Chinese company names allowed?	Only for OC
What is the regulatory body governing companies in this jurisdiction?	Registrar of Companies c/o Director of the MOBAA for offshore matters.
Is beneficial ownership disclosure required?	Beneficial ownership to be disclosed to the authorities (except for IC) but confidentiality protected by statute.
What is the incorporation fee? What is the annual fee?	Fees are payable to MOBAA. Incorporation fee: IC - USD100; OC - USD500 Annual fee: IC - USD100; OC - USD1500
Is foreign currency accounting allowed?	Yes
Is an annual return required?	Yes for OC
Is an audit required?	Yes for OC

MAURITIUS — Trust Law

Is there a trust law?	Offshore Trusts Act 1992; domestic trust legislation not applicable to offshore trusts.
What is the date of enactment?	9 June 1992
What is the perpetuity period?	100 years, except for charitable offshore trusts and purpose offshore trusts which have no limitation period.
Are there anti-Saunders v Vautier provisions?	Yes
Are purpose trusts permitted?	Yes
Are there fraudulent transfer provisions?	Trust property which has been charged or dealt with in breach of trust or property into which it has been converted may be followed and recovered in certain circumstances.
Are there anti-forced heirship provisions?	Yes
Are there private trust company provisions?	Yes. A trust company can be registered as an offshore company with MOBAA.
What are the registration requirements, if any?	Registration of a declaration of trust with the MOBAA. The trust deed not be disclosed to the MOBAA.
What are the exceptions to the registration requirements, if any?	None

MALTA — Treaty Networks

Mauritius has double taxation treaties for income tax, interests and royalties with the following countries:

France, India, UK, Germany, Zimbabwe, Sweden, Malaysia, Swaziland, Italy, China, Pakistan, South Africa, Madagascar, Luxembourg, Namibia, Belgium, Singapore, Botswana, Kuwait, Lesotho, Sri Lanka and Russia.

Treaties are presently being negotiated with Oman, Vietnam, Canada, Greece, Uganda, Malawi, Portugal and Ireland.

NETHERLANDS — *Corporate Regulations*

What are the types of companies allowed?	• Limited liability companies • General partnerships • Limited partnerships
Are there redomiciliation/corporate migration provisions?	Yes, transfer of management registration at the Chamber of Commerce
Is share repurchase allowed?	Yes, but limited
Is dual listing permitted?	Yes
How many directors are required?	At least one
Are resident directors required?	No
How many shareholders are required?	At least one
Are corporate directors allowed?	Yes
Are bearer shares permitted?	Yes, depending on type of company
Are no par value shares permitted?	No
Are nonresident companies permitted?	Yes
Is tax free status guaranteed? How long for?	No
Are Chinese company names allowed?	Yes, if written in Latin characters
What is the regulatory body governing companies in this jurisdiction?	Chambers of Commerce
Is beneficial ownership disclosure required?	Yes
What is the incorporation fee?	No official fees
What is the annual fee?	No official fees
Is foreign currency accounting allowed?	Yes, but Nlg accounts should also be available
Is an annual return required?	Yes
Is an audit required?	Depends on size

NETHERLANDS — *Treaty Networks*

The Netherlands has concluded double taxation treaties with:

Armenia, Australia, Austria, Azerbajan, Bangladesh, Belarus, Belgium, Brazil, Bosnia-Herzegovena, Bulgaria, Canada, China, Croatia, Czech Rep., Denmark, Estonia, Finland, France, Georgia, Germany, Greece, Hungary, India, Indonesia, Ireland, Israel, Italy, Japan, Kazachstan, Korea (S), Kyrgystan, Latvia, Lithuania, Luxembourg, Macedonia, Malaysia, Malawi, Malta, Mexico, Moldova, Morocco, Netherland Antilles (and Aruba), New Zealand, Nigeria, Norway, Pakistan, Philippines, Poland, Romania, Russia, Serbia, Singapore, Slovakia, Slovenia, South Africa, Spain, Sri Lanka, Surinam, Sweden, Switzerland, Tajikstan, Thailand, Tunisia, United States, Uzbekistan, Venezuela, Vietnam, Zambia and Zimbabwe.

SINGAPORE	Corporate Regulations
What are the types of companies allowed?	• Limited liability companies • Unlimited liability companies • Companies limited by guarantee • General partnerships
Are there redomiciliation/corporate migration provisions?	No
Is share repurchase allowed?	No
Is dual listing permitted?	Yes, if permitted by the relevant stock exchanges
How many directors are required?	Two (2)
Are resident directors required?	One (1) who is 'ordinarily resident'
How many shareholders are required?	Two (2) unless sole corporate shareholder (ie parent company of wholly owned subsidiary)
Are corporate directors allowed?	No
Are bearer shares permitted?	No
Are no par value shares permitted?	No
Are nonresident companies permitted?	Yes
Is tax free status guaranteed? How long for?	No grant of tax free status
Are Chinese company names allowed?	Yes
Contact details for the regulatory body governing companies in this jurisdiction	The Registry of Companies and Businesses (RCB) 10 Anson Road #05-01/15 International Plaza Singapore 079903 Tel: (65) 227 8551; Fax: (65) 2251676
Is beneficial ownership disclosure required?	No
What is the incorporation fee?	Minimum S$1,200, depending on nominal capital. S$600 no share capital.
What is the annual fee?	None
Is foreign currency accounting allowed?	No
Is an annual return required?	Yes
Is an audit required?	Yes

SINGAPORE — Trust Law

Is there a trust law?	English common law governs
What is the perpetuity period?	Common law rule
Are there anti-Saunders v Vautier provisions?	No
Are purpose trusts permitted?	Not unless charitable
Are there fraudulent transfer provisions?	No
Are there anti-forced heirship provisions?	No
Are there community property provisions in domestic law?	Yes
Are there private trust company provisions?	No
What are the registration requirements, if any?	None

SINGAPORE — Treaty Networks

Singapore has double taxation treaties with:

Australia, Bangladesh, Belgium, Canada, Chile, China, Denmark, Finland, France, Germany, India, Indonesia, Israel, Italy, Japan, Luxembourg, Malaysia, Mauritius, Mexico, the Netherlands, New Zealand, Norway, Pakistan, Papua New Guinea, Philippines, Poland, Saudi Arabia, South Korea, Sri Lanka, Sweden, Switzerland, Taiwan, Thailand, United Arab Emirates, United Kingdom, United States of America, Vietnam.

SWITZERLAND — Corporate Regulations

What are the types of companies allowed?	• Stock corporation • Limited liability company • Co-operative • Partnership with unlimited liability
Is share repurchase allowed?	Yes
Are resident directors required?	Yes
How many shareholders are required?	Minimum one
Are corporate directors allowed?	Yes
Are bearer shares permitted?	Yes
Is tax free status guaranteed? How long for?	Tax exemption applies in various cantons
What is the incorporation fee?	CHF5,500-7,000 for a company with capital of CHF100,000
Is an annual return required?	Yes, biannual in certain cantons
Is an audit required?	Annual audits are required but limited liability companies have the choice

SWITZERLAND — Treaty Networks

Switzerland has double tax treaties with:

Australia, Austria, Belgium, Canada, Denmark, Egypt, Finland, France, Germany, Greece, Hungary, Indonesia, Iceland, Ireland, Italy, Ivory Coast, Japan, Korea, Malaysia, Netherlands, New Zealand, Norway, Pakistan, Portugal, Singapore, Spain, Sri Lanka, South Africa, Sweden, Trinidad and Tobago, United Kingdom, and USA.

TURKS & CAICOS ISLANDS — *Corporate Regulations*

What are the types of companies allowed?	• Limited liability companies • Unlimited liability companies • Companies limited by guarantee • International companies (IC) • Limited partnerships • Exempt status companies • Hybrid companies
Are there redomiciliation/corporate migration provisions?	Yes, lodge memorandum and articles of association; shareholder consent; and appoint resident representative (S 205/206).
Is share repurchase allowed?	Yes
Is dual listing permitted?	Yes
How many directors are required?	One
Are resident directors required?	No
How many shareholders are required?	One
Are corporate directors allowed?	Yes
Are bearer shares permitted?	Yes
Are no par value shares permitted?	Yes
Are nonresident companies permitted?	Yes
Is tax free status guaranteed? How long for?	Twenty years
Are Chinese company names allowed?	Yes
Contact details for the regulatory body governing companies in this jurisdiction	Mr JDK Lawrence F.S.C. Superintendant PO Box 173, Post office Building Front Street, Grand Turk Tel: 8094 62791 Fax: 8094 62821
Is beneficial ownership disclosure required?	No. However companies that are licensed financial institutions do but for the sole purpose of regulatory cooperation.
What is the incorporation fee?	Exempt company – US$100 Ordinary company – US$275
What is the annual fee?	Exempt company – US$300 Ordinary company – US$250 (For min authorised share capital of US$5000)
Is foreign currency accounting allowed?	Yes
Is an annual return required?	Not of a financial nature
Is an audit required?	No

TURKS & CAICOS ISLAND	Trust Law
Is there a trust law?	Yes
What is the date of enactment?	1990
What is the perpetuity period?	No provision within ordinance but can be specified in the individual trust deed
Are there anti-Saunders v Vautier provisions?	No
Are purpose trusts permitted?	Yes
Are there fraudulent transfer provisions?	Yes
Are there anti-forced heirship provisions?	Yes
Are there community property provisions in domestic law?	No
Are there private trust company provisions?	No
What are the registration requirements, if any?	Settlor has the option to register the trust if he wants

URUGUAY — *Corporate Regulations*

What are the types of companies allowed?	International Companies with Limited Liability (S.A.F.I.)
Are there redomiciliation/corporate migration provisions?	Redomiciliation/corporate migration is technically possible but complicated
Is share repurchase allowed?	Yes
How many directors are required?	One
Are resident directors required?	No
How many shareholders are required?	One
Are corporate directors allowed?	Yes
Are bearer shares permitted?	Yes
Are no par value shares permitted?	No
Are nonresident companies permitted?	No
Are Chinese company names allowed?	Yes, but not Chinese characters
What is the regulatory body governing companies in this jurisdiction?	Inspección General de Hacienda
Is beneficial ownership disclosure required?	No
What is the incorporation fee?	Variable
What is the annual fee?	0.3% of taxable base
Is foreign currency accounting allowed?	Yes
Is an annual return required?	Yes
Is an audit required?	Yes

URUGUAY — *Treaty Networks*

Uruguay has signed taxation treaties with Germany and Hungary.

DIRECTORY

DIRECTORY

Anchor Trustees International Limited	7th Floor 70 Symonds Street Auckland 1 New Zealand PO Box 3639 Auckland 1 New Zealand	Tel (64) 9 373 4450 Fax (64) 9 366 0343 *see p 231*
Appleby Spurling & Kempe	2217 Jardine House 1 Connaught Place Central Hong Kong	Tel (852) 2523 8123 Fax (852) 2524 5548 *see p 65*
Basel Trust Corporation (Channel Islands) Limited	PO Box 484 Basel House St Helier Jersey JE4 5SS British Isles	Tel (44) 1534 601 900 Fax (44) 1534 607 876 Email baseltrustjersey@compuserve.com *see p 129*
Bryan Cave LLP	Suite 2106 Lippo Tower Lippo Centre 89 Queensway Central Hong Kong	Tel (852) 2522 2821 Fax (852) 2522 3830 *see p 243*

Caribbean Management & Trust Co Ltd	PO Box 2176 60 Nevis Street St John's Antigua	Tel (268) 462 2176 Fax (268) 462 3077 *see p 41*
Citco Barbados Limited	Whitepark House White Park Road PO Box 806E Bridgetown Barbados	Tel (246) 427 8716 Fax (246) 426 8913 Contact *Mary Ellen Bourque* *see p 53*
Citco (Luxembourg) S.A.	5 Boulevard Royal Royal Rome II B.P 332 L-2013 Luxembourg	Tel (352) 472 323 Fax (352) 472 473 Contact *Ariane Slinger* *see p 161*
Citco Nederland B.V.	World Trade Center Tower B, 17th Floor Strawinskylaan 1725 1007 XX Amsterdam The Netherlands	Tel (31) 20 572 2300 Fax (31) 20 664 7557 *see p 189*
Citco (Suisse) S.A.	19, Rue de la Croix-d'Or PO Box 3124 1211 Geneva 3 Switzerland	Tel (41) 22 317 7020 Fax (41) 22 317 7030 *see p 205*
Crump & Co.	18/F On Hing Building 1 On Hing Terrace Central Hong Kong	Tel (852) 2537 7000 Fax (852) 2804 6615 *see p 237*

Deacons Graham & James	3rd - 6th Floor Alexandra House Central Hong Kong	Tel (852) 2825 9211 Fax (852) 2810 0431 *see p 23*
Evans & Co	Shirley Street PO Box N-9298 Nassau Bahamas	Tel (242) 328 8510 1 (242) 322 5178 9 Fax (242) 322 5942 *see p 45*
International Company Services Ltd	Sovereign House St Johns Isle of Man IM4 3AJ British Isles	Tel (44) 1624 801801 Fax (44) 1624 801800 Email iom@icsl.com *see p 123*
International Company Services (Portugal) Lda	Parque Empresarial Algarve Apartado 246 8400 Lagoa Algarve Portugal	Tel (351) 82 342 601 Fax (351) 82 342 259 Email por@icsl.com *see p 169*
International Company Services (SA) Ltd	The Terraces 5th Flr 34 Bree Street Cape Town 8001 South Africa	Tel (27) 21 418 4237 Fax (27) 21 418 2196 Email isca@iafrica.com *see p 175*
International Company Services (TCI) Ltd	PO Box 107 Oceanic House Duke Street Grand Turk Turks & Caicos Islands British West Indies	Tel (809) 94 62828 Fax (809) 94 62825 Email tci@icsl.com *see p 211*

International Management (Mauritius) Ltd	Les Cascades Building Edith Cavell Street Port Louis Mauritius	Tel (230) 212 9800 Fax (230) 212 9833 Email imm@intnet.mu *see p 183*
John Koh & Co	8 Robinson Road 12th Floor COSCO Building Singapore 048544	Tel (65) 538 9880 Fax (65) 538 2221 *see pp 145 & 197*
Kleinwort Benson (Guernsey) Trustees Limited	PO Box 44 The Grange St. Peter Port Guernsey Channel Islands GY1 3BG	Tel (44) 1481 727111 Fax (44) 1481 728317 *see p 117*
KPMG Legal Services	Amcham Plaza 2/F 7th Avenue Sabana Norte San José Costa Rica PO Box 10208 San José Costa Rica 1000	Tel (506) 220 1366 Fax (506) 296 0269, (506) 220 0408 *see p 101*
LGT Bank in Liechtensten AG Representative Office Hong Kong	11th Flr Three Exchange Square 8 Connaught Place Central GPO Box 13398 Hong Kong	Tel (852) 2523 6180 Fax (852) 2868 0059 *see p 157*
Michael T Dabit & Associates	Al-Hindi Commercial Centre Shemesani PO Box 941389 Amman 11194 Jordan	Tel (962) 6 682 622 (962) 6 682 633 Fax (962) 6 682 644 Email mtdabit@nets.com.Jo *see p 135*

Mitchell's Chambers	PO Box 174 The Valley Anguilla British West Indies	Tel (264) 497 2391 Fax (264) 497 2050 Email mitchellm@anguillanet.com Web http://www.offshore.com.ai/mitchells *see p 31*
Morgan Guaranty Trust Company of New York	22/F Edinburgh Tower 15 Queen's Road Central Hong Kong	Tel (852) 284 11358 Fax (852) 284 11259 *see p iii*
Myers & Alberga	1 Regis Place PO Box 472 Grand Cayman Cayman Islands British West Indies	Tel (345) 949 0699 Fax (345) 949 8171 *see p 81*
Sovereign Trust International	1601-1603 Kinwick Centre 32 Hollywood Rd Central Hong Kong	Tel (852) 2542 1177 Fax (852) 2545 0550 Email hk@icsl.com Web http://www.icsl.com *see pp 61 & 105*
Stikeman Elliot	Cottons Centre Cotton Lane London SEI 2QL England UK	Tel (44) 171 378-0880 Fax (44) 171 378-0344, (44) 171 865-0226 *see p 221*
Triay & Triay	28 Irish Town PO Box 15 Gibraltar	Tel (350) 72020 Fax (350) 72270 Telex 2219 TRIBAR GK *see p 109*

TrustNet	Unit 1204A 12/F Peregrine Tower Lippo Centre 89 Queensway Hong Kong	Tel (852) 2525 9991 (852) 2526 8955 Fax (852) 2877 6852 *see p 95*
TrustNet (Brtitish Virgin Islands) Ltd	TrustNet Chambers PO Box 3444 Road Town Tortola British Virgin Islands	Tel (809) 494 5296 Fax (809) 494 5283 *see p 75*
The Winterbotham Trust Company (Uruguay) S.A.	PO Box 12.129 Blanes Viale 5910 11.500 Montevideo Uruguay	Tel (598-2) 61 65 44/5/6/7 Fax (598-2) 61 76 1 Email winterb4@adinet.com.uy *see p 217*